Habituation in German Modernism

Studies in German Literature, Linguistics, and Culture

Habituation in German Modernism

Embodied Cognition in Literature and Thought

Meindert Peters

Rochester, New York

Copyright © 2024 Meindert Peters

All Rights Reserved. Except as permitted under current legislation, no part of this work may be photocopied, stored in a retrieval system, published, performed in public, adapted, broadcast, transmitted, recorded, or reproduced in any form or by any means, without the prior permission of the copyright owner.

First published 2024
by Camden House

Camden House is an imprint of Boydell & Brewer Inc.
668 Mt. Hope Avenue, Rochester, NY 14620, USA
and of Boydell & Brewer Limited
PO Box 9, Woodbridge, Suffolk IP12 3DF, UK
www.boydellandbrewer.com

ISBN-13: 978-1-64014-162-9

Library of Congress Cataloging-in-Publication Data
CIP data is available from the Library of Congress.

Cover image: Untitled (1925–26), by László Moholy-Nagy. Private Collection c/o Sotheby's © 2024 Estate of László Moholy-Nagy / Artists Rights Society (ARS), New York.

The publisher has no responsibility for the continued existence or accuracy of URLs for external or third-party internet websites referred to in this book, and does not guarantee that any content on such websites is, or will remain, accurate or appropriate.

To Koos

Contents

Preface	ix
List of Abbreviations	xi
Introduction: "Habit Has Not Yet Done Its Work"	1
1: Martin Heidegger's *Sein und Zeit*: Situating Ourselves; Worlding the Body	21
2: Rainer Maria Rilke's *Die Aufzeichnungen des Malte Laurids Brigge*: Writing as Practice	48
3: Georg Kaiser's *Von morgens bis mitternachts* and Karlheinz Martin's Film Adaptation: Ecstatic Experience	72
4: Alfred Döblin's *Berlin Alexanderplatz*: The Affordances of Others	91
5: Walter Benjamin's *Einbahnstraße* and Its *Nachtragsliste*: Critical Responsiveness	120
6: Vicki Baum's *Menschen im Hotel*: Warmth	144
7: Evolving Form	173
Concluding Remarks	194
Appendix: Translation of "Duitsche Literatuur" (1929) by Chris de Graaff	201
Bibliography	205
Index	225

Preface

I WOULD LIKE TO START by thanking the institutions who have made (the research for) this monograph financially possible: the Faculty of Medieval and Modern Languages at Oxford, the New College Reynolds Fund, and the Jade Fonds of the Prins Bernhard Cultuurfonds of the Netherlands, and, indirectly, the John Fell Fund. A special thank you to the Association for German Studies in Great Britain and Ireland for their generous support toward the publication of this monograph. Thank you all very much!

Earlier versions of two chapters have been published elsewhere: chapter 1 appeared in a shorter version and open-access (Creative Commons CC BY license) in *Phenomenology and the Cognitive Sciences* 18, no. 2 (2019), and a different version of chapter 6 in a special issue entitled "Transatlantic Cognitive Cultures," edited by Shannon McBriar and me, of *Symbiosis: A Journal of Transatlantic Literary and Cultural Relations* 25, no. 2 (2021). I thank the editors of these journals for their permission to reprint here.

Thank you to New College, Oxford, and all its staff and academics, for housing and feeding me through the years and continuing to be the kind of dynamic academic environment one can only dream of—and Thomas Goodwin, Martin Hallmannsecker, Louisa Künstler, Felipe Soza, Alexandra Whelan, and Luca Zenobi for our friendships rooted there. Thank you to the Friedrich Schlegel Graduate School of Literary Studies at the Freie Universität zu Berlin for giving me an office for two years, for creating a warm and open academic community, and for all the feedback I have received in and out of their seminars. Thank you also to the Erasmus+ program of the European Commission for making this exchange possible; may it live a long life! Thank you to the librarians at the Taylorian in Oxford for their continued help and support (especially in those strange months in 2020 and 2021 during which access to libraries was online only), as well as those at the Philologische Bibliothek of the FU in Berlin, the Walter-Benjamin-Archiv in Berlin, and the DLA Marbach, for giving me easy access to so much wonderful material.

To all friends and colleagues who have read or listened to parts of this book and helped me with comments and suggestions: Patty Argyrides, Myrto Aspioti, Kevin Brazil, Robert Britten, Maggie O'Brien, Nicholas Courtman, Tom Goodwin, Marie Lindskov-Hansen, Sophie König, Daan Schneider, Byron Spring, Alexandra Whelan, as well as several peer reviewers of a different version of the Heidegger chapter. To those academics whom I have never met, but who when contacted, helped me out: Malte Herwig, Steffan Davies, thank you very much! Thank you to Sue Jones, Karen Leeder, Georgina Paul, and Naomi Rokotnitz for the different ways in which they have supported me through the years.

Thank you to Carolin Duttlinger, Barry Murnane, Michael Wheeler, and Stephan Besser, as well as several anonymous peer reviewers for their very helpful and much-needed comments and suggestions on various chapters and the overall structure of the monograph. All remaining issues are, of course, entirely of my own doing. To my editor, Jim Walker, for nurturing this project in a way that I had not thought possible, as well as everyone else behind the scenes at Camden House for making this monograph a material object in the world.

To Shannon McBriar, without whom I would not be the researcher I am, who gave me an undiminishing enthusiasm for research, and continues to be my favorite intellectual interlocutor. To Benjamin Morgan, whose questions will never leave me, without whom my research interests would not have found a fruitful base, and without whom this book would simply not exist. Thank you.

And finally, a thank you to my family, friends, and most importantly Koos, without whose warmth I do not flourish.

Abbreviations

BA	Alfred Döblin, *Berlin Alexanderplatz: Die Geschichte vom Franz Biberkopf*
BA2	Alfred Döblin, *Berlin Alexanderplatz*, translated by Michael Hofmann
BT	Martin Heidegger, *Being and Time*, translated by Joan Stambaugh
GH	Vicki Baum, *Grand Hotel*, translated by Basil Creighton
KGA	Walter Benjamin, *Kritische Gesamtausgabe*
MH	Vicki Baum, *Menschen im Hotel*
MLB	Rainer Maria Rilke, *Die Aufzeichnungen des Malte Laurids Brigge*
MM	Georg Kaiser, *Von morgens bis mitternachts*
N	Rainer Maria Rilke, *The Notebooks of Malte Laurids Brigge*, translated by Robert Vilain
OWS	Walter Benjamin, *One-Way Street*, translated by Edmund Jephcott
SW	Walter Benjamin, *Selected Writings*, translated by Rodney Livingstone and others
SZ	Martin Heidegger, *Sein und Zeit*
ZS	Martin Heidegger, *Zollikoner Seminare*
ZSS	Martin Heidegger, *Zollikon Seminars*, translated by Franz Mayr and Richard Askay

Introduction: "Habit Has Not Yet Done Its Work"

On September 11, 1906, Rainer Maria Rilke wrote to his friends Gudrun Baroness von Uexküll and her husband the biologist Jakob Baron von Uexküll about his trip to Marburg the day before. About his encounter with the city's *Elisabethkirche*, he writes: "wie genau wußte ich alles wieder; als ich den Glockengriff gegenüber vom Dom faßte, um den Küster zu rufen, da wars [*sic*], als wäre noch eine Spur in meiner Hand, in die er genau hineinpaßte" (how exactly I remembered everything; when I grabbed the bell handle opposite the cathedral to call the sexton, it was as if there was still a trace in my hand into which it fitted exactly).[1] Rilke conjures up a shared memory, that of their shared visit to the same church a year earlier.[2] He attempts to evoke this shared familiarity through a bodily sensation—notice the use of the word "genau" (exactly) for both the act of remembering and the physical sensation. His hand is attuned to the handle. The church is incorporated. Familiarity resides in his body. Rilke's letter testifies to the theme of this book, namely the interest of early twentieth-century German-language authors in bodily knowledge.

It is no coincidence that Rilke addresses this image of corporeal adaptation to the Baroness and Baron von Uexküll. The latter's work in biology explored the kind of pragmatic, corporeal knowledge that Rilke hints at here. Uexküll's concept of *Umwelt* understands animals' perception of the environment—and this includes humans' perception—not as objective, but as determined between the senses and abilities of these animals and their material environments. In his ecological theory, *what* we see is determined by our senses, and *how* we register it is determined in terms of our physical abilities.

An example: in one of Uexküll's most famous images, he describes how a tick cannot see or hear as humans do. But it can smell. It waits in a tree for a mammal to bite down on, which it perceives through the smell

---

1   Rilke, *Gesammelte Briefe*, 184. All translations are my own unless otherwise noted.
2   Rilke was first invited to Friedelhausen in 1904 by Luise Countess of Schwerin, Gudrun von Uexküll's mother. Uexküll, *Jakob von Uexküll*, 127. Gudrun von Uexküll writes in her biography of her husband that Rilke and the biologist soon connected on the topic of the right way to view nature (56).

of butyric acid. It then drops down, hopefully on the mammal, which it will recognize by the heat emitted by its body, and after finding a not-too-hairy spot via its sense of touch, the tick will know to bite down.[3] The *Umwelt* of the tick is shaped by its senses and its possibilities for action, and is thus completely different from how a human would perceive the very same forest. Humans would sense the approaching mammal predominantly through sound and vision, and would approach with curiosity or, if the animal is bigger, fear. In other words, our bodies—their senses and abilities—shape our worlds.

Rilke's letter describing the handle that fits right into his hand seems to point to Uexküll's theory of *Umwelt* while also moving beyond it to questions of habituation. Rilke's description of his hand and the handle that "genau hineinpaßte" (fitted exactly) anticipates one of Uexküll's more programmatic statements in *Umwelt und Innenwelt der Tiere* (1909): that every animal is "gleich vollkommen seiner Umgebung angepaßt" (perfectly adapted to its surroundings).[4] However, while Uexküll, especially in his writings on humans, suggests that practices may be dynamic, his picture of *Umwelt* is in the first place a static one.[5] Rilke's image, by contrast,

---

3   Uexküll and Kriszat, *Streifzüge*, 1–2. See also Giorgio Agamben's re-telling of it in Agamben, *Open*, 11. Georg Kriszat's contribution to the work would be fully erased from its recent English edition if it were not for Uexküll's original, generous introduction: "The authors have split up their tasks in such a way that one (Uexküll) wrote the text and the other (Kriszat) was responsible for illustrations." Uexküll, *Foray*, 43.

4   Uexküll, *Umwelt und Innenwelt*, 5. My translation. There is also a substantially revised second edition of the work from 1921. Only after this version, according to Mildenberger and Herrmann, did a wide reception of the work set in (7). This is also the version that both scholars have recently republished with extensive commentary (Jakob von Uexküll, *Umwelt und Innenwelt der Tiere*, ed. Florian Mildenberger and Bernd Herrmann (Berlin: Springer, 2014). The major differences between the two versions, they write, are a different final chapter and changes in the introduction, as well as that the chapter "Der Funktionskreis" (Functional Cycle) replaced "Der Reflex" (7; Reflex). The quotation to which this note refers reads, in the 1921 version: "alle Tiere sind in ihre Umwelten gleich vollkommen eingepaßt" (22; all animals are fitted perfectly into their environments: my translation).

5   Uexküll and Kriszat, *Streifzüge*, 63. Here Uexküll suggests that we can learn to see the world differently: "Am leichtesten wird man sich von der Verschiedenheit menschlicher Umwelten überzeugen, wenn man sich von einem Ortskundigen durch eine unbekannte Gegend führen läßt" (It is easiest to be convinced of the differences in human environments when one has a local guide take one through an unfamiliar area (translated by Joseph D. O'Neil: Uexküll, *Foray*, 98). David Herman, indeed, emphasizes these moments in Uexküll, stating that "Uexküll also stressed intraspecies variation." Herman, "Re-Minding Modernism," 265.

hints at a more dynamic picture in which habituation, the malleability of bodily practices to new circumstances, plays an important role. The body doesn't just fit the world, it adjusts itself to it. Through this more dynamic image, Rilke thus raises the question of how we become attuned to our environments. This is the question that animates this study: How do we habituate ourselves to environments that are not yet, or no longer, familiar? How does the hand adjust to the handle?[6]

Rilke's evocation of a corporeal, practical knowledge, what is often called "embodied cognition" today, is the starting point of my research into such questions of adaptations through German modernist texts. To do so, this book brings modernist texts into dialogue with contemporary accounts of embodied cognition. The flourishing research program that comes together under the name of "embodied cognition" today is one that draws from and feeds into work in a diverse range of disciplines, including philosophy, psychology, cognitive (neuro)science, and artificial intelligence. Turning away from Cartesian dualism and cognitivism, embodied cognition research understands cognition as occurring in the dynamic interplay of the mind, body, and environment, which are inextricable from each other. The present study brings theories of embodied cognition to six close readings of modernist texts: Martin Heidegger's *Sein und Zeit* (Being and Time), Rainer Maria Rilke's *Die Aufzeichnungen des Malte Laurids Brigge* (The Notebooks of Malte Laurids Brigge), Georg Kaiser's *Von morgens bis mitternachts* (From Morn to Midnight), Alfred Döblin's *Berlin Alexanderplatz* (Berlin Alexanderplatz), Walter Benjamin's *Einbahnstraße* (One-Way Street), and Vicki Baum's *Menschen im Hotel* (Grand Hotel). In setting up these dialogues, this book brings into relief German modernism's concerns over how to adapt to environments that are new, changed, and/or changing. Thus, although Uexküll's theory seems to have been an important starting point for the implicit and explicit discussions of embodied practices in some of the texts discussed in this book—Heidegger and Döblin, for example, engaged explicitly with Uexküll's work[7]—the aim of this study is not to trace his influence. The

---

6   There is an important difference to be made here between "habituation" and "attunement." In my use, the former refers to making certain behavior prereflective, easier, almost automatic, through repetition (that is, to make something habit). "Attuning" refers in a broader sense to adjusting our (sensing and moving) body to relevant parts of an environment. Thus, while the process of habituation (but not necessarily habits themselves) entails attunement, not all attunement needs to become habit, and attunement can thus be a more dynamic way of adjusting to environments (this more dynamic approach is the subject of chapter 5).

7   Giorgio Agamben also suggests that Benjamin, like Rilke, was personally acquainted with Uexküll, staying in his villa on Capri. But I have not been able to confirm this information. Agamben, *Open*, 39.

modernist texts that I discuss here explore questions of dynamic human embodiment that go beyond Uexküll's ideas and that situate them in the realm of explorations of cognition today.

This dialogue is fruitful because the field of embodied cognition research today focuses on *acquired* knowledge: on habits and skills, on our smooth engagement in familiar worlds.[8] These modernist texts, however, solicit an attention to what happens when smooth engagement breaks down and to how we learn new habits and skills. Their authors explore the moments in which our bodies are not attuned to our environments, when the world is recalcitrant, when our habitual actions fall flat. German modernism engages with an often hostile, unfamiliar, and/or new environment, one that is dynamic and in motion, one in which, to paraphrase Walter Benjamin, one should not rely on previous achievements.[9] The attention of these authors to the moments in which our corporeal knowledge falls flat as well as to the ways in which we can start to inhabit the unfamiliar, raises important questions within embodied cognition research that are often left underexplored in its focus on habit and skill, that is, on the familiarized body.

At the same time, this dialogue between German modernism and embodied cognition research opens up new ways of looking at the German modernist period. Namely, it presents a view of the modern urban environment as represented in these texts not as something inherently hostile to human (social) practices—as, for example, Uexküll's own writing suggests[10]—but as *as yet* unfamiliar. Rather than emphasizing the alienation and isolation that these texts investigate regarding the modern urban experience—a reading well-established in German literary studies—this dialogue focuses our attention on how modernist authors investigate agents exploring and adapting to their immediate environments.

The question of how we can come to inhabit environments that are not yet, or no longer, familiar, might be even more relevant now than it was one hundred years ago. The more global our societies and the more they change; the more people choose to work, study, and/or start a life in foreign countries; the more people are uprooted by the effects of war, or by economic or environmental destruction—the more these

---

8　See Maxine Sheets-Johnstone's critique of this focus on habitual use in Sheets-Johnstone, *Primacy of Movement*, 417.

9　*KGA* VIII, 90. "In diesen Tagen darf sich niemand auf das versteifen was er 'kann.' In die Improvisation liegt die Stärke" (These are days when no one should rely unduly on his "competence." Strength lies in improvisation: *OWS*, 27).

10　See, for example, Uexküll, "Umrisse einer kommenden Weltanschauung," 659–61. In this text, he puts forward a pessimistic approach to city life as an unnatural environment for humans, given our bodies. "Nature" is our natural habitat and it is here that we can flourish.

things happen the more the question of how one finds a place for oneself in unknown, changed, or changing societies determines our lives. In this book, by urging the study of embodied cognition away from habit towards questions of habituation, I aim to contribute to these important questions about how we can come to attune ourselves to new environments—like Rilke's hand—and thus how we might be able to manipulate such environments for our ongoing endeavors.

"Animation" and Enactivism

I use "embodied cognition" in this study to refer to a strand of research that is also often referred to as "4E cognition."[11] The four "E"s refer to the idea that cognition is not only embodied, but also embedded, extended, and enacted. Other determinations of (parts of) the field include "distributed cognition" and "situated cognition." The idea that groups these fields is that thinking does not happen (exclusively) in the brain, but that cognition is, at least to some extent, shaped by the body (beyond the brain) and by its environment. The theory of 4E cognition is therefore opposed to other theories of cognition such as cognitivism, computationalism, and Cartesian dualism.[12] I shall begin by explaining my terminology before focusing on how this broad discipline shapes my thinking in this study.

Because the human body is central to this study, I use "embodied cognition" to cover the field of 4E cognition more broadly. Indeed, the modernist texts that I discuss here explore the body's centrality to human understanding. Even if our bodies are animated by a shared environment, as I argue in this book, it is through the body that we gain knowledge of that environment. Thus the use of "embodied cognition" instead of "4E cognition" not only follows convention elsewhere—for example, in the Stanford Encyclopedia of Philosophy—but the words "embodied cognition" are also more evocative of the idea of the body's centrality than is the designation "4E cognition." Nevertheless, the other "E"s are also covered in this study (we will see how Rilke's Malte *extends* his thinking to pen and paper, Döblin's Biberkopf dynamically *enacts* a wall, and the behavior of Baum's Grusinskaja is clearly *embedded* in defunct cultures).

That said, I should note that even though I choose to use the term "embodied cognition," I bear in mind an important argument against it that was first put forth by Maxine Sheets-Johnstone. The term "embodied cognition," Sheets-Johnstone argues, suggests that there is something

11 See, for example, Newen, de Bruin, and Gallagher, *The Handbook to 4E Cognition*; and Shapiro and Spaulding, "Embodied Cognition."
12 For contemporary approaches to such theories of cognition see, for example, Scheutz, *Computationalism*; Lavazza and Robinson, *Contemporary Dualism*.

that we call cognition, which is only subsequently embodied. If, as theorists gathering around this term argue, knowledge is indeed first and foremost bodily knowledge, something that arises from, and is shaped and sustained by, a moving body, then "embodied cognition" is at best a confusing use of words. Such terms are the symptom of a field which, Sheets-Johnstone writes, "take[s] up a preeminently cognitive science . . . and tr[ies] to reshape it to match the realities of life itself through linguistic implants."[13] Instead of "embodied cognition," she proposes the term "animation." This term evokes both physical movement and physical "thinking"—although these might, as I shall show throughout this book, be impossible to disentangle. Moreover, the term "animation" not only emphasizes the centrality of movement to the living human body but also suggests that the body is animated by something, by the people and things in its environment. The term thus does justice to the idea that the world is essential to the body and the body essential to its environment. Moreover, the term "animation" marks a more pronounced shift away from the centrality of thought, thinking, cognition, contemplation, all of which point to brains and minds. "Animation" emphasizes movement over thought, and habit over knowledge. Rather than bringing thinking to the body, the use of the term "animation" starts off from the idea of a body that is open to its environment and then goes on to explore how thinking arises from that body. In addition to the use of "embodied cognition," as my preferred term for this field of research, I thus also use the term "animation" when thinking through the ways in which human movement plays a role in the philosophical and literary texts that are the objects of my study. Moreover, when I use the word "body," I thus refer to the body/mind package.

The fields of research subsumed under the name of "embodied cognition" have very different theoretical commitments. What they have in common is a belief in the idea that the body and its environment at least shape, if not realize, thinking. As these fields of research are diverse, accounts of, and approaches to, embodied cognition differ. This study uses an approach that is most closely aligned with so-called "enactive" approaches to cognition. The enactive approach, which was first explored by Francisco J. Varela, Evan Thompson, and Eleanor Rosch,[14] "understand[s]," as Shaun Gallagher writes, "the brain to be an integrated part of a larger dynamical system that includes body and (physical, social, and cultural) environments."[15] The relation between cognition and the body or the environment, then, is not merely causal

---

13 Sheets-Johnstone, *Primacy of Movement*, 496.
14 Varela, Thompson, and Rosch, *Embodied Mind*.
15 Gallagher, *Enactivist Interventions*, 11.

but constitutive.[16] Brain, body, and environment are "dynamically coupled"; the idea is that "significant changes in one part of the system will cause changes or adjustments in the other parts."[17] Enactivism focuses on know-how, on the ways in which we use the social and material environment, often transparently so. It argues that meaning is enacted: "a path," Varela, Thompson, and Rosch say, "exists only in walking."[18]

Enactive approaches are useful for this study because they close the gap between the humanities and the cognitive sciences. They both derive from and draw on a wealth of sources that, crucially, include phenomenology and ecological psychology. Gallagher, for example, draws heavily on insights from Merleau-Ponty and Husserl.[19] Enactivists also draw on insights that have their origin in early twentieth-century German thought. Julian Kiverstein and Erik Rietveld, for example, who have written on the concept of "affordances"—a term which has also gained traction in literary studies[20]—draw on Heidegger's work.[21] Indeed, many of the ideas of enactive cognition are aligned with (at least certain readings of) Heidegger's *Sein und Zeit* (1927), to which I turn in the first chapter of this book. Heidegger's emphasis on what he calls *Zuhandenheit* (readiness-to-hand)—that is, know-how—as the basis of knowledge of our environment, suggests a view of cognition as habitual. His concept of *das Man* is an early rendition of ideas, found in enactive cognition, of the environment as always already soliciting normative behavior. Moreover, the emphasis of enactivists on "affordances" (or possibilities for action), derives from accounts of ecological psychology, most notably from James J. Gibson's account, which in turn draws on Uexküll's

---

16 Adams and Aizawa critique enactivist and extended mind proposals by saying that they exactly confuse causality with constitution. See Adams and Aizawa, *Bounds of Cognition*.

17 Gallagher, *Enactivist Interventions*, 8.

18 Varela, Thompson, and Rosch, *Embodied Mind*, 241.

19 E.g., Gallagher, *How the Body*; Gallagher, *Enactivist Interventions*. The journal that Gallagher edits together with Dan Zahavi, *Phenomenology and the Cognitive Sciences*, shows a wealth and variety of work being done within the field, also beyond strictly embodied approaches.

20 See, for example, Terence Cave's *Thinking with Literature*, ch. 4. In July 2022, a conference was held in Berlin on the topic of literary form and affordances entitled "Form und Affordanz" by Jutta Eming and CJ Jones.

21 A volume of essays entitled *Heidegger and Cognitive Science*, edited by Julian Kiverstein and Michael Wheeler, shows the manifold ways in which dialogues between philosophers working on Heidegger and researchers working in the cognitive sciences can be mutually beneficial. Kiverstein and Wheeler, *Heidegger and Cognitive Science*. See also Wheeler, *Reconstructing the Cognitive World*.

theory of *Umwelt*.[22] Given this diverse set of approaches, Cecilia Heyes has suggested that enactivism would be better thought of as a philosophy of nature than a scientific project.[23] As Gallagher writes, drawing on Heyes, "a philosophy of nature takes seriously the results of science, and its claims remain consistent with them, but it can reframe those results to integrate them with results from many sciences."[24]

A Question of Attuning

This book draws on and extends this work in embodied cognition with a focus on questions of bodily adaptation. Within the cognitive sciences, much attention is being paid to "smooth coping," the everyday, habitual motions of a body familiarized with its environment, and the ways in which thinking is a part of such embodied engagements. By contrast, relatively little attention is being paid to what happens when we do not know how to proceed, when, for example, the environment responds unexpectedly to our actions.[25]

It is useful to bring the modernist texts discussed in this study into dialogue with theories of embodied cognition, because in them the everyday practices of agents are repeatedly challenged by an unfamiliar environment. Many of the characters explored in this study come from elsewhere into a city that is new and/or strange to them. Rilke's Malte (discussed in chapter 2) enters Paris with a map. With his parents deceased, he has no bridges back to his old, aristocratic culture. The city's street names, in French, stand out in the German text. In *Von morgens bis mitternachts* (chapter 3), the unnamed main character, a bank clerk, goes to a big city—probably Berlin—and gets immersed in new experiences. In Döblin's *Berlin Alexanderplatz* (chapter 4), Franz Biberkopf is released into Berlin after a lengthy stay in jail, a city that seems to have changed immensely in his absence, and one whose "freedom" stands in stark contrast to the rituals of jail.

As I show in chapter 5, Benjamin, in *Einbahnstraße* and its so-called *Nachtragsliste*, similarly thinks of the German bourgeoisie as being out of

---

22 Gibson, *Ecological Approach*. Indeed, Evan Thompson writes that the "sensorimotor world" of enactivist accounts "is none other than [ ] Uexküll's original notion of an *Umwelt*." Thompson, *Mind in Life*, 59.

23 Heyes suggested this in response to a paper given by Shaun Gallagher and drawing on the work of Peter Godfrey-Smith. Quoted in Gallagher, *Enactivist Interventions*, 22. See Godfrey-Smith, "On the Status."

24 Gallagher, *Enactivist Interventions*, 22.

25 Yet see, for example, the special issue of *Phenomenology and the Cognitive Sciences* on "choking" in sports, edited by Massimiliano L. Cappuccio. Cappuccio, "Unreflective Action."

tune with the advent of new technologies, stuck in the closed-off dynamics of its everyday habits and the interiors that shape them. The soldiers who come back from World War I, the war that exposed the most extreme face of new technology, have nothing to find in these interiors; the interiors afford them nothing. In Baum's *Menschen im Hotel* (discussed in chapter 6) only one character, Kringelein, is not familiar with the city, but it is through his eyes that we see it. The other characters, however, who are familiar with the ways of that particular world to different degrees, are clearly not at home in it either. The behaviors of Dr. Otternschlag and Baron von Gaigern, for example, are attuned not to contemporary life but to the horrors and rhythms of the war. Grusinskaja is a character whose life is embedded, as countless flashbacks suggest, within an old order of (Imperial) discipline. And finally, Heidegger, discussed in chapter 1, though primarily investigating smooth coping, is also interested in the moments when everyday engagements fail, when the material environment pushes back. The various forms of what he terms *Unzuhandenheit* (unreadiness-to-hand), which describes how objects come to stand out from the transparency of everyday use, together with his concept of anxiety, suggest that Heidegger was similarly interested in unfamiliar environments. Indeed, Heidegger, Benjamin, and Rilke all use words such as "Aufsässigkeit" (recalcitrance) or "Aufdringlichkeit" (obtrusiveness) to refer to the modernist material environment. Time and again in these texts, agents with habits situated elsewhere and/or in the past, run into the realities of modern environments. Whether change is elicited by technological, economic, material, or social shifts, they explore environments that are new, changed, or changing.

Crucially, their investigations of the dynamics between environments and humans do not end with the recalcitrance of the unfamiliar. The texts studied here are especially relevant because they explore how we can begin to re-inhabit our environments. They implicitly urge us to actively engage with our surroundings rather than contemplate our situation from a distance. By engaging responsively, our bodies will attune themselves to the specific circumstances of our environments and the situations we find ourselves in. But how exactly do we become responsive, and what is at stake in adaptation? In chapter 1, Heidegger starts us off by emphasizing that it is not merely a matter of *how* we adapt but also what for. In terms of "authenticity," he argues that we need a clear role for which the environment becomes meaningful and for which we can learn new habits and skills. Rilke's text also explores the importance of a guiding goal, but extends this by exploring play and experimentation, especially through writing, as ways of negotiating an unfamiliar environment. In chapter 3, Kaiser's work explores states of ecstasy (such as gambling, drinking, and sex) which might well provide us with a temporary sense of mastery but which ultimately prove unsustainable. In chapter 4,

Döblin's novel brings to the fore how an attentiveness to the behavior of others might teach us something about how we can negotiate new territories. And in chapter 5, Benjamin then explores the importance of a continued habituating—as opposed to rigid habits—through an innervation of the body. This innervation combines a heightened kinaesthetic awareness, a sensitivity toward the environment, and a readiness for action. Baum's novel extends these considerations about responsiveness by suggesting not only, as Döblin's novel does, that other people show us new ways into unfamiliar environments, but that the mere presence of the social warmth coming from others can make us more attentive to the (affective) possibilities of the environment. Finally, in chapter 7, a look at the various forms of these modernist texts (with a small detour through the early reception of Kafka), shows that these forms, too, although perhaps initially new and unfamiliar, are dynamic and invite participation and the learning of new ways of engaging. Through these modernist texts we can thus not only explore the recalcitrance of the unfamiliar, and what this recalcitrance does to our everyday practices, but also how we can re-situate ourselves in unfamiliar environments by being responsive to new possibilities for action.

Simmel, Benjamin, and a Disaffected Modernism

By exploring embodied cognition in these German modernist texts, this book also re-examines a particular reading of German modernism. Specifically, it aims to challenge the understanding of modernist texts as predominantly artefacts of the isolation, sensory overload, and alienation from the environment experienced by people in modernity, especially from the nineteenth century onwards. Regarding the kind of approaches to modernist German literature that I wish to challenge, Georg Simmel's *Die Großstädte und das Geistesleben* (1903; The Metropolis and Mental Life) is arguably the most influential theorization of agents in their modern environments. Indeed, Michael H. Whitworth refers to it as "enormously suggestive for literary critics."[26] In this sociological study, Simmel proposes the notion of *Reizschutz*, or stimulus shield: "der Typus des Großstädters,—der natürlich von tausend individuellen Modifikationen umspielt ist—[schafft] sich ein Schutzorgan gegen die Entwurzelung, mit der die Strömungen und Diskrepanzen seines äußeren Milieus ihn bedrohen: statt mit dem Gemüte reagiert er auf diese im wesentlichen mit dem Verstande . . ." (the metropolitan type of man — which, of course, exists in a thousand individual variants — develops an organ protecting him

---

26 Whitworth, *Modernism*, 182.

against the threatening currents and discrepancies of his external environment which would uproot him. He reacts with his head instead of his heart).[27] As the instincts of city inhabitants are dulled through overstimulation, they can only interact with their environments through their intellect. As Whitworth writes, "the idea of conscious intellect as a shield protecting the organism from stimuli is one [Simmel] shares with Henri Bergson and other late nineteenth-century psychologists."[28] On the one hand, this leads to "Blasiertheit" (a blasé attitude),[29] the essence of which is an "Abstumpfung gegen die Unterschiede der Dinge" (blunting of discrimination).[30] Aided also by the money economy, in which everything is understood in terms of its price, objects become interchangeable. Their different meanings and values are no longer of interest. Any excitement over objects disappears.[31] On the other hand, because the metropolitan agent becomes indifferent to his surroundings, he also turns inward. Together with intellectualism, then, there appears a flourishing of the inner life, of subjectivity. And it is this turn to subjectivity as Simmel diagnoses it, which is understood to anticipate the internal monologues characteristic of English-language literary modernist texts such as Virginia Woolf's *Mrs Dalloway* (1925) and James Joyce's *Ulysses* (1922).[32] In addition, this blasé attitude brought about by an overstimulation of the senses affects interpersonal relations, which atrophy. The sheer number of people that inhabitants of cities come across every day does not allow them to engage as they would in a small town. Simmel goes as far as to say that he suspects, in himself and other city dwellers, "eine leise Aversion, eine gegenseitige Fremdheit und Abstoßung, die in dem Augenblick einer irgendwie veranlaßten nahen Berührung sogleich in Haß und Kampf ausschlagen würde" (a slight aversion, a mutual strangeness and repulsion, which will break into hatred and fight at the moment of a closer contact, however caused).[33] Ultimately, Simmel's text suggests a preoccupation with a distance between people and their social and material environments, as well as with the consciousness that flourishes under that separation.

Benjamin's influential analysis of modernity is in many ways similar to that of Simmel. The famous figure of the stroller, the *flaneur*, from Benjamin's unfinished *Passagen-werk* (1927–40), resembles Simmel's

27 Simmel, *Großstädte*, 11. All translations of this source are by Kurt H. Wolff: Simmel, *Metropolis*, here, 410.
28 Whitworth, *Modernism*, 182.
29 Simmel, *Großstädte*, 19.
30 Simmel, *Großstädte*, 20; Simmel, *Metropolis*, 414.
31 Simmel, *Großstädte*, 20–22.
32 See, for example, Whitworth, *Modernism*, 181–82, and Williams, *Country and the City*, 243–45.
33 Simmel, *Großstädte*, 24; Simmel, *Metropolis*, 415–16.

(male) figures of modernity.[34] The *flâneur* is an individualized figure in an anonymous mass of people, "observing, and being observed," as Janet Wolff writes, "but never interacting with others."[35] Here too, then, we find an emphasis on individualism rather than interaction and on observation rather than participation. Benjamin's analysis of shock in his famous essay on the work of Charles Baudelaire, *Über einige Motive bei Baudelaire* (1939; On Some Motifs in Baudelaire), is equally interested in individual consciousness. Discussing Freud's theory of *Reizschutz*, Benjamin takes his cue from Simmel to write about the shocks of modernity, the overstimulation of nerves, and the ways in which people have adapted to them by developing a protective shield. The city dweller is both numb to sudden stimuli and continuously in a heightened state of awareness. "Daß das Auge des Großstadtmenschen mit Sicherungsfunktionen überlastet ist, leuchtet ein" (that the eye of the city dweller is overburdened with protective functions is obvious).[36] The more our lives are marked by shocks that are parried by a numb but alert consciousness, the more our lives are marked by short moments (*Erlebnis*) rather than by lived, that is, processed, experience (*Erfahrung*). Our lives become fragmented and we become reflective rather than absorbed in our interaction with the world around us. In Benjamin's view of modernity too, then, we find an emphasis on a barrier between human and urban environment and a retreat into the self.

To this day, Simmel's and Benjamin's analyses often shape discussions of human agency in modernist texts, especially those in German.[37] Unsurprisingly so, perhaps, since Simmel and Benjamin together with Siegfried Kracauer, as Andrew J. Webber writes, "established the terms of and the fundamental critical methods for the analysis of the modern urban condition."[38] Thus Lothar Müller, for example, states that German modernist literature's portrayal of people in the big city is best understood through Simmel: "Zum literarischen Portrait des Großstädters liefern Simmels Analysen . . . das soziologische Röntgenbild" (Simmel's analyses provide a sociological X-ray of the literary portrait of the city dweller).[39] Andreas Huyssen brings in Simmel and Benjamin to discuss Rilke's *Die Aufzeichnungen des Malte Laurids Brigge,* writing that its main protagonist "may represent one of the most persuasive poetic embodiments of

---

34 For an important critique of the figure of the *flaneur* in Benjamin's work and beyond in terms of gender, see Wolff, "Invisible Flâneuse."
35 Wolff, "Invisible Flâneuse," 40.
36 *GS* I.2, 649. Translation by Harry Zohn: Benjamin, *Illuminations,* 191.
37 Relatively recently, Tim Sparenberg has traced this influence back to an essay by Roy Pascal. Sparenberg, "Georg Simmels soziale Physik," 522; Pascal, "Georg Simmels *Die Großstädte.*"
38 Webber, Introduction, 3.
39 Müller, "Großstadt," 31–32.

Georg Simmel's metropolitan type of individuality, a figure that captures Simmel's intensification of nervous stimulation in the extreme."[40] As I will demonstrate in more detail in their respective chapters, the works of Döblin and Baum are also discussed in the terms laid out by Benjamin and Simmel.

A closer look at embodiment in modernist texts, however, allows us to shift our focus away from this emphasis on internal, closed off, and individual life towards an investigation of the responsive attempts at engaging with, and using, the socio-material environments that are also shown in these texts. The texts discussed in the following chapters explore bodies that become attentive to the possibilities of their material and social environments. They allow for a reading in more dynamic terms, focused more on cooperation than on interpersonal disconnection, more on trust than on irony or reserve, on corporeal action rather than on closed-off subjectivity, on responsiveness rather than bluntness. Thus, while dominant readings foreground how modernist texts depict closed-off and increasingly isolated individual subjects, this study shows how these texts also explore the human body's ability to be responsive to its surroundings and to other bodies.

Navigating the Unfamiliar

Yet an interpretation of modernism in the direction of responsiveness would not so much contradict Simmel's and Benjamin's analyses as it would refocus our attention on other aspects of their work. As Bernd Widdig writes, it would be a mistake to understand Simmel as a cultural pessimist: "Modern life for [Simmel] is defined as a careful and creative process of adaptation, one of accepting these fundamental dynamics and taking advantage of the enormous potential for personal freedom and social mobility, yet at the same time finding modes of resistance against their potentially overwhelming forces."[41] Indeed, in "Soziologie der Sinne" (1907; Sociology of the Senses), Simmel allows for the kind of dynamic engagement between agent and environment that the present study explores. Simmel here concedes that modern "individuals" continue to connect with their social environments, suggesting that these connections offer a way out of blasé indifference.[42] The dynamics of interaction as Simmel sees them become clear in a passage that is worth quoting in full:

---

40 Huyssen, "Notebooks," 76. See also Huyssen, "Paris/Childhood."
41 Widdig, *Culture and Inflation*, 67.
42 See also Bistis, "Simmel and Bergson," 397.

Daß die Menschen sich gegenseitig anblicken und daß sie auf einander eifersüchtig sind; daß sie sich Briefe schreiben oder miteinander zu Mittag essen; daß sie sich, ganz jenseits aller greifbaren Interessen, sympathisch oder antipatisch berühren; daß einer den andern nach dem Wege fragt und daß sie sich für einander anziehen und schmücken—all die tausend, von Person zu Person spielenden, momentanen oder dauernden, bewußten oder unbewußten, vorüberfliegenden oder folgenreichen Beziehungen, aus denen diese Beispiele ganz zufällig gewählt sind, knüpfen uns unaufhörlich zusammen. An jedem Tage, in jeder Stunde spinnen sich solche Fäden, werden fallen gelassen, wieder aufgenommen, durch andre ersetzt, mit andern verwebt. Hier liegen die, nur der psychologischen Mikroskopie zugänigen Wechselwirkungen zwischen den Atomen der Gesellschaft, die die ganze Zähigkeit und Elastizität, die ganze Buntheit und Einheitlichkeit dieses so deutlichen und so rätselhaften Lebens der Gesellschaft tragen.[43]

[The fact that people look at and are jealous of one another, that they write each other letters or have lunch together, that they have sympathetic or antipathetic contacts, quite removed from any tangible interests, that one person asks another for directions and that people dress up and adorn themselves for one another—all the thousands of relations from person to person, momentary or enduring, conscious or unconscious, fleeting or momentous, from which the above examples are taken quite at random, continually bind us together. On every day, at every hour, such threads are spun, dropped, picked up again, replaced by others or woven together with them. Herein lie the interactions between the atoms of society, accessible only to psychological microscopy, which support the entire tenacity and elasticity, the entire variety and uniformity of this so evident and yet so puzzling life of society.][44]

These "microscopic" dynamics of interpersonal contact thus suggest for Simmel ways out of the reserve that goes hand in hand with indifference and apathy. Relations between people are constantly established, reinforced, or dropped, suggesting a more dynamic picture than his initial analysis of the "blasé attitude" seems to allow. Later in the essay, Simmel concedes that other people's faces, gazes, and smells affect us whether we want them to or not, "bewußt oder instinktiv" (consciously or instinctively).[45] The body is moved, in other words, by those around it.

   43 Simmel, "Soziologie der Sinne," 1026.
   44 Simmel, "Sociology of the Senses," 110. All translations of this source by Mark Ritter and David Frisby.
   45 Simmel, "Soziologie der Sinne," 1029; Simmel, "Sociology of the Senses," 112.

He explores the ways in which our senses involve us in interactions with other people, and shape our perception of them, suggesting that these moments of contact may be a (partial) cure for blasé attitudes.[46]

Benjamin, too, is interested in exploring a more responsive engagement with the modern environment, one that takes leave from the ambiguous involvement of the *flâneur*. He suggests that we might be able to negotiate the scope and speed of change in modern life through habit, skill, and an innervation of the communal body. My fifth chapter, on Benjamin's *Einbahnstraße* and its *Nachtragsliste*, will shift attention away from the gaze of the *flâneur* to the skillful involvement of the expert. Benjamin reads expertise through Leon Trotsky's description of the sensitivity with which his father attends to manual labor. The expert, as read by Benjamin in Trotsky's description, treats every moment of his engagement with the world as new. The expert approaches the environment with careful steps and is sensitive and responsive to his surroundings.

Reading *Einbahnstraße* and the other German modernist texts treated in this study with a focus on embodied cognition, we can begin to move away from the limited and limiting discussion of the disconnection between the modern environment and its agent in terms of shock and shock resistance. That is, we can begin to see that the modernist attitude is not only that of a mind which has adapted to its environment by shielding itself against it, but also one of a body *as yet* unfamiliar with, and unattuned to, that environment. The distinction is essential. In the first of these accounts of the modernist attitude, the modern environment is seen first and foremost as a problem. It is *inherently* overwhelming and thus something to protect oneself against. In the account that I develop throughout this book, the environment, while anxiety-inducing and frustrating, is overwhelming only to the inexperienced agent. This inexperience then opens up the possibility for, and interest in, learning ways of usefully engaging with the modern environment. Important orthodox readings of modernist texts explain the alienation, disengagement, and blasé attitude of the modern "subject" by pointing to the overwhelming and alienating nature of the modern environment. By rereading both canonical and less canonical modernist texts, with an emphasis on bodily adaptation, I argue that this experience of disconnection and disaffection is, at least in part, also an experience of navigating the unfamiliar. In other words, I read this disconnection and disaffection as a lack of specific know-how, as part of an engagement with the not yet habituated. In the more established reading, distance is a way of adapting to the

---

46 In another essay, titled "Soziologie der Geselligkeit," Simmel discusses what he calls "sociability" (Geselligkeit), which offers for him a pure kind of social interaction in which business is left outside and in which more playful interactions can emerge. See also Bistis, "Simmel and Bergson," 397.

city environment; in my complementary reading this distance is a lack of attunement to the possibilities of the new environment.

Reanimated Modernism: Weak Modernism?

Through an exploration of embodied cognition in these modernist texts, this study draws on and extends current debates in both modernism studies and cognitive literary and cultural studies. The latter field of cognitive literary and cultural studies has blossomed over the past twenty years. The field ranges from neuroscientific studies of brain activity during reading to the ways in which cognitive studies can help re-think narration.[47] In cognitive approaches to modernism studies, two recent studies in particular have explored English-language modernist literature from the perspective of enactive cognition; they anticipate in their own field the arguments of this book.[48] David Herman, in his essay "Re-Minding Modernism" (2011), turns to enactive cognition research and Uexküll's work, to challenge historians and theorists of the novel who have argued that the collective interest of modernist authors in the workings of the mind marked an *inward* turn. Enactive cognition, Herman shows, challenges such a rigid inner/outer distinction. Thus he writes that modernist narratives took leave from realism not by turning inward but by highlighting the inextricability of the inner and outer, undermining the Cartesian dualism of mind and body.[49] Herman replaces the inner/outer distinction with a continuum "stretching between, at one pole, a tight coupling between an intelligent agent and that agent's surrounding environment, and, at the other pole, a looser coupling between agent and environment."[50]

This book further develops Herman's argument about this continuum, while rephrasing its terms slightly. Throughout this book, and starting from a discussion of Heidegger's *Sein und Zeit* in chapter 1, I

---

47 E.g., Zunshine, *Introduction to Cognitive Cultural Studies*; Zunshine, *Oxford Handbook*; Burke and Troscianko, *Cognitive Literary Science*; Morgan, Spolsky, and Park, "Situated Cognition"; McBriar and Peters, "Transatlantic Cognitive Cultures." See also "The Edinburgh History of Distributed Cognition" book series for Edinburgh University Press, edited by Miranda Anderson and Douglas Cairns. For embodied narratology see, e.g., Caracciolo and Kukkonen, *With Bodies*; and Bolens, *Style of Gestures*. For two recent special issues on literature and cognition in German Studies specifically see: Engler-Coldren, Knapp, and Lee, "Embodied Cognition around 1800"; and Lehleiter, "Reading Minds." For a cognitive approach to film, see Pisters, *The Neuro-Image*. For an approach to performance, see Rokotnitz, *Trusting Performance*.
48 But see also Bernini, *Beckett and the Cognitive Method*.
49 Herman, "Re-Minding Modernism," 253.
50 Herman, "Re-Minding Modernism," 249.

re-phrase Herman's continuum in more existential terms, to emphasize that something is at stake when agent and environment are too loosely coupled. The continuum developed here runs from, on the one pole, a recalcitrant environment that forces us into repeated (self-)reflection or into stubbornly repeating our habitual behavior, to, on the other pole, an environment to which we are habituated, one we largely cope with smoothly. It is the process of getting closer to this second state of smooth engagement, and the important complexities within, that is central to my reading of the German modernist texts I examine.

Dirk Van Hulle's *Modern Manuscripts* (2014) extends Herman's argument against the supposed "inward turn" of modernist literature, by focusing on the manuscripts of these texts as signs of an enactive mind, one that is constituted in action and interaction, in this case on paper. This process, Van Hulle writes, must have also influenced how modernist authors understood and thus represented the mind. Drawing on various texts, but in particular on Samuel Beckett's manuscripts, Van Hulle argues that "the constant enactive interplay of composition and decomposition, reading, writing, rereading and rewriting," as evident from the manuscripts, shows that "the modernist interest in the workings of the mind is not an internalist preoccupation or 'inward turn' but an early sensitivity to enaction and '*Umwelt*' research, prefiguring much of what cognitive sciences confirm today."[51] Van Hulle also explores what Herman also points out: the role of literature itself in the process of seeking to, in Herman's words, "transform unknown territories into negotiable places."[52] Focusing on the mind of the writer, Van Hulle argues that "if a writer's mind—like any other mind—consists of the interaction between an intelligent agent and his/her cultural as well as material circumstances, this cultural and material environment can also be, for instance, a book by another author."[53]

At various moments in this book, I turn to this question of literature as a cultural tool, as well. In the second chapter, Rilke starts us off on this question by showing how Malte's copying and rewriting of narratives, most notably that of the prodigal son, makes his environment more negotiable (to borrow Herman's phrasing). In *Berlin Alexanderplatz*, too, we read how Franz Biberkopf starts to enact his environment differently while being told a story (chapter 4). But I address modernist literature's interaction with the extratextual world in most detail in my final chapter on modernist form. Here, I return to the concept of "affordances," which is not only a concept frequently employed in discussions of embodied

---

51 Van Hulle, *Modern Manuscripts*, 171; 212.
52 Herman, "Re-Minding Modernism," 266.
53 Herman, "Re-Minding Modernism," 266; Van Hulle, *Modern Manuscripts*, 149.

cognition, but also one employed in literary studies. In Terence Cave's use of the term, which I explore in chapter 4, the term "affordance" connotes "agency, intention, purpose," but other literary scholars working in and beyond cognitive approaches have used the term to their advantages as well, authors such as Karin Kukkonen, Rita Felski, and, most extensively, Caroline Levine.[54] Yet while Levine's *Forms* offers insightful analyses on the connections between social and literary forms as well as their uses, my approach here is different. I use the term "affordance" to explore how modernist form as a set of affordances is a dynamically meaningful space not only mimicking the ongoing construction that is our built world but also bringing extratextual (linguistic) objects into its dynamically meaningful constellations. My aim is to show how modernist literature, like the city, consists of various elements that are arranged into surprising or unfamiliar constellations; how it stands in deliberate communication with, and revivifies, its extra-textual environment, and invites, and sheds light on, processes of familiarization, revivification, participation, and co-construction.

Within modernism studies more broadly, this study and its focus on adaptation may be thought of as following a path toward a weak, or weaker, modernism, such as Paul K. Saint-Amour has blazed in his special issue of *Modernism/modernity*.[55] If a narrative of "strong people exhibiting strength" about modernism has long been superseded in its studies, Saint-Amour attempts to move more decisively toward its opposite in "weakness."[56] The "weak" of weak modernism may refer, as Saint-Amour writes, to the "*woman, queer*, and *disabled*," whose supposed weakness is

---

54 Cave, *Thinking with Literature*, 51; Kukkonen, *Probability Designs*; Felski, *Hooked*; Levine, *Forms*.

55 Several monographs have recently explored modernism's interest in corporeality. Lucia Ruprecht's *Gestural Imaginaries* (2019) explores the dialogue between dance and cultural criticism focusing on the German-speaking realm and the critical potential of individual, intermittent gestures. In English-language modernism studies, Ariane Mildenberg's 2017 *Modernism and Phenomenology* explores literature, art, and phenomenology together to reveal a "deep-rooted openness to the world that turns us into 'perpetual beginners.'" Also focusing on the English realm, Lisi Schoenbach's *Pragmatic Modernism* (2011) equally brings literature and philosophy of the modernist period together, with a focus on the pragmatist philosophies of William James and John Dewey. Like the current monograph, Schoenbach's work treats habit as an important critical tool, but her project predominantly explores how shared habits are institutionalized rather than bodily habituation itself. Two monographs focusing on the English-language realm have recently explored the sense of touch specifically: Santanu Das (2006) explores touch and intimacy in First World War literature and Abbie Garrington (2013) investigates the sense of touch in modernist literature more generally. Das, *Touch and Intimacy*; Garrington, *Haptic Modernism*.

56 Saint-Amour, "Weak Theory, Weak Modernism," 437.

a "logic to dismantle."[57] It may also refer to its meaning as "pliant, flexible, readily bending" which cannot be viewed non-normatively either.[58] My study participates in this move away from strong masculinity and toward "weakness."[59] Yet, it aims only to participate in this move to the extent that such weakness—in this case the weakness of a responsive body that is always already entangled in, and influenced by, the dynamics of life—may be a strength. It aims to show that it is not knowledge but learning, not stubbornness but flexibility, not individuality or autonomy, but cooperation and participation, whether deliberate or not, which the texts that I discuss explore as solutions to experiences of disconnection and disaffection. My study thus also offers a counterpoint to Helmut Lethen's influential study of strong masculinity in Germany between the two World Wars in *Verhaltenslehren der Kälte* (Cool Conduct; 1994).[60] Drawing predominantly on texts from the *Neue Sachlichkeit*, Lethen paints the masculinist ideal of a cool conduct as a response to modernity: virile, stubborn, closed-off, rational, resistant, insensitive. My study paints a contrasting picture of "weakness," and indeed warmth, not by bringing in neglected voices—although this study makes a case for the importance of Baum's works—but rather by predominantly re-thinking texts that are still seen as central to the German modernist canon. This study aims to show that what was *seen* as strong may have always been more flexible and porous than the word suggests.

"Not Yet"

I conclude this introduction with a phrase from Benjamin's *Einbahnstraße*. In a vignette called "Verlorene Gegenstände" (Articles Lost), Benjamin writes about seeing an unknown town in the distance. The town can appear to him only once like this, he writes, because: "Noch hat Gewohnheit ihr Werk nicht getan" (*KGA* VIII, 47; Habit has not yet done its work: *OWS*, 63). We do not yet see what the town's inhabitants see, but as soon as we enter it, it starts to change. In the absence, so far, of a "stete, zur Gewohnheit gewordene Durchforschung" (*KGA* VIII, 47; a constant exploration that has become habit: *OWS*, 63) the town appears as an image that can never be restored "once we begin to find our way about" (*OWS*, 63).[61]

"Habit has not yet done its work," marks the argument of this book: that the modern environment is not, in these texts, objectively

---

57 Saint-Amour, "Weak Theory, Weak Modernism," 438.
58 Saint-Amour, "Weak Theory, Weak Modernism," 438.
59 Saint-Amour, "Weak Theory, Weak Modernism," 437.
60 Lethen, *Verhaltenslehren der Kälte*; Lethen, *Cool Conduct*.
61 "Haben wir einmal begonnen, im Ort uns zurechtzufinden, so kann jenes früheres Bild sich nie wieder herstellen" (*KGA* VIII, 47).

uninhabitable but is instead *as yet* unfamiliar. And it is the "Durchforschung" that I take to be an important part of the interest of the modernist writers I examine. The texts that follow investigate just how we can come to inhabit environments: what Benjamin's "constant exploration" might look like. Through these texts, this study traces a developing picture of how we can habituate ourselves to the unfamiliar. They bring into clear relief not only the problems and opportunities afforded by the unfamiliar, but also the ways in which we can become responsive to possibilities for action. My book shows how, even at a place and time of immense social and material change, like Europe in the early twentieth century, we can find new ways of adapting our behavior to as yet unfamiliar environments.

To do so, I first turn to Heidegger's *Sein und Zeit*, which provides a useful theoretical base on how our practices are embedded in our sociocultural environments and what happens when our practices start to fail. However, his text is far from meant as the ultimate theoretical horizon of this study. Instead, it functions as a first interlocutor for my questions about how we adapt to new environments and offers a first consideration, namely that it matters *why* we adapt.

1: Martin Heidegger's *Sein und Zeit*: Situating Ourselves; Worlding the Body

In *Die Grundprobleme der Phänomenologie*, Heidegger writes: "[Dasein] *findet sich* primär und ständig *in den Dingen*, weil es, sie betreuend, von ihnen bedrängt, immer irgendwie in den Dingen ruht" ([Dasein] *finds itself* primarily and constantly *in things* because tending them, distressed by them, it always in some way or other rests in things).[1] In the fundamental ontology as proposed in his *Sein und Zeit* Heidegger began painting this picture of human existence (*Dasein*) in which we are always already in the world, submerged in our environment. Rather than the Cartesian subject who takes a step back from the physical world, contemplating the world from a distance because thought is supposedly the only thing we can be sure of, in Heidegger we find ourselves already moving through the world, handling objects, and being among other people. Yet even though Heidegger's account of *Dasein* shows it as always already physically engaged with the world, *Sein und Zeit* has often been critiqued for not containing an explicit discussion of the body. For example, De Waelhens, in his introduction to *The Structure of Behaviour* by Merleau-Ponty, writes that Heidegger in *Sein und Zeit* only devotes ten lines to the problem of the body.[2] In a series of lectures held between 1959 and 1969 and published as the *Zollikoner Seminare* in 1987, Medard Boss confronted Heidegger with a similar critique by Jean-Paul Sartre: "[Es] wunderte [Sartre], daß Sie im ganzen 'Sein und Zeit' nur sechs Zeilen über den Leib geschrieben` hätten" (*ZS*, 292; [Sartre] wondered why you only wrote six lines about the body in the whole of *Being and Time*: *ZSS*, 231). Heidegger reacted to this criticism by stating that his idea of the body should not be seen in the light of a dichotomy between body and mind and that he was not talking about an object called body (Körper) but rather a living body open to the world (Leib; *ZS*, 116–17; *ZSS*, 89–90). His reluctance to provide a direct treatment of the body in *Sein und Zeit*, it seems, derived from his fear of turning the body into an object of contemplation, transforming it into a *Körper*, and thus once again setting

---

1   Heidegger, *Grundprobleme der Phänomenologie*, 226. All translations of this source by Albert Hofstadter: Heidegger, *Basic Problems*, here, 159.
2   De Waelhens, "Philosophy of the Ambiguous," xviii.

up the Cartesian dichotomy. Instead he chose to emphasize the world in which and with which the body as *Leib* is always already engaged.[3]

A similar interpretation of the absence of the body in *Sein und Zeit* underlies Gallagher and Jacobson's recent critique of Heidegger's treatment of intersubjectivity in the context of exploring the relationship of Heidegger's work to advances in the cognitive sciences.[4] For Heidegger, what he calls "being-in-the-world" (In-der-Welt-sein) is both being with other people as well as being with and handling objects. We are not only always already in the world with other things, we also already encounter other people in relation to these objects. Through this structure we are part of an intersubjective relation with others that he calls "being-with" (Mitsein; *SZ*, 114; *BT*, 111). Through being-with we have an everyday familiarity with other people in the shared world of objects and people we encounter. Gallagher and Jacobson critique Heidegger's treatment of intersubjectivity for overlooking what Trevarthen first defined as *primary* intersubjectivity, that is, direct, face-to-face relations,[5] which has been a central concept in a wide range of research in the cognitive sciences.[6] According to Gallagher and Jacobson, Heidegger's account is lacking because it only discusses indirect relations between people: relations that move from person to object to person.

In this chapter I argue that Gallagher and Jacobson's criticism, although opening up important questions about the place of immediate, emotionally rich, face-to-face encounters in *Sein und Zeit*, shares the same assumption that drove Merleau-Ponty's and Sartre's critiques: that because the body is not explicitly discussed as a *Körper*, that embodiment must therefore be insufficiently acknowledged in Heidegger's emphasis on being-in-the-world, rather than stressing the immediacy of experience. Through placing Gallagher and Jacobson's account of embodied practice (section 2 of this chapter) and intersubjectivity (sect. 4) alongside Heidegger's corresponding notions of *Leib* (sect. 1) and being-with (sect.

---

3   That said, in the *Zollikoner Seminare* Heidegger does admit to not having had a thorough understanding of the body at the time of writing *Sein und Zeit* and so could not say more about the subject (*ZS*, 292).

4   Gallagher and Jacobson, "Heidegger and Social Cognition."

5   Trevarthen, "Communication and Cooperation." Although Trevarthen coined the term "primary intersubjectivity," Mary Catherine Bateson had already shown the presence of it in the infant and their mother. Bateson, "Mother-Infant Exchanges." For more on primary intersubjectivity in the newborn see, for example, Meltzoff and Moore, "Imitation of Facial"; Trevarthen, "Foundations of Intersubjectivity"; Legerstee, "Role of Person and Object"; Meltzoff and Brooks, "Like Me."

6   E.g., Ratcliffe, *Rethinking Commonsense Psychology*; Butterworth, "Joint Visual Attention"; De Jaegher and Di Paolo, "Participatory Sense-making"; Colombetti, *Feeling Body*.

3), in this chapter I will try to develop a better understanding of these concepts central to *Sein und Zeit* and emphasize, in Heidegger, the extent of the body's immersion in the world. In so doing, I attempt to show that Heidegger's account of intersubjectivity is one of immediacy, thereby defending Heidegger against Gallagher and Jacobson's claim that he does not provide an account of the kind of immediate, face-to-face relation they call primary intersubjectivity.

In the larger context of this book, this dialogue brings into relief the kind of absorbed action whose absence is addressed by the other modernist texts. Heidegger explores the unreflected habitual performances that come to stand out when they are resisted by our socio-material environments. However, in the final part of this chapter, I also place Heidegger's analyses in *Sein und Zeit* within modernist concerns over how to adapt to new or unfamiliar environments. To do this, I turn to his analyses of "anxiety" and "authenticity." For Heidegger, anxiety is an affective state caused by, or at least linked to, a recalcitrant environment. His concept of authenticity, which he believes can come about through anxiety, investigates bodily adaptation—a "modified grasp" (*BT*, 172; SZ, 179)—as needing to center around an agent's purpose or role. Heidegger's text reminds us that it is important to think what we adapt *for*, for what purpose or role, not just about *how* we adapt. Thus this chapter situates Heidegger's thought within modernist concerns over bodies that run into socio-material resistance and over how we might consequently adapt anew to retrieve the kind of smooth performance with which Heidegger starts his analysis.

Heidegger's *Leib* as Being-in-the-World

In *Sein und Zeit* Heidegger argues that *Dasein* is always already in the world and that we are thus always already surrounded by objects. At the moment when we become conscious of the world, we already stand in relation to these objects. We are already familiar with them, we are already using them as tools. Rather than contemplating these objects from a distance, we already have knowledge of them in their usefulness, or what Heidegger calls their *Zuhandenheit* (*SZ*, 69; readiness-to-hand: *BT*, 69).[7] A fork, for example, is always already seen as a thing to eat with. I can,

---

7   This pragmatic engagement with the environment is in many ways reminiscent of Uexküll's *Umwelt*. Heidegger was clearly interested in Uexküll's work, as his discussion of the biologist in his lectures from the 1929/30 winter semester attests. In these lectures in which he discusses his own concept of *Welt* in much detail, he explores Uexküll's work as well. See Heidegger, *Grundbegriffe der Metaphysik*, §63b. For more information on Uexküll's influence on Heidegger, see Buchanan, *Onto-Ethologies*.

of course, see a fork as a piece of metal of certain measurements, I can rationalize it—this is what Heidegger states that science does—but that actually takes me a step back from how this thing has meaning to me in my everyday existence. Even if I have never seen a fork before, I will approach it pragmatically: I approach it as lacking a function, as having a "disruption of reference" (Störung der Verweisung), or approach it with assumptions about what its use may be (*SZ*, 74; *BT*, 74).[8] This is illuminatingly shown in the Walt Disney film *The Little Mermaid* (2013).[9] When Ariel comes across a fork for the first time in her life, she approaches it as the tool she thinks it most resembles: a comb. Particularly in these moments where we do not know the function of tools or where they simply do not function as they should, the extent to which we count on the world in its *Zuhandenheit* becomes apparent. The world according to Heidegger thus has meaning to us in its use: knowledge we have, first and foremost, through our physical using: "je weniger das Hammerding nur begafft wird, je zugreifender es gebraucht wird, um so ursprünglicher wird das Verhältnis zu ihm, um so unverhüllter begegnet es als das, was es ist, als Zeug" (*SZ*, 69; the less we just stare at the thing called hammer, the more we take hold of it and use it, the more original our relation to it becomes and the more undisguisedly it is encountered as what it is, a useful thing: *BT*, 69).

French phenomenologists and psychologists such as Sartre and Merleau-Ponty have criticized Heidegger, implicitly and explicitly, for his lack of discussion of how the body functions in this being-in-the-world.[10] Contemporary thinkers have uttered similar reservations in their discussion of *Sein und Zeit*. Krell, for example, asks: "Did Heidegger simply fail to see the arm of the everyday body rising in order to hammer the shingles on the roof?"[11] However, as David R. Cerbone and Søren Overgaard amongst others have argued, such a discussion of the body's functioning

---

8   According to Heidegger, when objects are not obviously *Zuhanden* because either 1) they are unuseful to us or we do not know their use (*Aufsässigkeit*), 2) they are broken (*Auffälligkeit*), or because 3) another tool to use it with is failing (*Aufdringlichkeit*), then they show themselves in their *Vorhandenheit* (objective presence). Yet the usual *Zuhandenheit* only becomes more apparent in this *Vorhandenheit*. He states: "Dabei wird aber das Zuhandene noch nicht lediglich als Vorhandenes *betrachtet* und begafft, die sich kundgebende Vorhandenheit ist noch gebunden in der Zuhandenheit des Zeugs" (*SZ*, 74; What is at hand is not thereby *observed* and stared at simply as something present. The character of objective presence making itself known is still bound to the handiness of useful things: *BT*, 73).

9   *The Little Mermaid*, directed by Ron Clements and John Musker (Walt Disney Pictures, 1989).

10   Sartre, *L'être et le néant*; De Waelhens, "Philosophy of the Ambiguous."

11   Krell, *Daimon Life*, 52. See also Franck, "Being and the Living."

as proposed by Krell removes this body from the world it is engaged in, by directing attention to the arm rather than the hammering.[12] It turns the arm into an objective thing—what Heidegger calls *Vorhandenheit* (objective presence)—or at least into the object of our objectifying thought, and therefore delineates the body from consciousness, bringing us back to the Cartesian dichotomy between body and mind that Heidegger is trying to overcome. In a series of lectures held from 1959 to 1969, published as the *Zollikoner Seminare* (Zollikon Seminars) in 1987, Heidegger also makes this point, and his explanations help illuminate his understanding of the body as being-in-the-world as earlier proposed in *Sein und Zeit*. In response to the criticism levelled by Sartre and other French thinkers, he states: "Bei den französischen Autoren stört mich immer noch die Mißdeutung des In-der-Welt-seins, wobei es entweder als Vorhandensein oder aber als Intentionalität des subjektiven Bewußtseins vorgestellt wird" (ZS, 339; As for the French authors, I am always disturbed by [their] misinterpretation of being-in-the-world; it is conceived either as objective presence or as the intentionality of subjective consciousness: ZSS, 272). Heidegger's idea of being-in-the-world overcomes this separation between body and mind, as he states in the *Zollikoner Seminare*, by foregrounding *Leib* over *Körper*, where the first is a living body and the second mere object.[13] *Leib* for him denotes the way in which the body is engaged with the world: "mein Sitzen auf dem Stuhle hier, ist seinem Wesen nach immer schon ein Dortsein bei etwas. Mein Hiersein zum Beispiel heisst: Sie dort sehen und hören." (ZS, 126–27; my sitting on the chair here, is essentially always already a being-there at something. My being-here, for instance, means: to see and hear you there: ZSS, 97). Thus taking *Leib* to mean being-in-the-world, Heidegger in *Sein und Zeit* does put forward his ideas on the body by describing the ways in which we are always already in the world and engaged with it, by describing the body's interactions rather than the body itself. *Leiben* (bodying-forth) for Heidegger—notice his use of a verb—just *is* being-in-the-world and *vice versa*. More focus on the body itself would only remove the body from the very situatedness Heidegger wants to put it in, strip it from its context, and, thus, take a step back from the fundamental ontology Heidegger is interested in. In other words, the Cartesian dichotomy that Heidegger is overcoming is not only that between body and mind, but also that between the (embodied) subject and their environment.[14]

---

12 Cerbone, "Heidegger and Dasein's 'Bodily Nature'"; Overgaard, "Heidegger on Embodiment." See also Aho, *Heidegger's Neglect*; and Levin, "Ontological Dimension of Embodiment."

13 Heidegger points out that the French language has a word for *Körper* (*le corps*) but not for *Leib* (ZS, 116; ZSS, 89).

14 See also Wheeler, *Reconstructing the Cognitive World*, 22–23.

Physical Being: Gallagher's "Body Schema" versus *Da-sein*

In *How the Body Shapes the Mind*, Gallagher offers a similar understanding of the body as *Leib*.[15] Combining neuro-scientific research with phenomenology—especially that of Merleau-Ponty—he proposes a productive new approach to thinking about the body-mind relation within the neurosciences. As in a variety of works ranging from Henry Head and Gordon Holmes to Merleau-Ponty, he makes a similar distinction to Heidegger's *Körper* and *Leib* in the distinction between "body image" and "body schema."[16] The difference between "body image" and "body schema" is the consciousness we have of the body. He states that when the body appears in consciousness it is clearly delineated from its environment. The "body *image*" is a system of such conscious images of the body that treat it as an object.[17] Yet it often focuses on one part of the body, such as a failing knee. Similar to the way in which in Heidegger a tool only becomes apparent to us in its *Zuhandenheit* when it fails in performing its function, the knee only becomes an image to the mind when it fails to do its job. These borders between body and environment are obscured, however, when one is immersed in experience. "The body *schema* functions in an integrated way with its environment, even to the extent that it frequently incorporates into itself certain objects."[18] Thus the fork or the hammer that we handle can become part of the "body schema." The constitution of this schema also involves what Gallagher calls a "prenoetic performance" of the body: "a prenoetic performance is one that helps to structure consciousness, but does not explicitly show itself in the contents of consciousness."[19] Much like Heidegger's idea of *leiben*, then, such a prenoetic performance gains knowledge of the world through embodied practice.[20] Thus, although Gallagher spends only a couple of lines on Heidegger in his book, highlighting Merleau-Ponty's philosophy instead, his distinction between "body image" and "body schema" is strikingly similar to Heidegger's distinction between *Körper*

---

15 Gallagher, *How the Body*.
16 Head and Holmes, "Sensory Disturbances"; Merleau-Ponty, *Structure of Behaviour*; Gallagher, *How the Body*, 19–25. For a comprehensive overview of the literature see Tiemersma, *Body Schema and Body Image*. In the first chapter of *How the Body Shapes the Mind*, Gallagher describes the "terminological and conceptual confusions" between the two terms. Merleau-Ponty's "schéma corporel," for example, was rendered into "body image" in Fischer's English translation of the work. Gallagher, *How the Body*, 17–39.
17 Gallagher, *How the Body*, 37.
18 Gallagher, *How the Body*, 37.
19 Gallagher, *How the Body*, 32.
20 Gallagher, *How the Body*, 36–37.

and *Leib*. Both make a distinction in order to emphasize the body in its active and practical position in the world.

However, although this distinction is apparent in both Heidegger and Gallagher, Heidegger's idea of *Leib* goes a step further than Gallagher's idea of the "body schema." Whereas "body schema" is the way in which the body is situated in the world, Heidegger's *Leib* does not just overcome the body-mind dichotomy by putting forward an idea of embodied practice, but it also overcomes the boundaries of that body by placing us *elsewhere*. The *da* of Heidegger's famous *Dasein* does not refer merely to a situatedness in our body in the world, but to being "there" rather than being, firmly positioned, here. Hence, he states in the *Zollikoner Seminare*: "Grenze des Leibens (der Leib ist nur insofern er leibt: Leib) ist der Seins-horizont, in dem ich mich aufhalte. Deshalb wandelt sich die Grenze des Leibens ständig durch die Wandlung der Reichweite meines Aufenthaltes" (*ZS*, 113; The limit of *Leiben* (*Leib* is only as it *leib*s: "*Leib*") is the horizon of being within which I sojourn. Therefore the limit of my *Leiben* changes constantly through the change in the reach of my sojourn: *ZSS*, 87). In *Da-sein* my *Leib* is oriented toward its world, and open to it.[21] So rather than contemplating the way in which my hand works, which would be to see it as *vorhanden*, rather than describing the experience of how my hand is hammering, as an intentionality of my consciousness, what Heidegger is trying to show is that when I am hammering a nail into the wall my preoccupation is with the hammer, the nail, and the wall which constitute the world that I am participating in. The major difference between Gallagher's "body schema" and Heidegger's *Leib* is that whereas the "body schema" may take a tool into its schema, still preoccupied with its own "schema," the openness and outward orientation of *Da-sein* toward the world constitutes a *Leiben* that is also always already elsewhere. That is not to say that a similar kind of absorption of the body in the world that we find in Heidegger is not also found in Gallagher—see for example his phenomenological description of grabbing a book to read

---

21 Heidegger states: "Entscheidend bleibt indessen dies, daß auch in aller Erfahrung des Leiblichen in daseinsanalytischer Sicht immer von der Grundverfassung des menschlichen Existierens—im transitiven Sinne—eines Bereiches von Welt-Offenständigkeit auszugehen ist; von Offenständigkeit also, von der her sich in deren Lichte die Bedeutsamkeiten des Begegnenden dem Menschen zusprechen." (*ZS*, 292; Nevertheless, from the Da-seinanalytic perspective, it remains decisive that in all experience of the bodily [*des Leiblichen*] one must always start with the basic constitution of human existing, that is, from being-human as Da-sein—as existing, in the transitive sense, of a domain of standing-open-toward-the-world; therefore, from this standing-open, in the light of this standing-open, the significant features of what is encountered address the human being: *ZSS*, 231).

out a passage in *How the Body Shapes the Mind*[22]—but to say that where Gallagher's "body schema" *can* be absorbed in the world, Heidegger's *Leib* exists only insofar as it is absorbed in the world.

World as Shaped by Others: "Intersubjectivity" in Heidegger

This difference in Heidegger's *Leib* and Gallagher's "body schema" carries through in their understanding of intersubjectivity, or what Heidegger calls being-with (*Mitsein*) and leads, or so I want to argue, Gallagher and Jacobson to critique Heidegger's account of intersubjectivity. In Heidegger's account we, in our engagement with objects, in our everyday familiarity with them, also stand in relation to, and come across, other people: "[d]as Feld zum Beispiel, an dem wir 'draussen' entlang gehen, zeigt sich als dem und dem gehörig, von ihm ordentlich instand gehalten, das benutzte Buch ist gekauft bei . . . , geschenkt von . . . und dergleichen. Das verankerte Boot am Strand verweist in seinem An-sich-sein auf einem Bekannten, der damit seine Fahrten unternimmt, aber auch als 'fremdes Boot' zeigt es Andere." (*SZ*, 117–8; The field, for example, along which we walk "outside" shows itself as belonging to such and such a person who keeps it in good order, the book which we use is bought at such and such a place, given by such and such a person, and so on. The boat anchored at the shore refers in its being-in-itself to an acquaintance who undertakes his voyages with it, but even as a "boat which is unknown to us," it still points to others: *BT*, 115). In my practical being in the world with objects I am thus also already surrounded by others. It might seem strange for Heidegger to start his discussion of other people with objects around us, but it points to Heidegger's belief that others cannot be understood away from the (shared) world and vice versa.

This statement needs unpacking. Just as Heidegger believes we engage with objects pragmatically, see them in their usefulness, so we engage with other people pragmatically, too. Like with tools, we always already know how to engage with other people, and do so. This fundamental way of always already being among others is what Heidegger calls being-with (*SZ*, §26). We might take a step back and think about what other people are thinking, but this is generally not how we deal with other people. "Most of the time," so Dreyfus writes, "Heidegger points out, we just work with and deal with others skillfully without having any beliefs about them or their beliefs at all."[23] At the same time, and this is why objects are relevant to how we come across others, we see others in their practical, meaningful engagement in the world too:

22 Gallagher, *How the Body*, 32.
23 Dreyfus, *Being-in-the-World*, 148.

"auch wenn die Anderen in ihrem Dasein gleichsam thematisch werden, begegnen sie nicht als vorhandene Persondinge, sondern wir treffen sie 'bei der Arbeit,' das heißt primär in ihrem In-der-Welt-sein" (*SZ*, 120; when others become, so to speak, thematic in their Dasein, they are not encountered as objectively present thing-persons, rather we meet them "at work," that is, primarily in their being-in-the-world: *BT*, 117). Other people are thus part and parcel of our meaningful environments. Their meaningful activities are part of the environments that our living bodies are immersed in: "'Welt' ist auch Dasein" (*SZ*, 118; the "world" is also Dasein: *BT*, 115).

But other people are also shaped by the world. While in *Sein und Zeit* our encounter with others stays on a certain level of abstraction, in the *Zollikoner Seminare*, Heidegger pays more attention to the fact that we encounter other people as living bodies and shows them as entangled in our meaningful, shared world. He argues against the understanding of another person's movement as expression (*Ausdruck*); instead reading movement as gesture (*Gebärde*) (*ZS*, 116; *ZSS*, 89). Movement always stands in relation to a meaningful environment, he argues, and therefore is not mere movement, or an expression of an inner thought or feeling, but rather a gesture:

> In der Philosophie müssen wir den Namen Gebärde nicht auf die Deutung "Ausdruck" beschränken, sondern müssen damit alles Sich-Betragen des Menschen als ein durch das Leiben des Leibes bestimmtes In-der-Welt-sein kennzeichnen. Jede Bewegung meines Leibes geht als eine Gebärde und damit als ein sich so und so Betragen nicht einfach in einen indifferenten Raum hinein. Vielmehr hält sich das Betragen schon immer in einer bestimmten Gegend auf, die offen ist durch das Ding, auf das ich bezogen bin, wenn ich zum Beispiel etwas in die Hand nehme. (*ZS*, 118)

> [Within philosophy we must not limit the word "gesture" merely to "expression." Instead, we must characterize all comportment of the human being as *being-in-the-world*, determined by the *Leiben* of the body. Each movement of my body as a "gesture" and, therefore, as such and such a comportment does not simply enter into an indifferent space. Rather, comportment is always already in a certain region [*Gegend*] which is open through the thing to which I am in a relationship, for instance, when I take something into my hand. (*ZSS*, 90–91)]

And when applied more directly to intersubjective relations:

> Aber was liegt in dem Phänomen des Errötens selbst? Es ist auch eine Gebärde, insofern der Errötende auf die Mitmenschen bezogen

ist. Damit sehen Sie, wie die Leiblichkeit diesen eigentümlichen ekstatischen Sinn hat. Diese betone ich so sehr, um Sie von der Ausdruck-Mißdeutung wegzubringen. Auch die französischen Psychologen mißdeuten alles als Ausdruck von etwas Innerem, statt das Leibphänomen in der mitmenschlichen Bezogenheit zu sehen. (*ZS*, 118)

[But what lies in the phenomenon of blushing itself? It too is a gesture insofar as the one who blushes is related to his fellow human beings. With this you see how bodiliness has a peculiar "ecstatic" meaning. I emphasize this to such a degree in order to get you away from the misinterpretation of "expression"! French psychologists also misinterpret everything as an expression of something interior instead of seeing the phenomena of the body in the context of which men are in relationship to each other. (*ZSS*, 91)][24]

Every movement of the human body for Heidegger is gesturing toward something, and should thus be seen as a gesture. He moves away from an idea of expression, of someone having a thought and then expressing that in her movement, toward the movement not gesturing backward, inside, but forward in regard to its meaning. In other words, we should not look at the movement of someone as something that comes from inside but indeed something that is always already ecstatic, connecting and reacting to a meaningful outside world. Just as we ourselves are *da*, then, preoccupied with the world in our *Leiben*, so others are always encountered as entangled in the world, as well. They, too, are animated by the world, and we see them as such. Hence, what we are engaging with in others is what Dreyfus calls their "directed, significant, concernful *comportment*," a totality of movements which points away from their bodies toward the things in the world they are preoccupied with.[25]

But while we are always already engaging with the way in which others are meaningfully engaging with the world, grow up doing so, we also

---

24 While Mayr and Askay have done a great job at the difficult task of translating Heidegger, I think the translation at times needs clarification, or the addition of the ambiguity from the original. In the second quoted line, for example, the English reads "It too" but the German "*Es ist auch*" also leaves open the possibility that Heidegger means to say that "It is also a gesture." The former makes more sense to how I understand Heidegger to think about blushing as a gesture, but the ambiguity of the original should be noted. "Misinterpretation of 'expression'" for "*Ausdruck-Mißdeutung*" seems to say that the word "expression" is misinterpreted, while I think Heidegger means that movements are misinterpreted as expression. "Of which men are in relationship to each other" is a rather clunky translation of "*mitmenschlichen Bezogenheit*," where something like "interhuman relation" would have sufficed.

25 Dreyfus, *Being-in-the-World*, 147.

always already engage with the world *as* others engage with it, according to Heidegger. The way in which I am made to engage with this world is just an image of how someone else is; while riding a bus, Heidegger says, anyone is like anyone (*SZ*, 126; *BT*, 123). How I eat with a fork is just how one eats with a fork. Through this shared world, being amongst objects referring to other people, we are shaped by the cultural and historical framework in place. This whole framework is what Heidegger calls *das Man*.[26] Aho writes, referring to *das Man* as "Anyone": "The anonymous 'They' or 'Anyone' refers to a totality of interconnected relations; customs, occupations, practices and cultural institutions as embodied in gestures, artifacts, monuments, and so forth. This totality of relations gives meaning to beings."[27] So not only am I always already in the world with objects, and with others using objects, I am also already with others using these objects as *one* uses them. Their gestures are my gestures; we have always already learned to be a body from others. Significantly, then, it is exactly because I am always already using objects as one uses them, because I am part of *das Man*, that I also already understand the actions, and thoughts in the actions, of other people. Their gestures are my gestures; our embodied existence is a shared one. It is because our meaningful world, and our gestures toward it, are shared that I can "count on" (*SZ*, 125; *BT*, 122) people doing things a certain way in a certain situation.[28] It is only because of this shared understanding of the world

---

26 Dreyfus famously translates "das Man" as "the one" rather than the usual "the They" which he finds misleading "since it suggests that *I* am distinguished from *them*, whereas Heidegger's whole point is that the equipment and roles of society are defined by norms that apply to *anyone*. But even translating *das Man* by 'we' or 'anyone' does not capture the normative character of the expression. *We* or *Anyone* might try to cheat the Internal Revenue Service, but still *one* pay's *one*'s taxes." Dreyfus, *Being-in-the-World*, 151–52.

27 Aho, *Heidegger's Neglect*, 20.

28 While Heidegger separates his treatment of being-with and *das Man* and never explicitly addresses their connection, I take them to be two sides of the same coin, connoting different aspects of the same understanding of intersubjectivity whereby we are always already with other people doing things with them, alongside them, against them, as *one* does them. But where being-with is emphasizing the way in which we engage with others, Heidegger's treatment of *das Man* focuses on the normative structures guiding our behavior, thereby doing away with a notion of a separate self: "*Zunächst*, 'bin' nicht 'ich' im Sinne des eigenen Selbst, sondern die Anderen in der Weise des Man" (*SZ*, 129; *Initially*, "I" "am" not in the sense of my own self, but I am the others in the mode of the they: *BT*, 125). It should be noted that, like Taylor Carman and Hubert L. Dreyfus, I take Heidegger to say that *das Man* is a basic constitution of *Dasein*, and that any authenticity modifies it. Frederick A. Olafson, in contrast, understands *das Man* in psychological terms, as something to be overcome through authenticity which is basic. But this, as Olafson himself also recognizes (but as a problem in

that I even can be surprised by other people's actions, and that I might feel the need to take a step back from my everyday interaction to contemplate the other person's beliefs. Hence we always already understand the other, because like us, they are animated by a shared world, indeed they derive their meaning from their engagement in it. All in all, in Heidegger, other people are far from the "ineffable and radical exteriority" that they are for someone like Lévinas.[29] Heidegger emphasizes that other people are those ontologically closest to us: "die Anderen sind vielmehr die, von denen man selbst sich zumeist *nicht* unterscheidet" (*SZ*, 118; Others are . . . those from whom one mostly does *not* distinguish oneself: *BT*, 115).

"Intersubjectivity" in Gallagher and Jacobson: Positioned Rather than "There"

At first view Gallagher's understanding of intersubjectivity, as shown in a number of his works, is similar to how Heidegger believes we are being-with and part of *das Man*.[30] Whereas the traditional accounts of how we attribute mental states to other people, "theory theory" and "simulation theory," state that we infer another person's mental state from the other person's behavior, turning them into theoretical problems, the "interaction theory" Gallagher proposes argues that our "immediate, non-mentalistic mode of interaction" with the world already gives us a sense of how other people think.[31] Gallagher and Jacobson state:

> Thus, what we call the mind of the other person is not something that is entirely hidden away and inaccessible. Rather, in our encounters with others we not only have perceptual access to another person's intentions, because their intentions are explicit in their embodied actions and expressive behaviors, but also their actions resonate in our own motor systems. Other persons elicit our enactive

---

Heidegger), takes away the shared world from being-with and opens up a need for "an agreement among human beings" which in Carman's and Dreyfus's accounts is taken up by *das Man*. Olafson, *Heidegger*, 242. Carman, "On Being Social"; Dreyfus, "Interpreting Heidegger"; Olafson, "Heidegger à la Wittgenstein."

29 Zahavi, "Beyond Empathy," 159. See, for example, Lévinas, Totalité et infini.

30 E.g., Gallagher, "Understanding Interpersonal Problems"; Gallagher, "Inference or Interaction"; Gallagher, *Enactivist Interventions*.

31 Gallagher and Jacobson, "Heidegger and Social Cognition," 217–19. In Gallagher and Jacobson's understanding, both in theory theory (TT) as well as simulation theory (ST) we attempt to understand others by "attempting to infer or 'mindread' the other's mental processes" (217). TT claims we do so through constructing a theory, thus applying folk psychology, whereas ST states we do not need such folk psychology as we have our own mind as a model.

response; they have an effect on us that is not reducible to a subjective simulation or an empathic response to the other's behavior but attunes our system to further possible interaction.[32]

Just as in *Sein und Zeit*, they propose a physical being with one another that gives us a non-mentalistic understanding of each other. Their analysis of intersubjectivity differs, however, from Heidegger's in that they make a distinction between primary and secondary intersubjectivity.[33] They adopt these concepts from Trevarthen, who intensively studied the interaction between infants and their mothers and who defines primary intersubjectivity as "direct face-to-face play."[34] In their article, Gallagher and Jacobson understand primary intersubjectivity as an immediate engagement with another person without the mediation from, or need of, other objects or people.[35] For example, they state that "[p]ersonal, face-to-face, emotion-rich relations [are] the kind of relations that depend heavily on primary intersubjectivity."[36] Later in the essay they talk of primary intersubjectivity as essential to relations such as friendship and love.[37] Secondary intersubjectivity, according to them, "supplements" and "enhances" primary intersubjectivity. Here, through shared attention to the world surrounding us, pragmatic contexts come into play and show us "what things mean and what they are for."[38] This leads them at the end of their discussion of secondary intersubjectivity to state that "our perception of the other person is never of an entity existing outside of a situation, but rather of an agent in a pragmatic context that throws light on the intentions, or possible intentions, of that agent."[39]

How does one square such a statement with the existence of an immediate relation in primary intersubjectivity? It is not that primary intersubjectivity is only present in early childhood (as their work in developmental psychology might suggest) for they make a point of stating that it remains present in adulthood,[40] nor is it, as the following description of

---

32 Gallagher and Jacobson, "Heidegger and Social Cognition," 220.

33 Gallagher and Jacobson, "Heidegger and Social Cognition," 119–23. There is a third aspect to intersubjectivity that Gallagher names "narrative competency," but this aspect is not further discussed in their article. For an account of narrative competency please refer to Gallagher and Hutto "Primary Interaction."

34 Trevarthen, "Foundations of Intersubjectivity," 327.

35 Gallagher and Jacobson, "Heidegger and Social Cognition," 219.

36 Gallagher and Jacobson, "Heidegger and Social Cognition," 225.

37 Gallagher and Jacobson, "Heidegger and Social Cognition," 238.

38 Gallagher and Jacobson, "Heidegger and Social Cognition," 221. See also the concept of "joint attention," for example in Turner, "Multimodal Form-Meaning Pairs."

39 Gallagher and Jacobson, "Heidegger and Social Cognition," 223.

40 Gallagher and Jacobson, "Heidegger and Social Cognition," 221.

their account of it shows, a mentalistic, disembodied interaction: "perceptions [of facial and body movements] give the infant, by the end of the first year of life, a non-mentalizing, perceptually-based embodied understanding of the intentions and dispositions of other persons."[41] In their account, then, primary intersubjectivity is embodied but does not seem to take the context, at least thematically, into account. The world only comes in explicitly in secondary intersubjectivity. So, whereas Heidegger's *das Man* is always already a *Da-sein*, being-there entangled in meaningful objects and persons meaningfully engaging with these objects, already taking part in the socio-historical practices of *das Man*, in Gallagher and Jacobson's account there is a significant difference between primary and secondary intersubjectivity, between direct contact with the other and mediated contact with them. It is from this position that they critique Heidegger for skipping over the former.

Unworldly Primary Intersubjectivity

In their article Gallagher and Jacobson critique Heidegger for ignoring primary intersubjectivity, for only paying attention to pragmatic encounters directed toward objects, and therefore for lacking a coherent understanding of immediate, emotion-rich, face-to-face relations.[42] They state that "[b]ecause Heidegger's account ignores the phenomenon of primary intersubjectivity, he is left with . . . a view that makes authentic relations with others, including relations of friendship and love, difficult to understand."[43] They have an abundance of evidence from developmental psychology for the presence of primary intersubjectivity in infants; as they show, infants discover (the body of) others first, and only through them the environment.[44] However, as Gallagher and Jacobson point out, Heidegger exactly "is not attempting to provide anything like a developmental account."[45] To a critique of a lack of an account of primary intersubjectivity in Heidegger it is therefore necessary to develop an account of primary intersubjectivity beyond the infant. Arguing for the existence of primary intersubjectivity in adults, Gallagher and Jacobson quote Wittgenstein and Scheler. The latter states: "for we certainly

---

41 Gallagher and Jacobson, "Heidegger and Social Cognition," 220.
42 Gallagher and Jacobson, "Heidegger and Social Cognition," 223–25.
43 Gallagher and Jacobson, "Heidegger and Social Cognition," 237–38.
44 Gallagher and Jacobson, "Heidegger and Social Cognition," 219–21. For evidence of the presence of primary intersubjectivity Gallagher and Jacobson cite, among other works, Allison, Puce, and McCarthy, "Social Perception from Visual Cues"; Johnson, "Recognition of Mentalistic Agents"; Gopnik and Meltzoff, *Words, Thoughts, and Theories*; Baldwin, "Infants' Ability."
45 Gallagher and Jacobson, "Heidegger and Social Cognition," 227.

believe ourselves to be directly acquainted with another person's joy in his laughter, with his sorrow and pain in his tears, with his shame in his blushing...."[46] However, is it not precisely the case that we need the shared world (in its mutually constitutive relationship with the meaningful gestures of others) to tell us about the feelings behind blushing or tearing up? Let us take the example of a student presenting a paper in an academic setting. If their face were to turn red here, everyone would think them to be nervous, even though they could be hot or have a fever. This does not need any mental reflection. Why? Because they are a student reading a paper, in front of a big group of people, in an academic institution, and so on. It is part of our shared understanding of the world that in this context one might be nervous. In other words, how can I understand the "expression" of an emotion without the shared, concrete context toward which it gestures? How can I understand tears, redness, and laughter without this context?[47]

Yet Gallagher and Jacobson might argue that context is indeed important but that it is just that: an unthematic context which supports the immediate engagement with the other. Indeed, I think that is exactly what the discussions of the body as *Leib*, and the gestures of the other person in Heidegger are pointing toward: both the immediacy of our engagement in the world (whether with an object or another person), and the inseparability of the other and objects from their contexts. To be embodied in the world for Heidegger means that we take in the whole situation, including its socio-historical background, in an *unmediated* and holistic way. To speak in the manner of Heidegger's *Dasein*, to be in the situation with the student also means to be "there" in the place of the nervous student. I would argue, therefore, that if there is anything missing in Heidegger's account of being-with and *das Man* it is not primary intersubjectivity but rather secondary intersubjectivity if understood as mediated by objects.[48] There is, in Heidegger, no mediation via either

46 Scheler, *Nature of Sympathy*, 260.
47 It bears mentioning that we are of course more familiar with some people's gestures than we are with others. Because we have, as mentioned earlier, always already learned to be a body from others (and continue to do so), within a meaningful, socio-cultural environment, we usually understand better the behavior in a context of close family and partners than of colleagues, and similarly better those gestures of the people within the same culture as of those without. In general, *the extent to which* gestures and our meaningful environments are shared also depends on our grain of analysis. For more on grains of analysis in the context of human behavior, see Rietveld and Kiverstein, "Rich Landscape," 329–30.
48 This is also the answer, I believe, to a problem posed by Overgaard in a recent article. He states—via Merleau-Ponty (190)—the following: "the meaning of the gesture is, as Merleau-Ponty says, 'not given but rather understood,' and that means we still need an account of how we understand it" (77). I would

my body, objects or other people, but rather one meaningful world, one "Verweisungsganzheit" (*SZ*, 70; totality of references: *BT*, 69), with which we, for the largest part, engage immediately. If there is anything like secondary intersubjectivity in Heidegger, in which others are *mediated* through objects, this secondary intersubjectivity marks a step back from our fundamental embodied existence in the world.[49]

Even so, these arguments take nothing away from Gallagher and Jacobson's concern that it seems that Heidegger is more interested in objects than other people. However, as I will argue in the following section, such a reading of being-with overlooks several paragraphs in which Heidegger concerns himself with our direct engagement to others. But not only does Heidegger indeed pay attention to something akin to the "face-to-face" but he is also concerned about an issue similar to the difference between primary and secondary intersubjectivity: Heidegger emphasizes in our engagement with others the difference between focusing one's (immediate) attention on others and focusing so on objects.

---

argue that in Heidegger we exactly find such an account, namely in his concept of *das Man*. Heidegger's answer, I believe, would be that the shared world we live in and the meaningful gestures that point toward it are mutually constitutive. Overgaard, "Heidegger on Embodiment," 77; Merleau-Ponty, *Phenomenology of Perception*, 190.

49 As an example of such a stepping back from our immediate relation to the other, Heidegger talks of empathy (*Einfühlung*). An attempt at empathy, Heidegger states, is a consequence of not recognizing that we are already in understanding of each other, are being-with, partly due to the fact that we hide our true feelings toward one another. Instead of our embodied being in the world, therefore, with empathy we consciously start to deliberate what the other might be feeling, and thus, according to Heidegger, we take a step back from the world again: "'Einfühlung' konstituiert nicht erst das Mitsein, sondern ist auf dessen Grunde erst möglich und durch die vorherrschenden defizienten Modi des Mitseins in ihrer Unumgänglichkeit motiviert." (*SZ*, 125; "Empathy" does not first constitute being-with, but is first possible on its basis, and is motivated by the prevailing deficient modes of being-with in their inevitability: *BT*, 121). Just as contemplating my arm while hammering takes me away from my involvement in a world disclosing task, such empathy artificially removes us from our being-in-the-world and being-with-others. Such empathy to Heidegger is not only a step away from the fundamental ontology of how we always already are in the world, but it also brings forth a disingenuous stance towards the other we encounter, he writes: "Dieses 'rucksichtloses' Mitsein 'rechnet' mit den Anderen, ohne dass es ernsthaft 'auf sie zählt' oder auch nur mit ihnen 'zu tun haben' möchte." (*SZ*, 125; "Inconsiderate" being-with "reckons" with others without seriously "counting on them" or even wishing "to have anything to do" with them: *BT*, 119).

The Face-to-Face in Heidegger: Authentic *Fürsorge*

Gallagher and Jacobson's critique of a lack of primary intersubjectivity in Heidegger's concept of being-with also points to the fact that he seems to pay more attention to objects than other people. Other commenters on Heidegger's account of being-with, too, have pointed out that he seems less interested in face-to-face relations than he is in people working *with* each other in their everyday concerns in the world; Sartre, for example, describes Heidegger's understanding of being-with as a "crew" (*équipe*).[50] However, such a description of being-with also leaves much of Heidegger's discussion of it in *Sein und Zeit* underexamined. This problem is largely caused by Heidegger himself; the fact that he starts, as we have seen, his analysis with objects instead of people certainly invites a reading which stresses objects. Nevertheless, Heidegger seems repeatedly worried about the ways in which, and the extent to which, we pay attention to others "face-to-face." He, for example, discusses "defizienten und indifferenten Modi . . . bis zur *Rücksichtslosigkeit* und dem Nachsehen, das die Gleichgültigkeit leitet" (*SZ*, 123; deficient and indifferent modes up to the point of inconsiderateness and the tolerance which is guided by indifference: *BT*, 119). This attention to the other is most clear in his discussion of *Fürsorge*, which Joan Stambaugh translates as "concern" (*SZ*, 121; *BT*, 118). *Fürsorge* is the way in which we engage with others, which stands in contrast to the way in which we "take care of" (*besorgen*) objects. *Fürsorge* is concerned with the other person as *Dasein*, as a being meaningfully engaged in the world; Heidegger opens his discussion of it with the statement that provision of "Nahrung und Kleidung, die Pflege des kranken Leibes ist Fürsorge" (*SZ*, 121; food and clothing, and the nursing of the sick body is concern: *BT*, 118). But to emphasize that our concern for others is often deficient, he immediately thereafter references the common meaning of "Fürsorge" in German, namely that as social welfare, a system he deems necessary only because of our deficient everyday caring for others (*SZ*, 121; *BT*, 118). Heidegger's treatment of *Fürsorge* thus shows that being-with for him is more than a working together with others as a crew to get things done, or a relation that focuses in the first place on objects; we are engaged with the needs of others too. Indeed, he continues with discussing the degree of our openness to others (in "Rücksicht" and "Nachsicht"). And, most importantly for our present discussion, he makes a difference between authentic and inauthentic *Fürsorge*, and through this a significant difference between whether we

---

50 Sartre, *L'être et le néant*, 303. See also Dreyfus, *Being-in-the-World*, 148–49; and Zahavi, "Beyond Empathy."

pay attention to objects, or to other people as they are engaged meaningfully with the world.

On the one hand, we can "leap in" (*einspringen*) for others, by which we take care of the things the other is meant to take care of for themselves. The other person, thereby, is "aus seiner Stelle geworfen" (displaced) and "kann ... zum Abhängigen und Beherrschten werden" (*SZ*, 122; can become someone who is dependent and dominated: *BT*, 118–19). This is, according to Heidegger, what happens when we focus our attention on the object that the other is taking care of instead of focusing on the other herself in her meaningful engagement in the world, as authentic *Fürsorge* does. This authentic form Heidegger calls "leaping ahead" (*vorspringen*): "diese Fürsorge, die wesentlich die eigentliche Sorge—das heißt die Existenz des Anderen betrifft und nicht ein *Was*, das er besorgt, verhilft dem Anderen dazu, *in* seiner Sorge sich durchsichtig und *für* sie *frei* zu machen" (*SZ*, 122; this concern which essentially pertains to authentic care—that is, it pertains to the existence of the other, and not to a *what* which it [the other] takes care of—helps the other to become transparent to himself *in* his care and *free* for it: *BT*, 119).[51] With this distinction between the inauthentic leaping in and the authentic leaping ahead of concern, then, which has something of the old proverbial "give a man a fish and feed him for a day; teach a man to fish and you feed him for a lifetime," we find exactly what Gallagher and Jacobson are looking for in Heidegger: an account of an immediate and meaningful engagement with the other. Even if this relationship still has something crew-like about it, and is certainly still pragmatic—Heidegger later describes this authentic relation in terms of "das gemeinsame Sicheinsetzen für dieselbe Sache" (*SZ*, 122; devot[ing] themselves to the same thing in common: *BT*, 119)—it is certainly a crew of people engaged with the others as who they are: meaningfully acting people.

A Pragmatic Encounter with the Other

Even if there is an account of the face-to-face in Heidegger, there still may be a fear that an immediate, pragmatic approach to the other person, especially in their own pragmatic engagements, may lead to a treatment of them as an object, to a lack of consideration for their feelings. This reservation is certainly found in Gallagher and Jacobson: "In an analysis of intersubjectivity which is made exclusively in terms of secondary intersubjectivity, and for Heidegger, that means in terms of the ready-to-hand

---

51 For more on "leaping ahead," especially in relation to authenticity in division II of *Sein und Zeit* see §60, in particular page 285. "Leaping ahead" (*vorspringen*) seems here, too, to be linked to "anticipation" (*vorlaufen*) as the possibility of helping others to become authentic.

contexts within which we find others, there is a certain kind of interchangeableness amongst others. The everyday public world is often characterized by Heidegger as a workplace filled with equipment, or as a world of commodities, where others are encountered in terms of their particular functions."[52] But why do people become interchangeable if we encounter them in their pragmatic encounters with useful objects? Do I not prefer one kind of shoe over another and therefore one shoemaker over another? Heidegger certainly makes sure to imply as much when he first talks about encountering others through the shared world: "Imgleichen begegnet im verwendeten Material der Hersteller oder 'Lieferant' desselben als der, der gut oder schlecht 'bedient'" (*SZ*, 117; the producer or "supplier" is encountered in the material used as one who "serves" well or badly: *BT*, 115). It is important to recognize that we not only discover the other person through the objects we engage with, but that we also discover their view of the world in this way.[53] Through a shoe we not only understand why a shoemaker is useful but also how he thinks a shoe should be made. Indeed, that we also find other people's hopes and dreams in the objects we uncover is what Heidegger implies in the quote that started this chapter: "[Dasein] *findet sich* primär und ständig *in den Dingen*, weil es, sie betreuend, von ihnen bedrängt, immer irgendwie in den Dingen ruht" ([Dasein] finds *itself* primarily and constantly *in things* because, tending them, distressed by them, it always in some way or other rests in things).[54] Thus we do not discover only the *usefulness* of another *Dasein* in the object, but also the way in which they regard the world, how they are occupied by it. In such an understanding of the objects we deal with, we also start to make distinctions between different people, distinctions that will lead to friendships and love.[55] Surely, we choose our friends and lovers for many different reasons but many of them have to do

---

52 Gallagher and Jacobson, "Heidegger and Social Cognition," 225.

53 Gallagher and Jacobson also critique Heidegger for a secondary intersubjectivity "that is just opposite to the way it is described by developmental psychologists" (227). In Heidegger, they state, we establish relations to objects and through them with other people, while for developmental psychology we rather give meaning to objects through others. However, this is again to not recognize that Heidegger is not interested in the process of the construction of meaning but rather in pointing out that the world we live in is already full of meaning that we encounter through objects (and people engaging with these objects) on a daily basis. See also Olafson, *Heidegger*, 146–50 for a similar critique to that of Gallagher and Jacobson, as well as Dreyfus, *Being-in-the-World*, 142–62 for an extensive reply to this critique.

54 Heidegger, *Grundprobleme der Phänomenologie*, 226; Heidegger, *Basic Problems*, 159.

55 While Gallagher and Jacobson acknowledge the possibility of distinguishing between people in terms of the quality of what they do, they dismiss this

with how they deal with objects. We like our friends because they react to objects in a certain way and because they like certain objects and dislike others. We like our friends because they like the same TV shows as us and we might like our lovers because they fidget constantly with their clothing. I have already tried to show that there is no lack of primary intersubjectivity in Heidegger if it means an *immediate* engagement with the other, nor does he lack an account of the face-to-face, but neither does his pragmatic approach take away from such things as love and friendship, it just makes these relationships less abstract and more engaged. Of course, it is significant to human relationships how the other thinks and feels, but all this is a thinking and feeling about the world, in meaningful situations. This view of love and friendship may seem pragmatic, and it is, but that is exactly why we can never reason our way into love. A step back from this pragmatism, however, is only a denying of a relation we are always already in.

Reasserting Roles through Anxiety

Yet it is exactly in this stepping back that Heidegger's discussion of a worldly-animated body moves decisively into German modernist concerns, in the resistance *Leiben* meets in what he calls "anxiety" (Angst; SZ, §40). Heidegger's discussion of anxiety explores the experience of the world as recalcitrant, an experience that will reappear in the texts discussed in the subsequent chapters. For Heidegger, such a resistance to an absorbed *Leiben* is an opportunity for a reevaluation of our practices and to think about how we, as socio-historically shaped beings, can live authentically.

In Heidegger's understanding of anxiety the world both becomes meaningless and comes to stand out. Heidegger writes: "*das Wovor der Angst ist die Welt als solche.* Die völlige Unbedeutsamkeit, die sich im Nichts und Nirgends bekundet, bedeutet nicht Weltabwesenheit, sondern besagt, daß das innerweltlich Seiende an ihm selbst so völlig belanglos ist, daß auf dem Grunde dieser *Unbedeutsamkeit* des Innerweltlichen die Welt in ihrer Weltlichkeit sich einzig noch aufdrängt" (*SZ*, 187; that *what anxiety is about is the world as such.* The utter insignificance which makes itself known in the nothing and nowhere does not signify the absence of world, but means that innerwordly beings in themselves are so completely unimportant that, on the basis of this *insignificance* of what innerwordly, the world in its wordliness is all that obtrudes itself: *BT*, 181). How are we to understand such a statement? Dreyfus rightly points to the link Heidegger here makes between the obtrusiveness (Aufdringlichkeit)

---

possibility as an account toward love or friendship as soon as it arises ("Heidegger and Social Cognition," 225).

of anxiety and the obtrusiveness found in the *Unzuhandenheit* of tools.[56] The *Unzuhandenheit* of a tool makes it, by being broken, missing, or "in the way," stand out because it cannot be used without thought: these tools become obtrusive in their *un*usefulness (*SZ*, 72–76; *BT*, 72–75). This duality of meaninglessness and standing out, then, is not so strange when we remember that objects have meaning through our practical use. Hence, exactly when our practical engagement fails, we become aware of how it always already had meaning through our use of it, and now this tool and its meaning, as well as our practices, come to stand out. What is shown, then, is not the world both as nothing and as obtrusive, but rather two worlds; on the one hand the world-in-itself, a world independent from meaning "we" have always already given it through the practices of *das Man*, and on the other hand the world as *Umwelt* ("die Welt in ihrer Weltlichkeit": *SZ*, 187; *BT*, 181), as always already experienced in a *certain* way. The very difference between these two worlds then shows the second, and our embodied practices that shape it, as historically constructed, and causes anxiety.

For Heidegger, the question that arises out of this moment of recalcitrance that causes anxiety is not so much about *how* we can come to inhabit this situation, but rather *for what*. He sees anxiety as an opportunity to re-assert our roles. Heidegger believes that faced with anxiety we usually just "flee" into *das Man*, whereby anxiety is thus not a long-term problem. But anxiety also opens up a space for authenticity. What Heidegger calls "Eigentlichkeit," usually translated as "authenticity,"[57] describes for him the way in which we can come to own, take responsibility for, our actions. It is useful, as John Haugeland points out in essay on the topic, to think of Heidegger's discussion of authenticity in terms of truth.[58] "Truth" in Heidegger is not an absolute, transcendental version of the truth. Rather, truth for Heidegger is the historical way in which we are always already engaged with objects and other people in the world. Truth's reference, therefore, can only be the (social-historically shaped) agent. Falsehood, in this picture, rests on inconsistency; doing something one way one time and differently another time. The only way in which we can be consistent in our actions, then, is to be consistent in who we are, that is, in our identity or role.[59] This consistency in who we are

---

56 Dreyfus, *Being-in-the-world*, 178–80.

57 John Haugeland's translation of the term as "ownedness" is a notable exception. See Haugeland, "Truth and Finitude"; and Haugeland, *Dasein Disclosed*.

58 Haugeland, "Truth and Finitude," 50.

59 It might be useful here to think of Uexküll and his statement that each animal has its environment (or indeed Kiverstein and Rietveld's comparable statement that a form of life implies a niche and *vice versa*; see chapter 4 of this book). Consistency in the *Umwelt* depends on the consistency of the animal (identity).

Heidegger calls "Entschlossenheit," usually translated as "resoluteness" (*SZ*, 297; *BT*, 284). Thus, as Dreyfus sums it up, "resolute Dasein takes over a *determinate identity* that it is ready steadfastly to maintain even in adversity. . . ."[60] Truth of entities and actions in the world are made possible by such resoluteness.

To get a better grip on the concept of resoluteness and its place in modernist thought, it is useful to see what such resoluteness aims to counter. The kind of everyday behavior that Heidegger calls "inauthentic" (Uneigentlichkeit) is defined by a constant "falling prey" (Verfallen) to the world. Heidegger describes this in terms of constant movement. Dasein is tempted, curious, and constantly busy (*SZ*, §38). It wants new experiences, reassured by *das Man* that this is what a full life looks like (*SZ*, 177; *BT*, 171). Yet for Heidegger this makes Dasein "bodenlos" (*SZ*, 177; groundless: *BT*, 170) and—not unlike Theresa May's infamous "citizen of nowhere"—"überall und nirgends" (*SZ*, 177; everywhere and nowhere: *BT*, 170). Heidegger is thus arguing against cosmopolitanism and distraction. He writes that while we might think that encountering foreign cultures might lead to a "erst echten Aufklärung des Daseins über sich selbst" (*SZ*, 178; first genuine enlightenment of Dasein about itself: *BT*, 178), such encounters only give us more meanings, more ways of doing things, without asking what all these different ways of seeing are *for*. From the standpoints of the texts discussed in the following chapters, Heidegger's dismissal of encounters with foreign environments seems curious, as encounters with unfamiliarity are precisely what cause anxiety in these other texts. If Heidegger thinks that anxiety provides a road to authenticity, engagements with unfamiliar cultures might exactly be a way into authenticity. Even if he believes that foreign cultures do not offer useful new possibilities for action, they would nevertheless offer an understanding of "die Welt in ihrer Weltlichkeit." Instead, how anxiety comes about remains unclear in Heidegger's account, and foreign cultures, for him, merely feed into inauthentic distraction.

Opposed to this inauthentic distracted reacting and searching, for Heidegger, stands authentic attentive acting. In authenticity, new meaning, learning, is only of interest to the agent to the extent that it develops their chosen role or identity.[61] Only in light of such a role can we engage with objects and other people meaningfully and attentively. Because

---

The *Umwelt* can only change if we become a "different animal," that is, are inconsistent in our identity/practices. Rietveld and Kiverstein, "Rich Landscape."

60 Dreyfus, "Responses," 311.

61 Heidegger also puts this distinction in terms of (his lengthy discussion of) time, when he writes that authentic Dasein has a clear aim or goal and is thus preoccupied with the future, while an aimless inauthentic Dasein is preoccupied by the present, by what is next (*SZ*, 346–49).

we become attentive to what matters in our roles—in the same way in which, as we saw earlier, authentic being-with-others is attentive to the comportment of others—the role or identity that is taken on in this way shapes the way in which we develop further. We become better at our roles, more skilled practitioners of the tasks that are meaningful to that role. Such a role thus gives shape to the way in which the world appears to us. Heidegger differentiates between inauthentic Dasein finding itself in a general situation (Lage) and resolute, authentic Dasein begetting a concrete one (Situation: *SZ*, 299–300; *BT*, 287). The former loses itself in accidental opportunities that arise because everything is a possibility, whereas the latter begets possibilities, it "is . . . *acting*" (*BT*, 287; *handelt*: *SZ*, 300). In other words, authentic Dasein, by taking on a guiding role or purpose, gives the environment definition.

This is all not to say, however, and Heidegger is very clear about this, that authentic Dasein is not socio-historically shaped, or that in authenticity we get out of our worldly-animated body somehow. In beautiful terms of embodied adaptation, he writes that authenticity is only a "modifiziertes Ergreifen dieser" (*SZ*, 179; modified grasp of everydayness: *BT*, 172). It also does not seem to be the case that authentic Dasein comports itself in the same way as inauthentic Dasein does but with awareness.[62] Rather, authentic Dasein commits itself to its historicity—at an arbitrary point, it seems—and behaves in accordance with this history. Haugeland writes: "insofar as Dasein is owned, it is owned as historical. This means, among other things, that resolute Dasein discloses its current possibilities from out of a heritage that it takes over—that is, takes responsibility for."[63] In other words, at the point where inauthentic and authentic Dasein diverge we might still be acting in the same way, but their further development differs. Through their focused attention on their identities, rather than fleeing blindly into what happens around us, the direction of further learning differs. Heidegger's solution to anxiety, to our realization that we are worldly-animated bodies, is thus not an adjustment of our goals to whatever else is happening in the environment. Rather, it is an inflexibility in light of one's own identity that one takes on and takes responsibility for. Authentic *Dasein* holds onto its identity as much as possible no matter the consequences or problems.[64] Bodily adaptation, the learning of new skills, only develops around that center.

---

62 See e.g., Morgan, "Benjamin, Heidegger," 101.
63 Haugeland, "Truth and Finitude," 70. Cf. *SZ*, 383.
64 As Haugeland explains it, Heidegger's concept of "being-toward-death" (*Sein-zum-Tode*; *SZ*, 234) is meant to assure that if and only if we can no longer sustain our identity in the world, we give it up. Haugeland, "Truth and Finitude," 67–69.

Heidegger's emphasis on authenticity thus focuses our attention on the fact that in thinking about adaptation we should not only think of the "how" but also of the "why." What is it we want to achieve in adaptation? What are the goals that the socio-material environment can become meaningful for? What skills are relevant for which roles? Heidegger suggests that it is important to have a clear sense of purpose as a direction around which the world gains its meaning and in light of which skills and habits can adapt and develop to that environment. As we will see in the next chapter, we find this emphasis on purpose also in Rainer Maria Rilke's *Die Aufzeichnungen des Malte Laurids Brigge*.

Conclusion

Gallagher and Jacobson raise important questions about Heidegger's attention to face-to-face encounters. He certainly seems more interested in how people ride a bus together than in these people having meaningful conversations. It is at least peculiar that he starts his discussion of being-with with the observation that we encounter the farmer through the field we walk past. Nevertheless, his account of *das Man* shows that he certainly believes that we do not only encounter others in objects but also that others are central to how we understand objects. Moreover, his discussion of *Fürsorge* opens up a space in Heidegger's *Sein und Zeit* beyond an analysis of being-with as merely a crew of people acting together, toward the immediate face-to-face relations Gallagher and Jacobson are looking for. In authentic *Fürsorge* we do not engage with the objects of the other person's engagement but, in line with how Heidegger describes our understanding of the other's physical movement in the *Zollikoner Seminare* as gesture, we engage exactly with the other person *as* engaging meaningfully with our shared world, as always already "tied into" a meaningful context. If there is anything missing from Heidegger's fundamental ontology of the other, then, it is not the immediate, "face-to-face" relation of primary intersubjectivity but rather a *secondary* intersubjectivity, the *mediation* of our relation to the other through objects.

Gallagher and Jacobson's critique of Heidegger's lack of an account of primary intersubjectivity shares, therefore, the same assumption that drove the critiques of Merleau-Ponty and Sartre: that the lack of a discussion of the body as a *Körper*, rather than being an indication of a more radical position on embodiment, means that embodiment is insufficiently acknowledged in Heidegger's account of being-in-the-world. An attention to Heidegger's understanding of the body as *Leib*, as laid out in the *Zollikoner Seminare*, reveals the extent to which *Dasein* is always already immersed in its world. In Heidegger's view, embodied practice goes beyond the situated subject *into* the world: it is already always also elsewhere. When I am sitting here I am with the birds that I hear outside, with the table that I feel in front of me, and with the audience that I am addressing. Far from being self-contained, I am "there," and in so being I am also always already involved in the socio-historical framework constituted by these objects and people, or what Heidegger calls *das Man*. In such a view of intersubjectivity, the other *Dasein* is always already engaged with immediately and in a meaningful context. The model of ecstatic involvement we can take away from Heidegger, then, is one of immediacy where the division between primary and secondary intersubjectivity that underlies much research on intersubjectivity in the cognitive sciences since Trevarthen is replaced with the (ethically important) distinction between paying attention to objects and paying attention to other people. This model opens up a space for thinking about intersubjectivity away from mediation toward a holistic picture, different parts of which we focus on in our embodied involvement. We might focus on objects but they are still shaped and made meaningful by others, and we may focus on others but they equally are shaped by a shared environment. This model also helps us investigate literary characters anew. It helps turn our attention, in subsequent chapters, to how the bodies of characters in literature show how their environments are meaningful to them, and how these bodies therefore might show us new worlds of meaning.

The fear caused by Heidegger's radical stance on embodiment stems from the assumption that defining human relationships in terms of practicality results in our relationships becoming impersonal and interchangeable. How do we account for love and friendship when usefulness is understood as the primary way of relating to people? A pragmatic relationship with another person, however, does not mean that they become interchangeable. As argued, to see someone as the maker of my shoe, does not mean I cannot prefer him as a shoemaker over all the others. Love and friendship, indeed, may be more grounded in physical "in-the-world" relations than we would like to think. The way we watch a Disney movie together may indeed be a more fundamental relation than staring into each other's eyes. But even if this is so, Heidegger never states that we cannot take a mental step back from our pragmatic being-in-the-world, from our *Dasein*, but such a position just may obscure more than it reveals.

Anxiety, as caused by the environment's recalcitrant resistance of exactly this kind of everyday meaningful comportment, of our *Leiben*, situates Heidegger's thought in German modernist concerns. I take the texts discussed in this book to be concerned with the loss of this everyday meaningful comportment described in *Sein und Zeit*, as well as the anxiety that this loss causes and the attempt to find this comportment anew. Heidegger, too, finds in anxiety an opportunity to re-situate oneself anew. But it is not enough, Heidegger reminds us, to merely adapt. For the environment to become truly useful again, we need to know *for what*.

Thus we need to choose a role or purpose that can be the center of meaning, *for which* we do what we do.

Heidegger's analysis (rather than being the ultimate theoretical horizon of this monograph) provides us with questions that will be brought into further relief and complexity by the more poetic explorations in the texts discussed in the following chapters. What exactly causes anxiety and what does it feel like? How can we adhere to our roles and goals instead of getting distracted, even through adversity? How do we adapt physically? And what might be the role of others and of literature itself in finding our way in new or no longer familiar environments? The texts of the following chapters explore these and other questions of the how and why of adaptation through the nuanced particularity their authors offer in their (literary) texts.

In 1927, the same year that *Sein und Zeit* was published, Heidegger gave the set of lectures known as *Die Grundprobleme der Phänomenologie* in which he also discusses Rilke's work.[65] In the text, in which Heidegger further develops some of the ideas central to *Sein und Zeit*, Heidegger quotes in full a famous passage from Rilke's *Die Aufzeichnungen des Malte Laurids Brigge* in which its main character looks at the remains of a destroyed house on the wall of the remaining neighboring house. Heidegger uses the scene to argue that poetry can disclose our existence as situated in the socio-material world. Rilke's text, according to Heidegger, shows the environment as *Umwelt*. In the chapter that follows, I turn to this text. Rilke's vivid poetic descriptions of a particular experience of the recalcitrance of an unknown Paris and the anxiety that it causes offers a microscopic rendering of the kind of modernist mismatch between bodily habits and unfamiliar environments that Heidegger's concept of anxiety hints at. In this move from Heidegger to Rilke's text, the latter's literary poetics viscerally attend us to the particularities of an experience of anxiety: what it feels like. It is not that philosophy cannot, or does not, do this. Benjamin's work is a great example of philosophy using (literary) particularity.[66] But Heidegger, despite his linguistic playfulness with neologisms such as *Zuhandenheit*, mainly does not. And Rilke does. It is no coincidence that Heidegger does not merely point to Rilke's passage in his lecture but quotes it in its entirety. Heidegger clearly recognizes that there is something to be gained from this kind of close attention to

---

65 Heidegger, *Grundprobleme der Phänomenologie*, 244–46.

66 I want to avoid oversimplifying the relation between philosophy and literature by generalizing it. As Toril Moi writes: "attempts to define the relationship between philosophy and literature have often been formalistic in the sense that they set out a list of binary oppositions (universal versus particular, reason versus imagination, insight versus emotion, argument versus form) intended to settle the question once and for all. Such lists often disappoint." Moi, "Adventure of Reading," 126. See also Eldridge, introduction, 5.

the particularity of individual experience. Rilke's text, as a set of diary entries, sometimes taken from his own life, is testament to the nuances of human experience and its seemingly ambiguous, even contradictory, nature. It explores the difficulty of making sense of experience and putting it into words; at times it raises questions without answering them. Rather than conceptualizing anxiety as Heidegger does, Rilke makes it viscerally palpable. Hence Rilke's text does not function here as a mere illustration of philosophical theories (nor do any of the other literary texts that follow Rilke's in this monograph). Instead, Rilke's text helps us dive further into the complexities of the experience of a recalcitrant world and possible ways of overcoming it. Indeed, Rilke's text is particularly relevant for my discussion because it explores writing and literature themselves not as merely exposing the way in which our perception of the environment is historically structured (as Heidegger reads that particular scene from Rilke's text), but also as tools for trying to negotiate unfamiliar environments.

2: Rainer Maria Rilke's *Die Aufzeichnungen des Malte Laurids Brigge*: Writing as Practice

> *Aber sieh nur, was für ein Schicksal, ich, vielleicht der armsäligste von diesen Lesenden, ein Ausländer: ich habe einen Dichter.*
>
> [But see what good fortune I have, I, perhaps the most paltry of all these readers, a foreigner: I have a poet.]
>
> —Rainer Maria Rilke[1]

> *The word curious derives from the Latin cura, which also gives us both cure and care. Curiosity is a cure for self-absorption, the cure being to care about the world and lay down roots in it again. Reading and writing sentences is a means of laying down these roots, of achieving absorbedness.*
>
> —Joe Moran[2]

THAT EMBODIED HABITS shape animals' perceptions of the world is fascinatingly illustrated by a scene from Rilke's *Die Aufzeichnungen des Malte Laurids Brigge* (The Notebooks of Malte Laurids Brigge, 1910)—a fictional collection of found notes written by its titular character. The scene is set at Malte's maternal family home. In the words of the mother to her son, it was customary in summer that the Brahe family would have tea outside on the terrace. At a certain hour, the post would arrive and would be brought out by Ingeborg—whose relation to the Brahe family remains unclear. Malte's mother explains that during Ingeborg's fatal illness the family had time "sich ihres Kommens zu entwöhnen" (*MLB*, 77; to get used to her not being there: *N*, 52). But on the Thursday after Ingeborg's funeral "da kam sie" (*MLB*, 77; she came: *N*, 52). All the people at the table were quietly awaiting Ingeborg's arrival with the mail, Malte's mother was about to ask what was keeping her, when one of the dogs ran towards Ingeborg:

---

1   *MLB* 35; *N*, 23.
2   Moran, *First You Write a Sentence*, 210; emphasis original.

Dann raste er auf sie zu, wie immer, Malte, genau wie immer, und erreichte sie; denn er begann rund herum zu springen, Malte, um etwas, was nicht da war, und dann hinauf an ihr, um sie zu lecken, gerade hinauf. Wir hörten ihn winseln vor Freude, und wie er so in die Höhe schnellte, mehrmals rasch hintereinander, hätte man wirklich meinen können, er verdecke sie uns mit seinen Sprüngen. Aber da heulte es auf einmal, und er drehte sich von seinem eigenen Schwunge in der Luft um und stürzte zurück, merkwürdig ungeschickt, und lag ganz eigentümlich flach da und rührte sich nicht. (*MLB*, 78)

[Then he raced towards her, as he always did, Malte, just as he always did, and he reached her, because he began to leap up all around, Malte, around something that wasn't there, and then he climbed up her, to lick her face, right up. We could hear him whimpering with joy, and the way he bounded up high, several times in a row, quickly, one might really have thought that he was obscuring her with his jumping. But then all of a sudden there was a howl and he twisted round in the air midway through one of his leaps and fell back, oddly clumsily, and just lay there, peculiarly flat, and wouldn't move. (*N*, 54)]

In this scene, Rilke thus sets up a habitual situation: the summer days where the Brahes all have tea around the table on the terrace and where at a certain predictable hour, Ingeborg would come and bring the mail. Even after an apparently lengthy illness, they have not completely lost the habit of expecting her to arrive. But only the dog's habits are so rigid as to fail to notice the change immediately. If Uexküll only shortly discusses such false perceptions, sensorimotor failures based on false expectations run through Rilke's novel.[3] Like the dog in his changed surroundings, the work's titular character is thrown off by an unfamiliar environment time and again. The dog's debilitated position at the end of the scene, flat and motionless, mirrors Malte's own debilitation as he describes it in his notes.

Socio-culturally situated as Malte's habits are in the Danish aristocracy from which he hails, they are met with difficulty in the city of Paris. His engagements with the for him unfamiliar environment of Paris are resisted by its objects, which, like Heidegger's recalcitrant objects, "make attempts to escape from their applications" [*N*, 105; "machen Versuche, sich ihren Anwendungen zu entziehen: *MLB*, 153). Because the objects are no longer transparently bending to his use, he is distracted in his task. At the same time, the new environment elicits old, often negative, habits and memories; for example, he sees a destroyed wall which reminds him of masturbation or wet dreams and elicits the former. Malte's description

---

3   He calls this "magic" and indeed talks of reports of dogs' magic experiences but does not elaborate. Uexküll and Kriszat, *Streifzüge*, 84–91.

of his relationship to his material environment in these notes, the way in which his sensorimotor expectations turn out to be mistaken, how it inhibits certain habitual movements and elicits others, and the pragmatic terms he uses to do so, opens up a space from which to consider Malte's engagement and experience in light of theories of embodied cognition.

An embodied approach to the socio-material environment in *Malte Laurids Brigge* helps explore the novel's treatment of individuality, what it discusses as "life" (e.g., *MLB*, 171; *N*, 118). "Life," for Rilke, is that which is opposed to "fate." It is, as Robert Vilain explains, "being itself, beyond historical contingency . . . a mode in which [individuality] can be fully realized."[4] This concept of "life," understood to be Malte's existential goal, has the potential to challenge any reading of *Malte Laurids Brigge* that reads Malte's existence in socio-culturally contingent terms only. Writing in 1997, Manfred Engel understands such sociological readings as a general problem of Rilke scholarship. In his afterword to the text, referring to the 58th entry of the work in which the distinction between "fate" and "life" is discussed, he writes that (personal and socio-historical) context is only important to Rilke as it obscures access to the actually real ("eigentlich Wirklichen").[5] "Fate," or the ways in which the socio-material environment shapes, sustains, and inhibits different kinds of behavior, is thus only interesting to Rilke, according to Engel, as far as it obstructs the individuality of "life."

This chapter, however, shows that Rilke makes this idea of an individual life itself part of Malte's socio-cultural past. The histories that Malte rewrites as examples of attempts at finding individuality, are exactly stories he remembers from a little green book he read as a child. In other words, the idea of individual agency is itself, the novel shows, one that is socio-culturally provided.

Thus Malte's underlying engagement with these stories offers a way of thinking about how we might be able to negotiate our goals with and through a given socio-cultural environment. What underlies the fictional space of the heroes, namely, is Malte's more interesting dynamic manipulation of literature and history as part of his socio-material environment. In rewriting these histories through the perspectives of its heroes, Malte reenacts these heroes' actions, while at the same time reshaping his understanding of his own situation. Especially in his retelling of the prodigal son, it is hard to tell where Malte begins and the prodigal son ends. If Paris is debilitating, Malte nevertheless finds an involved engagement in literature (a motif of the absorbing potential of art that runs through the novel).

---

4   Vilain, explanatory notes, 181.
5   Engel, afterword, 341, n. 39.

This chapter draws out Malte's manipulation of these histories through more contemporary discussions of play (Di Paolo, Rohde, and De Jaegher) and so-called niche-building (Gibson) in the cognitive sciences and ecological psychology. Moreover, it explores the text's pragmatic attitude to literature through contemporary philosopher and cognitive scientist Alva Noë's conception of artworks as "strange tools." Noë's Heideggerian approach to art as objects that "re-organize" us, helps us explore the ways in which literature is used by Malte in restructuring his own environment. Through this dialogue with Noë's thought, in this chapter I argue that Malte, in rewriting these histories, attempts to materially create a nevertheless virtual, because fictional, environment that can support and sustain his attempt at individuality. Even if this attempt fails, Malte's manipulation of fictional others does provide agency and involved engagement. It helps him overcome, if only on paper, the claustrophobia, debilitation, and self-reflection induced by the recalcitrant objects that oppose everyday movements. His manipulation of these histories thus offers a picture of how we might leverage our environments, and literature more specifically, in such a way as to support our goals.

By reading *Malte Laurids Brigge* in dialogue with Uexküll's *Umwelt* as well as more dynamic, contemporary theories of embodied cognition, in this chapter I bring into relief the fraught relationship between Malte's embodied expectations and the material realities of the city of Paris.[6] But the chapter also shows that Rilke's text offers a solution to this problem of a recalcitrant environment. In moving away from a focus on Malte's self-reflection, in this chapter I investigate the way in which the novel thinks about literature not as something to contemplate but as something which can be leveraged to support us in our projects. *Malte Laurids Brigge* therefore suggests by way of literature how we can find agency not in turning away from our socio-material environments but precisely through manipulating them.

A Recalcitrant World

Rilke's apparent interest in "embodied cognition" comes to the fore in what happens when our habits are not in tune with our environment. Maxine Sheets-Johnstone states in *The Primacy of Movement* that many contemporary theorists of embodied cognition focus on what they call transparent "coping," in which the familiar world is aligned with our

---

6 Recently, Robert Britten has shown the productiveness of reading *Malte Laurids Brigge* in dialogue with embodied cognitive science. The current chapter complements his work with a focus on the third part of the novel. Britten, "Blick und Gebärde."

everyday habitual projects and thus becomes transparent.[7] Cups, pens, and jackets are ready to be used without having to be thought about. Rilke's interest in *Malte* lies, initially at least, in the opposite direction. Malte's world is, as in Heidegger's version of anxiety, opaque and claustrophobic. Objects are recalcitrant, "in-his-face," and "out-of-his-hands." Moreover, Malte's own behavior is not transparent but rather endlessly reflected on in his notes. In one scene, disturbed by noises coming from a neighboring apartment, Malte imagines a tin lid that gains its own agency, becomes disobedient, uncontrollable. Is it the lid, falling to the floor, clattering loudly, that causes the noise, or is it caused by his neighbor's eyelids failing to stay open? In any case, Malte contemplates that objects like the tin lid, no longer interested in their "natürlichen, stillen Zweck" (natural, quiet purpose; translation altered)—that is, in the case of the lid, fitting neatly on top of a tin—want to withdraw from their everyday use: "Sie machen Versuche, sich ihren Anwendungen zu entziehen, sie werden unlustig und nachlässig." (*MLB*, 153; they make attempts to escape from their applications, they become listless and sloppy: *N*, 105). Similarly, the first entry of the notebooks, in which Malte is finding his way around Paris with a map, is scattered with names of buildings whose French names stick out in the otherwise German text: "Maison d'Accouchement," "rue Saint-Jacques," "Val-de-grâce, Hôpital militaire" (*MLB*, 7; *N*, 3). These beginning pages are also marked by what Manfred Engel has described as the "Elend und Armut, Krankheit und Tod, Häßliches und Widerwärtiges" (misery and poverty, disease and death, ugliness and disgust) of the city in this novel; a sick-looking child, for example, sleeps with its mouth open, breathing in the toxic air (*MLB*, 7; *N*, 3).[8] In these various ways, everyday familiarity is replaced by an obtrusive and opaque city.

This recalcitrance of the city stands in contrast to the kind of "smooth coping" that Rilke might have found in Uexküll's theory of *Umwelt*.[9] Uexküll investigates precisely the ways in which animals understand their environments in pragmatic terms, based on their physical abilities. Uexküll sums up his own position nicely when, in 1934, he writes: "soviel Leistungen ein Tier ausführen kann, soviel Gegenstände vermag es in seiner Umwelt zu unterscheiden" (an animal is able to distinguish as many objects as it can carry out actions in its environment).[10] He calls this way in which the object is understood its "Wirkton" (effect tone),

---

7 Sheets-Johnstone, *Primacy of Movement*, 468–69.
8 Engel, afterword, 341. All translations of this source are mine.
9 For a good overview of Rilke's engagement with Uexküll as well as Uexküll's influence on other twentieth-century authors such as Aldous Huxley, see Herwig, "The Unwitting Muse."
10 Uexküll and Kriszat, *Streifzüge*, 61; Uexküll, *Foray*, 96.

which we might call, after James J. Gibson, an "affordance."[11] The tin lid in *Malte Laurids Brigge* wants to get away precisely from such limited use. It disturbs such use, emphasized by the obtrusive noise it produces when falling to the floor. The tin lid as well as the French names within the German text, the poverty, the dirt, and the ugliness in and of the city, suggest, in their obtrusiveness, the way in which the everyday transparency of affordances has disappeared. In a different scene, Rilke indeed contrasts the recalcitrant "objects" with the familiar (and familial). Here Malte wonders what it would have been like being a poet somewhere in an inherited country house: "O was für ein glückliches Schicksal, in der stillen Stube eines ererbten Hauses zu sitzen unter lauter ruhigen, seßhaften Dingen" (*MLB*, 39; what a happy lot it must be, to sit in the quiet parlour of an ancestral home amongst nothing but peaceful things that are comfortably settled there; *N*, 25). In contrast to how Malte imagines the tin lid, the objects of this inherited house are stable and silent. The tin lid is suggestive of how Malte's everyday physical engagements, the "affordances" of his familiar—inherited—environment, are challenged by Paris. When Malte comes to the city he has no family left, nor does he have a home or money. His position as a Danish aristocrat is in danger. A return to the transparency of home seems out of the question.

A particularly potent scene shows what such an "unruly" environment feels like for Malte. The scene illustrates how the new situation is unsettling at the most basic corporeal level. In a scene from the 18th entry, Malte experiences what we would today call "vection." Vection is the illusion of self-motion that occurs when we think we are moving when in fact it is much or all of our visual field that is moving instead.[12] We tend to know this phenomenon from when we are seated in a train at the station: while we believe our train is starting to move, it is rather the train next to us that has started to move. Malte's experience, however, is induced by a large group of people celebrating carnival. In a claustrophobic sequence, he recounts getting entangled in the masses and consequently experiencing vection:

> An den Ecken waren die Menschen festgekeilt, einer in den andern geschoben, und es war keine Weiterbewegung in ihnen, nur ein leises, weiches Auf und Ab, als ob sie sich stehend paarten. Aber obwohl sie standen und ich am Rande der Fahrbahn, wo es Risse im Gedränge gab, hinlief wie ein Rasender, war es in Wahrheit doch so, daß sie sich bewegten und ich mich nicht rührte. Denn es veränderte sich nichts; wenn ich aufsah, gewahrte ich immer noch dieselben

---

11 Uexküll and Kriszat, *Streifzüge*, 59. Gibson. *Ecological Approach*, 120.

12 Vection was first described by Ernst Mach in 1875 and termed "vection" in 1930 by M. H. Fischer and A. E. Kornmüller. Mach, *Grundlinien der Lehre*; Fischer and Kornmüller, "Optokinetisch ausgelöste Bewegungswahrnehmungen."

Häuser auf der einen Seite und auf der anderen die Schaubuden. Vielleicht auch stand alles fest, und es war nur ein Schwindel in mir und ihnen, der alles zu drehen schien. (*MLB*, 44)

[At the corners people were wedged firmly together, one jammed into another, and for them there was no motion forwards, just a soft, gentle back and forth, as if they were copulating in a standing position. But even though they were standing and I was running like a madman along the edge of the roadway where there were cracks in the crush, the truth was that they were moving and I was stock still. For nothing changed: when I looked up I could still see the same houses on one side of the street and the fairground booths on the other. Perhaps in fact everything was fixed and it was only a dizziness in me and in them that made everything seem to turn around. (*N*, 29; translation altered)]

The specifically urban environment with its masses of people thus tricks Malte into believing he is moving, when in fact he is not. The experience is disorienting and induces dizziness. Yet it also importantly points to the absence of a corporeal understanding, that is, the way in which we are used to an environment responding in a certain way. A key to understanding how vection shows our experience to be subject to expectations based on familiarity can be found in discussions of vision in the cognitive sciences.

In his cognitive approach to visual perception in *Action in Perception*, for example, Alva Noë argues that our perception is based on a familiarity with the world.[13] "Perceptual experience," he argues, "is something we enact, it is more akin to a skill, based on our familiarity with the world. We perceive objects as three-dimensional, for example, because we expect that if we walk around it, or grab it, our sensory stimulation changes in accordance with the object's three-dimensionality.[14] "To be a perceiver," Noë writes, "is to understand, implicitly, the effects of movement on sensory stimulation."[15] Noë does not discuss vection in his book, but it is easy to see how it might fit into his argument. Vection is based on the non-conscious, embodied knowledge, based on familiarity, that much or all of the visual field moves if and only if we ourselves move or are moved. The scene brings to the surface the way in which Malte's experience is subject to his corporeal familiarization, contingent on his non-conscious, embodied expectations. The basic level of corporeal and environmental transparency, the ability to reliably tell whether you are

---

13 Noë, *Action in Perception*, 63.
14 Noë, *Action in Perception*, 67.
15 Noë, *Action in Perception*, 1.

moving or not, is lost by Malte. His know-how is again thwarted by an unfamiliar and thus recalcitrant environment.[16]

The World as *Umwelt*

If objects become recalcitrant, what then happens to the subject? The recalcitrance of Malte's environment is also distracting. If Heidegger discusses the inauthentic response to anxiety as "falling prey" to the world, to distraction (see chapter 1), Malte discusses the recalcitrant objects in similar terms. He links the recalcitrance of objects like the tin lid to the self-indulgence of people: "die Leute sind gar nicht erstaunt, wenn sie sie auf einer Ausschweifung ertappen. Sie kennen das so gut von sich selbst" (*MLB*, 153; The people are not in the least surprised to catch them behaving intemperately. They know this so well from themselves: *N*, 105; translation altered). Especially when they encounter a hard-working student like Malte's neighbor, they try to distract him: "wo . . . einer ist, der sich zusammenhält, ein Einsamer etwa, der so recht rund auf sich beruhen wollte Tag und Nacht, da fordert er geradezu den Widerspruch, den Hohn, den Haß der entarteten Geräte heraus, die, in ihrem argen Gewissen, nicht mehr vertragen können, daß etwas sich zusammenhält und nach seinem Sinne strebt" (*MLB*, 153–54; where there is one who braces himself, a solitary, say, who was content to rest roundly on himself day and night, it's as if he provokes protest, scorn and hatred from those denatured objects that, with their consciences grown spiteful, can no longer tolerate anything else holding together in pursuit of its true meaning: *N*, 105–6). In the next note, Malte writes that he now understands the paintings in which a saint—he is probably referring to portrayals of the temptation of Saint Anthony by Hieronymus Bosch, Gustave Flaubert, and/or Paul Cézanne—is led into temptation by animated "objects."[17] The world is not only unfamiliar and out of grip for Malte, but it also distracts. He states that the objects are found "zuckend in der ungefähren Unzucht der Zerstreuung" (*MLB*, 154; convulsing in the casual debauchery of dissipation: *N*, 106). The objects thus do not only suggest a lack of a grasp on his environment, but also an imprecision and dissipation on the side of the agent. In the absence of a clear path forward through a recalcitrant environment, our "activity at hand," Rilke's text illustrates, is

---

16 This "explanation" of vection, which would also apply to the scene with the dogs that I opened this chapter with, is not to be understood as a denial of the gothic elements in the novel, to deny the presence of ghosts. Rather, it is meant to present a way of thinking about Rilke's exploration of ghostly appearances.

17 See Vilain, explanatory notes, 177–78; Engel, afterword, 269.

thus also under question. And if it is our nature to acquire habits, then we nevertheless need a goal in line with which to acquire them.[18]

This distraction is not only a psychological phenomenon, a lack of focus, but it also manifests itself as different behavior. The city of Paris elicits in Malte long-forgotten practices. In one of the most famous scenes from the notebooks also in entry 18—and the one that Heidegger draws on (see chapter 1)—Malte describes a no longer existing house (*MLB*, 40–43; *N*, 26–28).[19] The house has been demolished, but the remnants of one of its walls can still be seen on the outside of its formerly neighboring building. He writes that his description of it is ". . . Wahrheit, nichts weggelassen, natürlich auch nichts hinzugetan" (*MLB*, 41; truth, with nothing left out, and naturally nothing added either: *N*, 27). In a long section and in rather horrifyingly vivid terms, he describes what can still be gleaned from this wall. First, he describes the visible aspects, such as the remnants of rusty toilet plumbing and the grey and dusty traces of gas pipes. Then, he turns to the immaterial aspects of the lives lived there, "das zähe Leben dieser Zimmer" (the tenacious life of these rooms) that had refused to be erased (*MLB*, 42; *N*, 27): "Da standen die Mittage und die Krankheiten und das Ausgeatmete und der jahrealte Rauch und der Schweiß, der unter den Schultern ausbricht und die Kleider schwer macht, und das Fade aus den Munden und der Fuselgeruch gärender Füße" (*MLB*, 43; there lay the midday meals and the illnesses and the exhalations and year-after-year's-worth of smoke and the sweat that oozes out from the armpits and makes your clothes thick, and stale breath from people's mouths and the cheap-liquor smell of festering feet: *N*, 28). Malte thus turns to the ugly and the unsettling, the dirty and old, and traces that hint at the most physically intimate parts of human life such as sweat and toilet use. In later sentences he directly refers to urine and alludes to masturbation or wet dreams ("das Schwüle aus den Betten mannbarer Knaben" (*MLB*, 43; the mugginess of the beds of older boys: *N*, 28). What stands out here is that Malte's view of the wall is one of the lives of other people. He "sees" the smell of "vernachlässigten Säuglingen" (neglected nursing babies) and "der Angstgeruch der Kinder, die in die Schule gehen" (*MLB*, 43; anxious smell of children going to school: *N*, 28). In the objects, he sees the historical affordances for others. He sees in these objects other people's meaningful engagement. His seeing of the wall is thus the opposite of Malte's mother watching the family dog engage with the deceased Ingeborg. The dog's habitual movements conjured up its "direct object," a ghost from the past, while here the objects conjure up the past engagements of other people.

---

18 Noë, *Strange Tools*, 7.
19 See, most recently, Craig, "Rainer Maria Rilke's Dark Ecology," 268–70.

The affordances that Malte reads in the remnants of this wall, however, are not the "effect tones" as they relate to the factical, historical use by others. He is not reading other people's use from these walls as if reading a book. You cannot, of course, actually see the smell of neglected babies. Rather, the affordance that surfaces here is Malte's own picture of what such private spaces afford. Malte's discussion of the "house" is exactly a discussion of the most private lives that come to the surface, that are literally exposed to the world on this wall. Thus, what he sees in this wall, the nervous student, the muggy beds of adolescent boys, are the embodied memories they elicit in him. Indeed, Malte says as much when two notes later (note 20) he talks of his newly acquired "illness":

> Diese Krankheit hat keine bestimmten Eigenheiten, sie nimmt die Eigenheiten dessen an, den sie ergreift. . . . Männer die einmal in der Schulzeit das hülflose Laster versucht haben, dessen betrogene Vertraute die armen, harten Knabenhände sind, finden sich wieder darüber, oder es fängt eine Krankheit, die sie als Kinder überwunden haben, wieder in ihnen an; oder eine verlorene Gewohnheit ist wieder da, ein gewisses zögerndes Wenden des Kopfes, das ihnen vor Jahren eigen war. (*MLB*, 56)

> [This illness has no specific features of its own, it adopts the features of the person it takes hold of . . . Men who during their schooldays tried the vice that cannot be helped, whose deceived intimates were the poor hard hands of boys, find themselves tempted by it again, or an illness that they overcame as children takes hold again; or a habit they thought they had lost is back, a certain tentative twisting of the head that they used to do years ago. (*N*, 37)]

The reappearance of "masturbation" here, alongside other apparently long-lost habits and illnesses, suggests that this seeing of the environment is marked by a seeing in terms of the affordances that it has for the perceiving Malte. In other words, the wall does not challenge Malte's habits, in presenting to him practices that are unfamiliar to him, but rather, it presents Malte with the traces of a house which for him afford certain practices. Indeed, he writes at the end of the passage about the wall: "Ich erkenne das alles hier, und darum geht es so ohne weiteres in mich ein: es ist zu Hause in mir" (*MLB*, 43; I recognize everything around here, and that's why it enters into me so easily: it is at home in me: *N*, 28). However, as this second longer quotation suggests, the affordances he finds in the wall do not just remind him of old practices: it elicits them too. Habits such as masturbation and physical ticks return. The material environment that constitutes Malte's surroundings in Paris thus is not only recalcitrant and distracting but also reminds Malte of former experiences and practices and, indeed, elicits their return. Thus, more than the wall being exposed, its affordances bring to the surface Malte's most intimate practices.

This scene thus stands in contrast to Rilke's "poetic seeing," developed in his so-called *Dinggedichte*.[20] Certainly, Malte announces a different way of seeing in the notebooks: "Ich lerne sehen. Ich weiß nicht, woran es liegt, es geht alles tiefer in mich ein und bleibt nicht an der Stelle stehen, wo es sonst immer zu Ende war" (*MLB*, 8; I'm learning how to see. I don't know what the reason is, but everything enters into me more deeply and no longer stops at the point where it used to come to an end: *N*, 4). But if Rilke's "poetic seeing," for example in his texts on Cézanne and Rodin, is a disposition, a mode of seeing that needs to be cultivated, in *Malte Laurids Brigge* this seeing is not searched for, but triggered by a disrupting environment.[21] The vection, the recalcitrant objects, the wall, in all their disruptiveness show that this "seeing" is not a choice but the result of an environment responding in unexpected ways, which distracts. The lid is not actively looked at in a certain way, but a noise triggers Malte's reflection on it. The wall is not sought out but "erkannt." This "recognition" is also important because it suggests that the "seeing" of the wall is not a "pure," unadulterated seeing either. "Poetic seeing," as Manfred Engel and Luke Fischer describe, for example, is self-less and ecstatic. As Engel describes it, in Rilke's poetic seeing the distinction between object and subject, outside and inside, collapses: "in dem Augenblick, in dem das Ich ganz nach Außen gewandt, ganz aufnehmend ist, stellt sich in ihm . . . der dem Objekt korrespondierende Seeleszustand her" (at the moment when the I is completely turned outward, completely absorbing, the state of mind corresponding to the object is established in it).[22] The scene with the wall, however, does the very opposite. Rather than cancelling out the subject, the wall shows the world as an *Umwelt*, indeed as the non-dualistic, implicitly meaningful environment contingent on our physical bodies and its (socio-culturally shaped) habits—those that do not stand out in our everyday engagements. This scene exactly reflects on the *Umwelt* as *Umwelt*—this is why Heidegger describes the scene in detail—and reflects on the practices of a body that make it so.[23] The wall as perceived by Malte takes the *Umwelt* out of its transparency and makes it opaque. The "seeing" in this scene is exactly a reflection on, and an elicitation of, a body of habits and experiences which in a truly non-dualistic picture would be left hidden and unreflected in everyday coping.

---

20 See especially his "new poems." Rilke, *Neue Gedichte*.
21 See Rilke, *Auguste Rodin*; Rilke, *Briefe über Cézanne*.
22 Engel, afterword, 330. See also Fischer, *Poet as Phenomenologist*, 109.
23 Heidegger, *Grundprobleme der Phänomenologie*, 244–46.

Writing as Exploration

Underneath Malte's descriptions of an opaque and frictional relationship with his environment nevertheless lies a productive engagement with that same environment, namely through writing. The irony at the center of *Malte Laurids Brigge* is that while Malte struggles with writing, what we are reading is his writing. As Rilke's early French-language summary of the novel suggests, Malte's writing takes an important place within the dynamic between him and his environment: "il écrit, il est très attentive, il aperçoit beaucoup sans s'en rendre compte d'abord" (he writes, he is very attentive, he sees a lot without realizing it at first).[24] Malte does not just write down his experiences: writing becomes an active exploration of them. As Rilke tells his Polish translator, the writing importantly allows Malte to "grasp" his experiences, and keep them alive:

> ... wie etwa Ibsen ... für das in uns unsichtbar gewordene Ereignis sichtbare Belege aufsucht, so verlangt es auch den jungen M. L. Brigge, das fortwährend ins Unsichtbare sich zurückziehende Leben über Erscheinungen und Bildern sich faßlich zu machen; er findet diese bald in den eigenen Kindheits-Erinnerungen, bald in seiner Pariser Umgebung, bald in den Reminiszenzen seiner Belesenheit.[25]

> [... as for instance Ibsen ... seeks out visible pieces of evidence of the event that has become invisible to us, so too young M. L. Brigge longs to make life, which is continually withdrawing into the invisible, intelligible to himself through evocations and images; these he finds now in his own childhood memories, now in his Paris surroundings, now in the reminiscences of his wide reading.]

Malte "grasps" these events, that are otherwise disappearing, through writing. The words "sans s'en rendre compte d'abord" in the French summary suggest that the writing is not a mere jotting down of what is previously contemplated, but that the "grasping" happens in the act of writing. Only through writing do his experiences become understandable.[26] As Robert Britten writes "language is not an optional add-on to

---

24 Bern, Schweizerische Landesbibliothek, Ms. B 6, 74. The full note is reproduced in Engel, afterword, 326–27.

25 Rilke, *Briefe aus Muzot*, 319. *Letters*, 371.

26 Richard Menary writes in "Writing as Thinking" that "[c]reating and manipulating written sentences are [*sic*] not merely outputs from neural processes but, just as crucially, they shape the cycle of processing that constitutes a mental act. Completing a complex cognitive, or mental, task is enabled by a coordinated interaction between neural processes, bodily processes, and manipulating written sentences." Menary places emphasis here on mental tasks. However, if we get away from such a mind-focused language, we might say that writing helps

Malte's perceptual activities, ... to understand 'seeing' we must ask questions about writing, too."[27] Read in this way, the notebooks are the material remains of Malte's active process of working through his experiences. This manipulative aspect of writing is also suggested by the German title *Die Aufzeichnungen*, in what Huyssen calls the "visual connotation of drawing" of the German word "zeichnen."[28] Malte is sketching, exploring, and experimenting with imagery and language that might give meaning to his experiences, allow him to get a grip on them. The novel as a collection of notes highlights that if Malte is debilitated by his environment, he is also always already involved with his environment through writing. In other words: we must imagine Malte active.

But if writing about his experiences in Paris seems to get him into a more active practice, this is not where it ends for Malte. In entry 18, directly following the scene of vection, Malte describes the complete collapse of his everyday meaningful environment. He does so in terms that seem to allude to Uexküll's theory of animals' environments. Malte writes:

> Wenn meine Furcht nicht so groß wäre, so würde ich mich damit trösten, daß es nicht unmöglich ist, alles anders zu sehen und doch zu leben. Aber ich fürchte mich, ich fürchte mich namenlos vor dieser Veränderung. Ich bin ja noch gar nicht in dieser Welt eingewöhnt gewesen, die mir gut scheint. Was soll ich in einer anderen? Ich würde so gerne unter den Bedeutungen bleiben, die mir lieb geworden sind, und wenn schon etwas sich verändern muß, so möchte ich doch wenigstens unter den Hunden leben dürfen, die eine verwandte Welt haben und dieselben Dinge. (*MLB*, 47)

> [If my fear were not so great I would console myself that it isn't impossible to see everything differently and to carry on living nonetheless. But I am afraid, I have a nameless fear of that transformation. I haven't yet by any means settled down in this world, which seems to me to be good. What should I do in another? I would so dearly love to stay amongst the meanings that I have grown fond of, and if something does have to change, then let me at least live amongst the dogs, who have a world akin to ours and the same things in it. (*N*, 31)]

---

us attune our bodies to environments. Menary, "Writing as Thinking," 622. See also Andy Clark and David Chalmers' defining essay "The Extended Mind," in which they discuss writing (including the use of notebooks) as a form of extended cognition.

27 Britten, "Blick und Gebärde," 82.
28 Huyssen, "Notebooks," 75.

What, in the consequent paragraph Malte calls "die Zeit der anderen Auslegung" (*MLB*, 48; the age of the other interpretation: *N*, 31), is thus a big change in the way in which the environment has meaning to him. Seemingly alluding to the concept of *Umwelt* through his description of "Welt" as habitual and meaningful, this different topology, for Malte, constitutes a different *Welt*. He brings up a different animal to qualify the change. According to Malte, dogs thus have, perhaps, as Fick argues, "durch den Umgang mit dem Menschen" (by interacting with humans), a related world.[29] The ecology that Malte is going to, however, is far removed from such a similarly meaningful environment. Rilke employs a version of *Umwelt* to think through and qualify the change Malte is going through in terms of how his environment is meaningful to him, while also, by showing this radical change in the same person, taking leave of Uexküll's emphasis on the static character of our environments.

Tools, Toys, Niches, and Virtual Worlds

Malte's active engagement with his experiences, turning them into material objects through writing, comes to full fruition in his retelling of the histories he read in childhood. In entries 54 and 55 as well as 61 and 62, Malte rewrites the histories of several historical figures: False Dmitry I also known as Grigoriy Otrepyev; Charles the Bold; Charles VI of France; Pope John XXII né Jacques Duèze; Pierre de Luxembourg; and Charles VI the Holy Roman Emperor.[30] What Malte writes down in each case is not so much an accurate (or inaccurate) historical account of the lives of these figures. Rather, Malte writes down the imagined lived experiences of these figures as they are relevant to his current situation. Indeed, reading these rewritten histories within a development from Malte "simply" copying the Book of Job and Baudelaire's *Le Spleen de Paris* to his retelling of his own life as the prodigal son, we can see how these stories are increasingly inhabited by Malte. His increasingly involved engagement opens up a space from which to explore these stories as part of Malte's more dynamic engagement with his environment. That is, these histories become tools, or better yet, emphasizing Malte's exploration and experimentation, toys. Reading these stories as memories relevant for his present situation shows how stories live on dynamically within us, forgotten until they can be revivified for new purposes. Rilke reminds us of the dynamic afterlives of literature.[31]

29 Fick, *Sinnenwelt und Weltseele*, 314.
30 For a discussion of Malte's rewriting of these histories in terms of larger discussions of doing history see Hillard, "Rilke and Historical Discourse."
31 See, for example, most of the essays in the third part of Burke and Troscianko, eds., *Cognitive Literary Science*.

Embodied approaches to reading explore the roles that our bodies play in how we read stories. An important concept in this approach is that of "embodied simulation." The hypothesis of embodied simulation, as Raymond W. Gibbs Jr. writes, "asserts that people ordinarily attempt to construct imaginative embodied re-enactments of what the situation described by some specific discourse must be like to participate in given their own bodily capacities and experiences."[32] Moreover, as empirical research suggests, these are not operations that happen after the act of reading, after the text is understood, but are "an immediate part of people's moment-by-moment processing of linguistic meaning."[33] When I read about someone kicking a soccer ball, the hypothesis is, I am always already participating—to greater and lesser degrees, and in a variety of different ways—in this activity too.[34] Thus, the hypothesis holds, "literary experiences of all types are fundamentally grounded in embodied simulation processes."[35]

Malte's engagement with the historical figures as if he were them—that is, not in objective, historical terms, but as "relentlessly perspectival"—suggests such "embodied simulation" in writing.[36] Malte slips into the embodied perspectives of these heroes on their situations; he imagines their lived experiences. This physical mimicry is particularly apparent in the final retelling of the prodigal son, which cannot be separated from Malte himself. The dogs and the house in Malte's retelling of the prodigal son suggest that it is his own life that is being retold through the parable. This slippage between Malte and his historical figures also becomes apparent at the beginning of note 61: "Ich weiß, wenn ich zum Äußersten bestimmt bin, so wird es mir nichts helfen, daß ich mich verstelle in meinen besseren Kleidern. Glitt er nicht mitten im Königtum unter die Letzten?" (*MLB*, 177; I know that if I am destined for the worst it won't help me to disguise myself in my best clothes. Did he not slip down amongst the lowest of the low even in the midst of his kingship?: *N*, 123). Like Charles VI of France sliding down amongst the lowest, so Malte slips from himself into "er," into Charles VI's lived perspective.[37]

However, Malte's rewriting of these stories points beyond mere simulation towards a more dynamic engagement with narratives, especially in their mnemonic afterlives. It is not just that Malte's "bodily capacities

32   Gibbs, "Embodied Dynamics," 223.
33   Gibbs, "Embodied Dynamics," 224.
34   See Caracciolo, "Embodiment at the Crossroads," 247.
35   Gibbs, "Embodied Dynamics," 236.
36   Hillard, "Rilke and Historical Discourse," 303.
37   Not only does a slippage take place between Malte himself and historical figures, he also cannot separate his aunt Abelone from Bettina von Armin, whose letters she was reading. Abelone is described as having been "absorbed" by the writer (*N*, 117; aufgegangen: *MLB*, 170).

and experiences" shape the way he engages with a static literature. Rather, the literature is itself already a dynamic part of his experiences—"Vorräte seines Gemüts" (supplies of his mind)—and manipulated and put to use for his engagement with his environment.[38] As Rilke explains the historical figures to his Polish translator, his use of them is not concerned with these histories, but with the way in which they give shape to Malte's experiences: "Der Leser kommuniziere nicht mit ihrer geschichtlichen oder imaginären Realität, sondern durch sie, mit Maltes Erlebnis" (the reader should not be in communication with their historical or imaginary reality, but through them with Malte's experience).[39] Moreover, he writes in the same letter that they give shape to his problems: "Sie sind nicht historische Figuren oder Gestalten seiner eigenen Vergangenheit, sondern *Vokabeln seiner Not*" (they are not historical figures or characters of his own past, but *vocabula of his distress*).[40] These histories thus become tools for giving shape to his own life: dynamic, manipulable, "objects" that have become significant because they can be put to use for Malte's concerns. Like a hammer which lies dormant until something needs to be nailed, so Malte's readings become relevant to a situation they may offer insight into, or help for. That is, these stories, and not just that of the prodigal son, are parables. They offer Malte ways into understanding his own life.[41]

Malte's *use* of literature for his concerns is in some ways suggestive of pragmatic approaches to art and literature. In *Strange Tools*, Alva Noë takes a Heideggerian/embodied approach to art.[42] He sees art as a "strange tool" within the flow of our everyday organized activities. Tools or technologies, he explains, generally help us organize ourselves in our worlds. "There is an intimate link," he writes, "between technology and organized activities. Roughly, a tool (such as a hammer or a computer) is the hub of an organized activity. Technology is not mere stuff. It is the equipment with which we carry on our organized activities. Technologies organize us; properly understood, they are *evolving patterns*

---

38 Rilke, *Briefe aus Muzot*, 319. *Letters*, 371.
39 Rilke, *Briefe aus Muzot*, 318–19. *Letters*, 371.
40 Rilke, *Briefe aus Muzot*, 320. *Letters*, 371; translation altered.
41 Mark Turner uses the word "parable" as "*the projection of a story,*" as "a general and indispensable instrument of everyday thought." Turner, *The Literary Mind*, 7. See also Turner's concept of "blended classic joint attention" in which the "classic joint attention" in which "people are jointly attending to something they can perceive in the same environment," is blended across time and/or space to go "far beyond our local experience." Turner, "Multimodal Form-Meaning Pairs," 1–2.
42 Noë, *Strange Tools*. An important antecedent to Noë's discussion from the modernist period is American philosopher Dewey's pragmatist approach to art in *Art as Experience*. Dewey, *Art as Experience*.

of organization."[43] Art, by contrast, is a *strange* tool because rather than letting us organize ourselves, or organizing us, it lets us *reflect* on the ways in which we are organized.[44] Like Rilke's recalcitrant tin lid, art, in Noë's view, disrupts the daily flow of our activities and therefore makes us conscious of the ways in which we are organized. Moreover, because it makes us conscious of our organization, of our practices and habits, art, in Noë's thinking, allows us to reorganize ourselves, as well. In short, according to Noë, "[art] is a practice for bringing our organization into view; in doing this, art reorganizes us."[45]

Malte's engagement with literature aligns with Noë's emphasis on reorganization if not with his emphasis on reflection. Malte uses these histories as a kind of tool for enabling a different way of engaging with his environment, giving it (a new) meaning. The prodigal son is a new way for Malte of seeing his own history and future. However, what Rilke shows here is that art does not need to make us reflect on our practices for it to reorganize us. It can just be used in the dynamic of our engagements to change our organization in the same way that a doorknob, a hammer, or a load of cash (see the next chapter) allows us to reorganize our lives in smaller or larger ways. These histories do not make Malte reflect on his life but merely help him try out different ways of engaging, help him reshape his *Umwelt*. As Noël Carroll points out in his response to *Strange Tools*, the reflective aspect of Noë's considerations might fit well with a certain kind of postwar, avant-garde art—one that is "self-consciously phenomenological"—but not others.[46] Like Carroll's argument that religious art, for example, is often "produced to engender devotion," and any reflective stance produced would counter such a goal, Malte's use of these histories exactly overcomes reflection in favor of a, be it virtual, realignment with his environment.[47] Indeed, *Malte Laurids Brigge* repeatedly connects art to absorption, for example in a scene with girls looking at tapestries (*MLB*, 112; *N*, 76).[48] Art, as Carroll also points out, thus does not have

---

43   Noë, *Strange Tools*, 19.
44   Noë, *Strange Tools*, 16.
45   Noë, *Strange Tools*, 29.
46   Carroll, "Comments on *Strange Tools*," 219. See also Noë's response to Carroll and others: Noë, "Art and Entanglement."
47   Carroll, "Comments," 218.
48   In another scene, Malte as a child is drawing heroes when he drops his pencil. In a rather frightful scene, he is feeling for the pencil in the dark when he loses all sense that his arm is his, and to heighten this feeling he comes across a completely different arm looking for the pencil, too (*MLB*, 80–82; *N*, 54–55). This suggests, again, though in more frightful terms, the link between art and losing oneself (cf. Høffding's account of what he calls "ex-static absorption": *Phenomenology of Musical Absorption*, 85–87). For a very different interpretation of

to be a strange tool, it can just be a tool. Reorganization, or so Rilke shows here, does not need self-reflection.

Malte's use of these histories is creative and experimental; he *re*-writes these stories. This creative use does not create a different view of his own environment directly, but it creates a fictional, a virtual, reality through which his view of his own environment is altered. Literature becomes a special kind of tool: a toy. Creativity and virtual meaning underlie the discussion of play in an article on enactive cognition by Ezequiel A. Di Paolo, Marieke Rohde, and Hanne de Jaegher.[49] They turn to play because it is an embodied activity that allows for ambiguity of, and creation of new, meaning.[50] What they consider crucial in play is that it "relies . . . on the *combined similarity and difference* between two situations: one concrete, tied to physical events, and the other in terms of manipulated meaning."[51] The toy (e.g., a doll) is both an object in the here and now and stands in for a virtual world (e.g., a person). Equally, Malte's rewriting of these histories is both a material manipulation of existing stories and the creation of a virtual world in which Malte inserts himself. Crucially, play for Di Paolo and his colleagues exposes the way in which meaning is embodied and enacted: "When a child skillfully supplements the perceptual lack of similarity between a spoon and a car by making the spoon move like a car, he or she has grasped in an embodied manner the extent to which perception can be action-mediated."[52] Malte, however, has already been made to grasp this, for example through vection. For him, play is a way of virtually experimenting with reenacting his environment. If Malte's rewriting of literature is a tool, reshaping immediately his *Umwelt*, that is, without the need for reflection, then literature does so as a toy, through playing and experimenting in a virtual reality. If Stephen D. Dowden has recently argued that "what is crucial to modernism is the thought that art is . . . an active way of exploring, understanding, and knowing the world, of actively situating ourselves in it," Malte's rewriting of these histories is doing just that.[53]

At stake in Malte's dynamic manipulation and putting to work of history/literature is Malte's identity, and the idea of authenticity itself.

---

this scene from childhood in terms of embodied cognition, see Caracciolo et al., "Promise of an Embodied Narratology," 446–48.

49 Di Paolo, Rohde, and De Jaegher, "Horizons for the Enactive Mind."
50 Di Paolo, Rohde, and De Jaegher, "Horizons for the Enactive Mind," 74–5.
51 Di Paolo, Rohde, and De Jaegher, "Horizons for the Enactive Mind," 76.
52 Di Paolo, Rohde, and De Jaegher, "Horizons for the Enactive Mind," 32. Rilke's "Puppen" ("Dolls"; 1914) exactly describes playing with puppets as a way for children to assert themselves when they cannot in the presence of adults. Rilke, "Puppen," 1066.
53 Dowden, *Modernism and Mimesis*, 9.

We have seen how Malte thinks of his transition to a new *Umwelt*, in Uexküll's terms, as qualified beyond the practices of dogs. The concept of the "niche," a more dynamic rendering of *Umwelt* as proposed by James J. Gibson, will help us further explore Malte's transition. The concept of the niche, used in the cognitive sciences today, emphasizes animals' creative natures. The term was made central by Gibson, to mean a "set of affordances."[54] Niches are onto- and phylogenetically shaped environments which afford us a way of life. Just as each animal has its *Umwelt*, so each niche has its way of life. The idea of the niche, however, takes as its premise that animals do not just adjust to their environments but actively shape it over time to be able to do more, better. Rhetorically, Gibson asks: "Why has man changed the shapes and substances of his environment?" He answers: "To change what it affords him. . . . Over the millennia, he has made it easier for himself to get food, easier to keep warm, easier to see at night, easier to get about, and easier to train his offspring."[55] At stake in the niche are thus the practices of humans, their culture, and thus, as shaped by what we do, identity itself. It is this kind of dynamic relation which, as I argued above, marks Malte's engagement with these histories. Indeed, the idea that Malte's writing is akin to the manipulation of a supporting niche is suggested in the text just before the copies of Baudelaire and the Book of Job, when Malte writes: "da liegt es vor mir in meiner eigenen Schrift, was ich gebetet habe, Abend für Abend. Ich habe es mir aus den Büchern, in denen ich es fand, abgeschrieben, damit es mir ganz nahe wäre und aus meiner Hand entsprungen wie Eigenes" (*MLB*, 48; what I prayed for, evening after evening, lies before me in my own handwriting. I have copied it out of the books in which I found it, so that I would have it close, issued from my hand as if they were my own words: *N*, 31). He manipulates his environment, he re-writes these stories, to support himself and, as we will see, to sustain a different way of life. Indeed, attempts at sustaining ways of life are the very topics of Malte's rewriting of these histories.

The histories as retold by Malte importantly discuss various ways in which the chosen ways of life of historical figures clash with, or are sustained by, their (social) environments. Engel points out that the histories describe either individuals who are trying to uphold their "identities" faced with the strange and unfamiliar, or "individuals" who attempt to maintain a new identity in the face of their social surroundings.[56] However, these histories especially trace the ways in which ways of life are shaped, sustained and/or challenged through the environment of

---

54 Gibson, *Ecological Approach*, 120.
55 Gibson, *Ecological Approach*, 122.
56 Engel, afterword, 344.

objects and other people. About Grigory Otrepyev, for example, pretending to be the rightful Tsar of Russia, Malte suggests that it was the freedom and boundlessness of his possibilities that sustained his deception, made possible by the fact that he lost his parents (*MLB*, 158; *N*, 108–9). Yet, when the real Tsar's mother recognizes Otrepyev to be her son, her statement "beschränkte ihn auf ein müdes Nachahmen; sie setzte ihn auf den Einzelnen herab, der er nicht war: sie machte ihn zum Betrüger" (*MLB*, 158; restricted him to being a weary imitator; she reduced him to the level of the one person that he was not; she made him into an imposter: *N*, 109; translation altered). It is the restriction to his freedom of identity by Marie Nagaia that defeats him; he wants to be able to live however he wants, and thereby never be seen as an impostor. To be an impostor would mean that there is an essential truth to how he should live. At the same time, however, it is his guards' belief in his identity as Tsar which sustains his practice as Tsar. In the final note 71, the prodigal son wants to get away from the love of his family, from his "Gewohnheiten" (customary practices), from an environment in which even in front of the dogs he could do nothing without either "zu freuen oder zu kränken" (*MLB*, 206; pleasing or offending: *N*, 144). Charles the Bold, in note 55, although introduced as having a stable and strong identity, wants and needs to convince his body (especially his blood) of a way of life that he wants to assert by building up an environmental niche of objects and people around him that confirm his desired status as emperor:

> Für dieses Blut schleppte er alle die Dinge mit, auf die er nichts gab. Die drei großen Diamanten und alle die Steine; die flandrischen Spitzen und die Teppiche von Arras, haufenweis. Sein seidenes Gezelt mit den aus Gold gedrehten Schnüren und vierhundert Zelte für sein Gefolg. Und Bilder, auf Holz gemalt, und die zwölf Apostel aus vollem Silber. Und den Prinzen von Tarent und den Herzog von Cleve und Philipp von Baden und den Herrn von Château-Guyon. Denn er wollte seinem Blut einreden, daß er Kaiser sei und nichts über ihm: damit es ihn fürchte. (*MLB*, 160–61)

> [For this blood he dragged round with him all the things that didn't matter to him. The three huge diamonds and all the precious stones; the Flanders lace and the Arras tapestries, piles of them. His silken pavilion with the cords of twisted gold and four hundred tents for his entourage. And pictures, painted on wood, and the twelve solid silver apostles. And the Prince of Taranto and the Duke of Cleves and Philipp of Baden and the Lord of Château-Guyon. For he wanted to persuade his blood that he was an emperor with nothing above him—so that it would fear him. (*N*, 111)]

Charles the Bold creates an environmental niche of people and objects that sustain the way in which he wants to live. The force of his own body, his blood, his habits, is attempted to be controlled with objects and people who confirm the identity Charles the Bold wishes to assert. Not by a strong will, but by manipulating his environment, can the would-be-*Kaiser* convince his body to act out the role he wants to have.

What I submit is that, through these histories, Malte is building his own socio-material *niche*, one that does not shape and sustain one particular way of life, but rather allows him to believe that it is possible to live "freely," that is, without the pressure to have an authentic, stable practice. Like Charles the Bold collecting objects and people around him that assert a way of life against the pressure from his own blood, Malte builds a space of historical figures whose "freedom" he can imitate. Ironically, in this niche, Malte uses stories from his past that allow him to understand he need not be tied to that same past, its habits and its social pressures. It is this kind of structuring of a new environment to overcome "modern" models of identity, which Rilke seems to get at in his French summary of *Malte Laurids Brigge*, written around 1908. In a rather complex sentence, talking about the moment after Malte experiences the breakdown of his *Umwelt*, Rilke writes: "il faut en avoir une abondance des choses faites pour supprimer le sujet ainsi conçu par la réalité des documents ingénus qui prouvent sans le vouloir" (there must be an abundance of things that are made to suppress the subject as conceived by the reality of ingenuous evidence which proves without meaning it).[57] An abundance of "objects" is needed to do away with the otherwise overwhelming documents in favor of the idea of a (stable) subjectivity. This niche-building is thus not merely an attempt at doing away with the socio-material pressures to act *a certain way*, but also more fundamentally, to do away with the very idea of stable subjectivities in favor of a free choice of a way of life. In other words, Malte is trying to create a socio-material niche, be it a virtual one, out of characters from history to do away with the overwhelming structures that tell him to have a stable self, that tell him to act authentically in a narrowly conceived way. Malte's creative rewriting of these histories underpins a more creative understanding of selfhood. *Malte Laurids Brigge* thereby ties into recent reformulations of "authenticity" as dynamic, creative, and "relational."[58] In particular,

---

57   Rilke, MS. B 6, 74. I want to thank Myrto Aspioti for helping me make sense of this complex French sentence. In a letter to Lou Andreas-Salomé from the summer of 1903, Rilke asks a similar question: "Wo giebt es ein Buch, das stark genug gewesen wäre, mir über das fortzuhelfen was in mir war" (repr. in *MLB* 295; Where's a book that'd have been strong enough to help me get past what was inside me?: my translation).

58   Gallagher, Morgan, and Rokotnitz, "Relational Authenticity."

Malte's creative rewriting resonates with Naomi Rokotnitz's exploration of role-playing as a dynamic way into identity-formation: "*authenticity supporting* role-play results from *choosing* some roles, or aspects of these roles, over others; and of creatively amalgamating and/or *shaping* them to suit one's own preferences."[59] Yet, in Malte, it is not just that playing allows him to creatively experiment with different ways of life, but also that the stories he plays with themselves support such a playful, dynamic vision of self.

Ultimately, Malte's engagement with literature, rewriting stories from his memory, gives us a more dynamic understanding of our engagements with literature and its afterlife in memory than contemporary theories of embodied simulation suggest. Malte uses these stories and manipulates them in a way that allows him to look at his own environment differently. A clear task underlies this dynamic engagement with his "environment," that is, being "free," making certain stories relevant, allowing him to use them in a way that contributes to this task. Literature is thus not, *Malte Laurids Brigge* suggests, merely a static object which we *receive* in embodied ways, but it is itself something we can use dynamically in our meaningful engagements in the world. The stories we have read can be revivified for new projects, creatively and experimentally, and can shape, support, and sustain our chosen projects. Hence Malte can say before he starts rewriting the histories: "Aber diesmal werde ich geschrieben werden" (*MLB*, 48; but this time I will be written: *N*, 31).

Conclusion

What Malte attempts to do, then, is to sustain a dynamic, practical, and involved engagement through constructing a niche. Like Mieze in *Berlin Alexanderplatz*, who, as we will see, constructs her own, cute and comfortable little space away from the violence of a male-dominated society, Malte attempts to shape his own refuge in literature. While this is successful to the extent that he finds an absorbing practice away from debilitating self-reflection, it still marks a turn away from his environment that is the city of Paris. Indeed, the form of life he ends up with, that of the prodigal son, is not only fictional but also never engages with his life in the city. Like the generic inspirational quotes some people hang on their walls—often equally about freedom, and, indeed, often with people running with arms spread wide in a field, not unlike the image of the prodigal son leaving his home (*MLB*, 207; *N*, 144)—it might work well in the confined space of our living room, but less so in the real world. The question we are left with is how much support this fiction would offer

---

59 Rokotnitz, "Colluding in the Conspiracy," 207.

Malte in the city. The novel, ending as it does in this virtual space, offers little hope of it being successful.

Nevertheless, the novel offers important ways of getting out of perpetual self-reflection into a more dynamic engagement with our environments. It suggests that ways of re-organizing might always already be at offer. The stories, like Malte's masturbatory practices, are not so much searched for as that they arise as meaningful in the current situation. Indeed, the whole set of notebooks as "Aufzeichnungen," as sketches, may be seen more as manipulating, exploring, and practicing with his situation—albeit in a space of language—than as moments of deliberation and self-reflection. It is when Malte directly copies the texts of Baudelaire and the Book of Job, an activity that is especially suggestive of an action requiring little thought, that he describes that as a "Hülfe" (*MLB*, 48; a rescue: *N*, 31). When the rewriting of the histories suggests that he becomes increasingly absorbed in playing with these texts, this absorption is an affordance of literature that he has already pointed at talking about the readers in the *bibliothèque nationale*: "Sie sind in den Büchern. Manchmal bewegen sie sich in den Blättern, wie Menschen, die schlafen und sich umwenden zwischen zwei Träumen" (*MLB*, 35; they are in the books. Sometimes they move amongst the pages like people asleep who turn over between two dreams: *N*, 22). In *re*-writing, Malte enters into a playful, embodied engagement that is situated in the real world, in writing, as well as in the virtual worlds of these histories, whereby Malte and the prodigal son ultimately become indistinguishable.

The fact that the novel presents a disparate set of found texts suggests the idea of the environmental niche. Both in form and content the text takes literature out of a purely linguistic realm into a material world in which, as objects, they become tools that can be manipulated and used—anticipating the "material" forms of both Döblin's *Berlin Alexanderplatz* and Benjamin's *Einbahnstraße*, which I return to in the final chapter. Like Noë, Rilke's text suggests that literature can be productively understood as a tool for re-organizing our lives. Yet in contrast to Noë, the text shows that literature does not need to do so through reflection. *Malte Laurids Brigge* thus shows the recalcitrant and distracting aspects of unfamiliar environments, how everyday task-oriented movements and expectations are disturbed, as well as the ways in which these environments themselves may already be offering new tools for organizing our lives. As Malte attempts to do through restructuring his environment by rewriting these histories from memory, we can *use* literature, or be guided by it, to reorganize the way in which we engage with our environments, like a handle that gives us access to a previously closed door. And we can do so without having to consciously reflect on its meaning.

Rilke's text thus introduces us to the problem that this monograph traces through these texts: the recalcitrance of an unfamiliar environment.

Although it lets Malte's reorganization through literature remain virtual, *Malte Laurids Brigge* nevertheless suggests ways in which we can construct niches that support our goal-oriented actions. Moreover, its focus on how we might "use" other people, even if fictional, to resituate ourselves in foreign environments anticipates the social solutions given in the texts that are discussed in the following chapters.

3: Georg Kaiser's *Von morgens bis mitternachts* and Karlheinz Martin's Film Adaptation: Ecstatic Experience

THE "TEXTS" DISCUSSED in this chapter, Georg Kaiser's drama *Von morgens bis mitternachts* (*From Morn to Midnight*; [1912]), which premiered as a play in April 1917 at the Munich *Kammerspiele*, and its 1920 silent film adaptation by Karlheinz Martin, are in important ways outliers in the developing narrative of this monograph.[1] Like many of the other texts that I discuss in this book, they follow a (male) character into an unfamiliar city. The unnamed man, a bank clerk known as "the cashier," steals money from the bank and goes to the big city (presumably Berlin). But his experiences are far from the anxieties experienced by Malte or by those of Franz Biberkopf in *Berlin Alexanderplatz*, discussed in the next chapter. While some of the practices are marked as unfamiliar, the cashier does not have trouble immersing himself in the city. He easily manipulates his environments with the use of his new-"found" wealth. For the cashier, the city is not predominantly a place that needs habituation; instead, it offers opportunities for the kind of wild and ecstatic experiences that are caught in the famous phrase about Weimar culture (a period which the drama precedes): "dancing on the volcano." The cashier whips the spectators at a cycling race into a frenzy by upping the prize money repeatedly, he tries to do the same with women at a dancehall, and he almost loses himself in religion.

The experiences that the cashier encounters in these texts, such as alcohol, religion, dancing, gambling, sports, and sex, are the kind of experiences in which people all but lose themselves, that is, *ecstatic* experiences. These experiences correspond to the activities that psychologist Mihalyi Csikszentmihalyi describes in his book-length discussion of what he calls "flow": experiences in which "people become so involved in what they are doing that the activity becomes spontaneous, almost automatic;

---

1   Kaiser himself dated his writing of the play to 1912. But as Rhys W. Williams notes, Kaiser tended to date his texts earlier than they were written "to give the impression of a prodigious talent, unjustly neglected and discovered only later in his career." Wiliams argues that *Von morgens bis mitternachts* could have been revised as late as 1916, and even written as late as 1915. Williams, "Culture and Anarchy," 365. See also Groeneveld, "Modernist Medievalism," 89.

they stop being aware of themselves as separate from the actions they are performing."[2] At first sight, Csikszentmihalyi's understanding of flow aligns directly with how Heidegger understands our everyday habitual performance as absorbed in activity and lacking in self-awareness. Indeed, flow has been brought into discussions of Heidegger's ready-to-hand.[3] Yet reading *Von morgens bis mitternachts* in dialogue with Csikszentmihalyi's concept of flow allows us to make two important distinctions between various forms of uninhibited action. First, the cashier leaves the kind of everyday habitual life for a much more exciting one in the city. Both these experiences are marked by "smooth coping," by a body smoothly manipulating its environment. Yet where the former movements are robotic, marked by "automatic" movements that lack interest and attention, the latter is more fully engaged body and mind, in what Csikszentmihalyi has called a "merging of action and awareness."[4] Second, despite the fact that Csikszentmihalyi discusses, as we will see, the kind of experiences that the cashier participates in as "flow activities," a difference arises here between flow and ecstasy. Csikszentmihalyi's analysis places flow in relation to skill, that is, on hard-fought abilities. But the cashier's mastery of the environment relies rather on money. Indeed, the skillful, more careful "flow" of Csikszentmihalyi is more sustainable than the cashier's temporary, and wilder, ecstatic experience in the drama and silent film.

Reading Kaiser's text, and its film adaptation, in dialogue with Csikszentmihalyi's concept of flow thus continues to bring questions around immersive engagement into relief. It reminds us that everyday life, and its habitual motions, can be boring. Rather than being absorbing of attention, these everyday skilled movements can be accompanied by a feeling of restlessness, of wanting to find new and exciting paths. For those for whom everyday life is boring, the modern city might not be an overwhelming place but might rather offer new and exciting experiences. The city becomes an opportunity. Moreover, the texts allow us to make an important distinction within states of absorbed engagements, namely the difference between temporary states of ecstatic experience—such as might be precipitated by gambling, alcohol, sex, and religion—and a more sustained involvement, underpinned by habit, skill, and/or training, which the cashier does not find. Turning to both the drama and the film, and attending to the constraints and possibilities of these different

---

2 Csikszentmihalyi, *Flow*, 54.

3 E.g., Dreyfus, *Being-in-the-World*, 66; 94. See also, for example, Simon Høffding's *A Phenomenology of Musical Absorption*, in which he uses Dreyfus's Heidegger-inspired "smooth coping" alongside Csikszentmihalyi's understanding of "flow."

4 Csikszentmihalyi, *Applications of Flow*, 134. That is, action and awareness merge *toward* the same goal.

media, including silent film's visual highlighting of the human body and its engagement with the material world, adds depth to this argument about physical skill. But I begin with Kaiser's choreography.

Boredom

Kaiser's drama traces a human who wants to feel again. At work in the village, the cashier is bored. He is despondent working in the bank. Rhys W. Williams calls him an "automaton, wholly submerged in his function."[5] And until his hand is (accidentally) touched by a Florentine lady visiting the bank, initiating his ecstatic journey, the text introduces him through repetitive hand gestures: he knocks; he writes; he takes and hands over papers; he counts, bundles, and seals money. It is a hand choreography underlying a long stretch of dialogue between the bank director, a gentleman client, and the Florentine lady, during which the cashier says nothing. The abrupt brevity of the stage directions makes the gestures sound mechanical: the cashier "schreibt, holt Geld unter dem Schalter hervor, zählt sich in die Hand—dann auf das Zahlbrett" (*MM*, 5; writes, takes money from under the counter, counts it in his hand—then onto the payment tray).[6] This mechanical repetition is repeated in a later scene at the cashier's home. His daughters, mother, and wife have conversations in which they repeat the same phrases (*MM*, 30).[7] And when the cashier looks around the room, he thinks of the routines that await him until he dies and the table will be put aside for the casket (*MM*, 34). When his mother suddenly dies then and there, he feels very little: "keine vollständige Lähmung im Schmerz—kein Erfülltsein bis in die Augen" (*MM*, 35: no complete paralysis in pain—no being overwhelmed up and into the eyes). If the cashier is highly attuned to his environment at work and at home, he is also despondent. This brings to the fore an important difference between states of immersion, and between the cashier's and Malte's trajectories, that can be developed further via Csikszentmihalyi's concept of "flow."

5   Williams, "Culture and Anarchy," 369.
6   All translations of this source are mine.
7   "Frau *(kommt zu Mutter)*. Wir haben heute Koteletts. / Mutter. Bratest du sie jetzt? / Frau. Es hat noch Zeit. Es ist ja noch nicht Mittag. / Erste Tochter. Es ist ja noch lange nicht Mittag. / Frau. Nein, es ist noch lange nicht Mittag. / Mutter. Wenn er kommt, ist es Mittag. / Frau. Er kommt noch nicht. / Erste Tochter. Wenn Vater kommt, ist es Mittag. / Frau. Ja. *(Ab.)*" [Wife *(comes to mother)*. We'll have chops today. / Mother. Are you frying them now? / Wife. There's still time. It's still not noon yet. / Oldest daughter. It's still a long way from noon. / Wife. Indeed, it's a long way from noon. / Mother. When he comes, it will be noon. / Wife. He's not coming yet. / Oldest daughter. When father comes, it will be noon. / Wife. Indeed. *(Leaves.)*]

Csikszentmihalyi places flow in a careful balance between person and environment, that is between skill and challenge. In his popular book on the subject, a useful graph shows the flow channel that cuts through anxiety on the one hand and boredom on the other. That is, flow occurs when challenges and skills are in balance.[8] "When all a person's relevant skills are needed to cope with the challenges of a situation, that person's attention is completely absorbed."[9] However, when one's skills are no match for the challenges of the environment, anxiety occurs. Vice versa, if one's skills outmatch the challenges, boredom ensues. Importantly, however, this can have very little to do with *actual* skills and challenges. One can be perfectly matched for a challenge in terms of skills, but if one does not perceive one's skills as such, the feeling of anxiety will creep up anyway. Vice versa, one might be bored if one perceives one's skills to more than up to a task, even if in reality they are not.[10] In other words, flow, as Csikszentmihalyi understands it, occurs when *perceived* skills match *perceived* environmental challenges.

Csikszentmihalyi's analysis brings into focus how Kaiser's *Von morgens bis mitternachts* presents us with an example of "smooth coping" that is unsatisfying, as skill is not matched by a challenge. In the texts by Rilke and Döblin most notably, the main characters are overwhelmed by their new environments, they don't know how to proceed, they become anxious. Their perceived skills need to be developed for the unfamiliar environments of Paris and Berlin. And they long for the familiar environments they cannot return to. The cashier, however, reminds us that environments that are overly manageable, that do not surprise or challenge us, can lead to despondency, to mere robotic gestures, smooth but disinterested. The kind of "smooth coping" in familiar environments that is sought by Malte or Franz Biberkopf can also be boring. For the cashier the city, then, is a place that is exciting and challenging rather than overwhelming. The mark of his ecstatic experiences in the city is that it is immersive of both action *and* attention.

Games and Anarchy

The cashier's mechanical hand choreography and silence at work only end when the Florentine lady touches his hand. As Leanne Groeneveld

---

8 Csikszentmihalyi, *Flow*, 74.
9 Csikszentmihalyi, *Flow*, 53.
10 As Csikszentmihalyi points out about competitive games especially, absorption can also be disturbed by extrinsic goals: "if intrinsic goals—such as beating the opponent, wanting to impress an audience, or obtaining a big professional contract—are what one is concerned about, then competition is likely to become a distraction." Csikszentmihalyi, *Flow*, 73.

writes: "he becomes newly conscious and his senses become engaged."[11] The stage directions first say that he smiles and then: "Büsche des Bartes wogen—Brille sinkt in blühende Höhlen eröffneter Augen" (*MM*, 14; bushes of his beard billow—spectacles sink into blooming caves of opened eyes). His body blossoms, opens up, starts to move. This blossoming is emphasized sonically by the explosive alliteration of the letter "b" and the repetition of the open sounds of long stressed vowels throughout the sentence. Soon after that, the cashier's blossoming presents itself also in a first attempt to speak: "(durch Heiserkeit sträubt sich der Laut herauf) Holen Sie—Glas Wasser!" (*MM*, 15; (through hoarseness the sound strains upwards) Get me—glass of water!). The hoarseness suggests that it is a body that has forgotten how to speak; the request for water is the attempt to restore this ability. From this moment, the cashier is revitalized, "agile" (*MM*, 23) even: "Plötzlich sind Fähigkeiten ermittelt und mit Schwung tätig" (*MM*, 25; suddenly abilities are obtained and vigorously active). This is a physical awakening, of both one's perception to the environment and the abilities of one's own body, that we see throughout the modernist texts discussed in this monograph, most notably in Benjamin's *Einbahnstraße* and Baum's *Menschen im Hotel*. And as in Baum's text especially, it is a moment of intercorporeality—in this case, the touch of two hands, sexually charged—that is described as setting this physical thawing in motion. Yet Kaiser's text lets us know very little about why or how such human closeness might have this effect on someone (an aspect that will be central to my discussion of Baum's novel in chapter 6). However, what *Von morgens bis mitternachts* does describe is the kind of extreme "flow" that the cashier experiences in the city of Berlin: that is, ecstasy.

To open up the complexity in these states of ecstasy in the texts, it is helpful to contrast Csikszentmihalyi's concept of "flow" with Jules Evans's recent discussion of "ecstasy." "Ecstasy" is described by Jules Evans recently as a "peak experience" and a way to forget the self; to lose oneself; go beyond ourselves, and connect to something outside of ourselves.[12] He discusses experiences like religion, drugs, sex, war, and extreme sports. Positive sides to ecstasy, he writes, are its healing, inspiring, and connecting (that is, social) qualities and the sense of meaning it can give to our lives.[13] Negatively, it can lead to ego-inflation, suggestibility, and an unhealthy obsession with, or addiction to, such peak experiences.[14]

---

11   Groeneveld, "Modernist Medievalism," 91.
12   Evans, *Art of Losing Control*, x–xi.
13   Evans, *Art of Losing Control*, xxiii–xxiv.
14   Evans, *Art of Losing Control*, xxiv.

Csikszentmihalyi discusses "flow" as an "optimal" experience, but comes close to Evans's discussion of "ecstasy" when he states that "flow" has the characteristic of "a sense of discovery" and of "a new reality" opening up.[15] One way to think about the distinction between ecstasy and flow is to think of the former as a more extreme version of the latter. In Csikszentmihalyi's words to Evans: "flow is kind of a toned-down ecstasy, something that does have some of the characteristics of ecstasy—feeling that you're losing yourself in something larger, the sense of time disappears—but flow happens in conditions that are usually rather mundane. Of course, they happen also in arts or sports or extreme physical situations, but they can happen washing the dishes or reading a good book or having a conversation. It's a kind of experience which culminates in ecstasy."[16] That is, for Csikszentmihalyi, ecstasy is merely an extreme condition of the flow that occurs in everyday settings.

But there is something more at stake in the distinction made by Evans and Csikszentmihalyi, namely between a skillful control in flow and a letting go in ecstasy. As Evans writes at the end of his interview with Csikszentmihalyi: "[Csikszentmihalyi's] way of talking about ecstasy also appeals more to the autonomous self of capitalist society—hardworking, self-controlled, diligent, competent. Indeed, flow states are described as moments of supreme control and competence, rather than as a surrender of your ego to something Other." This difference between Csikszentmihalyi's "optimization" of experience through skill and control (in which ecstasy is a culmination) and Evans's more mystical letting go in ecstatic experience helps to productively complicate this reading of the cashier's experience. I will return to this difference below. For now, however, I turn to Csikszentmihalyi's analysis in *Flow* of the kind of activities that support flow, activities that align with the cashier's experiences in the drama and its adaptation, but which, in fact, do not always rely on the skill that Csikszentmihalyi is set on exploring.

In what Csikszentmihalyi discusses as "flow activities," that is, activities that are "*designed* to make optimal experience easier to achieve," there is a clear overlap with the kind of ecstatic activities that the cashier seeks out.[17] "Flow activities," Csikszentmihalyi writes, "have rules that require the learning of skills, they set up goals, they provide feedback, they make control possible. They facilitate concentration and involvement by making the activity as distinct as possible from . . . everyday experience."[18] He places these flow activities in the realm of games and play by discussing

---

15   Csikszentmihalyi, *Flow*, 74.
16   Qtd. in Evans, "Mihalyi Csikszentmihalyi on Flow and Ecstasy," n.p. See also Csikszentmihalyi, *Applications of Flow*, 134–35.
17   Csikszentmihalyi, *Flow*, 72.
18   Csikszentmihalyi, *Flow*, 72.

French anthropologist Roger Caillois's *Les jeux et les hommes* (*Man, Play, and Games*; 1958) which divides the world's playful activities into four broad classes. Caillois distinguishes *agôn, alea, ilinx,* and *mimicry* as the main four classes. *Agôn* marks competitive games such as soccer; *alea* games of chance such as gambling; *ilinx* refers to activities that change perception such as children do when they spin around; and *mimicry* refers to those activities in which we create alternative realities, such as the arts (Malte's writerly mimicry would fall squarely into this category). These are not mutually exclusive categories. Rather, a particular game's classification depends on the dominant aspect. Bringing this classification to bear on Kaiser's text and Martin's film, brings to the fore the central, but never fully explored, place of ecstatic experience in these texts.

In *Von morgens bis mitternachts,* the so-called *Sechstagerennen* (six-day race) is probably the clearest example of such a "flow activity." It has rules; it takes skill; there is a clear goal; and there is feedback and control. And it is separated in the stadium from "everyday" experience.[19] It is easily categorized as *agôn,* that is, a game of competition. Cyclists compete against one another. Yet, all this tells us very little about the role it takes in Kaiser's drama or the film. The role of the cyclists is not centered in the drama, even if a cyclist does appear "confessing" in the religious experience at the end. Rather what is relevant here is the audience's involvement. The cashier is spending money to heighten the audience's involvement by heightening the stakes: "Das Publikum kocht in Erregungen. Das muß ausgenutzt werden. Der Brand soll eine nie erlebte Steigerung erfahren" (*MM*, 44; The public is seething with excitement. This must be exploited. The fire shall experience an unprecedented intensification). The announcement of the prize money funded by the cashier leads to ecstasy (*MM*, 46). This ecstasy seems an instance, in Caillois's classification of games, of *ilinx,* activities that change perception. This distortion of perception is especially apparent in the film's famous scene of the cyclists. Here the camera's distorted view—the cyclists are horizontally stretched when they come into and go out of frame—emphasizes the speed and circular motion of the cyclists. The scene shows what the new medium of film offered, especially in terms of our discussion: making the relation between movement and visual perception immediately visible. One could read this as a distortion of the perspective of the cyclists, if it weren't for the fact that these scenes are intercut with a view of audiences turning their heads and bodies in circles, seemingly following the cyclists. The main goal of this aesthetic experimentation, then, is to show

---

19 When Csikszentmihalyi discusses ecstasy, as opposed to flow, in most detail, he discusses that the architecture that remains of older cultures (e.g., theatres, sports arenas, and temples) all center around the experience of ecstasy. Csikszentmihalyi, *Applications of Flow*, 134.

the distortion of the view of the spectators. Caillois writes about *ilinx*, in line with Evans's discussion of ecstasy as losing oneself, that [the person] lets himself drift and becomes intoxicated through feeling directed, dominated, and possessed by strange powers."[20] The cashier and his money indeed heighten the "strange power" over the group in which group behavior seems to allow for individual agency to be possessed by the social environment.

A similar social intoxication seems to be the cashier's goal in his interaction with the masked women in the private room of a dancehall. He encourages them to dance: "Tanze. Drehe deinen Wirbel. Tanze, tanze. Witz gilt nicht. Hübschheit gilt nicht. Tanz ist es, drehend—wirbelnd. Tanz. Tanz. Tanz!" (*MM*, 52; Dance. Spin your whirl. Dance, dance. Wit does not count. Being pretty doesn't count. Dance it is, spinning—whirling. Dance. Dance. Dance!). He describes dancing as being at the opposite corner of life to death (*MM*, 52). It is no coincidence that both Kaiser's text here and Csikszentmihalyi's when discussing *ilinx* mention dervishes, the members of Sufi fraternities, many of whom have the practice of getting into states of ecstasy by turning around in circles (*MM*, 52).[21] As with the audience of the cycling race, the cashier here attempts to encourage the intoxication of the people around him. He succeeds: the audience of the cycling race and some of the masked women in the dancehall do find the kind of immersive experience that the modernist authors of this book explore. Moreover, their experiences rely less on skill than on losing themselves in the experience, aligning more with Evans's analysis. But the cashier himself does not take part. If there is intoxication in his own behavior, it is only his excitement about getting the others intoxicated.

In his excitement about getting other people excited, but without participating in their excitement, he seems to be playing a different kind of game. The form that play takes in the cashier's behavior, and in which he connects to Malte, has more to do with *mimicry*, that is, it is a form of play-acting. Although the cashier *is* a rich man now, he also takes on the role of a rich man. He takes on new behaviors; in the film he buys a new suit. It is a performance then, which is also an experiment, a probe. The cashier is trying to see what effect money has on the world. What happens when money is brought into situations; or what effect can the cashier achieve with his money? Huder calls it a "Testreihe" (a series of tests): ". . . ein Kassierer [wird] plötzlich vom bürokratischen Lenker des Geldtransfers zum bravourösen Tester der Geldsubstanz" (a cashier changes suddenly from a bureaucratic steerer of money transfers into a

20 Caillois, *Man, Play, and Games*, 78.
21 Csikszentmihalyi, *Flow*, 73.

bravura tester of the substance of money).[22] The cashier's performance is akin to Malte rewriting histories as a kind of performance; they are both trying to see what it would be like if one took on a certain role.

But perhaps the most relevant difference that Caillois's classification of games makes in relation to this discussion of *Von morgens bis mitternachts* is not his classification of the dominant role of competition, chance, simulation, or vertigo, but rather how within each set of games there is a continuum between the opposite poles of *paidia* and *ludus*, or anarchy and rule.

> At one extreme an almost indivisible principle, common to diversion, turbulence, free improvisation, and carefree gaiety is dominant. It manifests a kind of uncontrolled fantasy that can be designated by the term *paidia*. At the opposite extreme, this frolicsome and impulsive exuberance is almost entirely absorbed or disciplined by a complementary, and in some respects inverse, tendency to its anarchic and capricious nature: there is a growing tendency to bind it with arbitrary, imperative, and purposely tedious conventions, to oppose it still more by ceaselessly practicing the most embarrassing chicanery upon it, in order to make it more uncertain of attaining its desired effect. This latter principle is completely impractical, even though it requires an ever greater amount of effort, skill, or ingenuity. I call this second component *ludus*.[23]

The cashier is clearly after the anarchy of *paidia*. He is looking for, and looking to increase, the turbulence and anarchy in the audience of the cycling race as well as in the masked dancers. And his own behavior, his mimicry of a rich man, is marked not by careful steps but by a complete loss of self-control, by such "uncontrolled fantasy" and "carefree gaiety." This emphasis on anarchy sets the cashier in *Von morgens bis mitternachts* apart from the other characters in the other modernist texts I discuss in this book, and their attempts at overcoming unfamiliarity. If Malte is testing the waters through mimicry of historical figures, he does so in a controlled way. He begins with merely copying other texts and only subsequently rewrites histories, to finish with the open story of the prodigal son, which he fills with his own experiences. And Malte does so in the relative safety of his own room. Here, however, the cashier dives right into life—Huder, calling the cashier an "Ekstatiker" (ecstatic person) and a "Lebenswilderer" (wildcat), writes that "er überschätzt, überfährt, und überbietet ... alles" (he overestimates, overruns, and overbids

---

22   Huder, afterword, 82. My translation.
23   Caillois, *Man, Play, and Games*, 13.

. . . everything).[24] We are closer here to Evans's ecstasy than to the hard work, self-control, and competency of Csikszentmihalyi's flow.

Indeed, the cashier's anarchy ties into Kaiser's interests in political anarchy. Williams has argued that anarchy, especially Gustav Landauer's (1870–1919), had a major influence on Kaiser's work and on *Von morgens bis mitternachts* in particular. Especially Landauer's analysis of the difference between the true value of things and the monetary value they have in a capitalist society is subject to Williams' discussion.[25] Landauer's questions tie into the cashier's experiments with what money can buy him. But there is also a social element to Williams's analysis. He argues that the group excitement at the *Sechstagerennen* comes close to Landauer's idea of "Geist" (spirit) a "living, socially cohesive force," but ultimately fails in Kaiser's text because he attempts to bring it about through money.[26] And if Landauer's interest in medieval social relations might indicate a more positive reading of the Emperor's appearance at the end of the *Sechstagerennen*, Williams argues that the Emperor is only a sign of the "surrogate unifying force" of nationalism, a nationalism also present in the "most intense outcry" that followed the win of a German rider as well as the German anthem that plays when the cashier leaves.[27]

More generally, the text's exploration of the "impulsive exuberance" of ecstatic experience ties into understandings of German culture in the Weimar Republic and the years leading into it as a culture of ecstasy. Most notably, Walter Benjamin, as we will see in chapter 5, discusses ecstatic experience in various of his writings also as a potentially revolutionary force. Two further examples show that the "ecstasy" was often a charge and laid at a variety of feet. Thomas Mann, for example, writing against fascism in 1930, asked whether this "Fanatismus, die Glieder werfende Unbesonnenheit, die orgiastische Verleugnung von Vernunft, Menschenwürde" (fanaticism, all this bacchantic frenzy, that orgiastic denial of reason and human dignity) was really German.[28] Writing in 1921, Carl Ludwig Schleich, a surgeon and writer, argues that the "ecstatic longing for intensification" (ein Rausch . . . der nach Steigerung giert) grabbed hold of their culture before World War I.[29] He connects

---

24 Huder, afterword, 84.
25 Williams, "Culture and Anarchy," 369.
26 Williams, "Culture and Anarchy," 367, 369. See also Landauer, *Aufruf zum Sozialismus*.
27 Williams, "Culture and Anarchy," 367, 369. Landauer states: "der Staat ist das Surrogat des Geistes" (the state is the surrogate for spirit). Landauer, *Aufruf zum Sozialismus*, 19; Landauer, *Call to Socialism*, 41.
28 Mann, *Deutsche Ansprache*, 19. Translated by H. T. Lowe-Porter: Mann, "Appeal to Reason," 154.
29 Schleich, "Kokainismus," 1311. All translations of this source by Don Reneau: Schleich, "Cocainism," here, 723.

gambling and sports to the use and abuse of weaker and stronger narcotics, from caffeine and nicotine to opium and, especially, cocaine. He then asks rhetorically about those addicted to cocaine: "kann man es den Mühseligen und Beladenen, den Gescheiterten und Gebrochenen, den hoffnungslosen Parias dieser Erde allzusehr übelnehmen, wenn sie in diesem Nirwana verfallen? Mögen sie eine Art des schönen Sterbens, ihre Euthanasie, hier suchen und finden, den Selbstmord auf dem Wege der Lust begehen . . ." (can one really hold it against those afflicted with toil and burdens, the failed and the broken, the hopeless pariahs of this earth, if they fall victim to this nirvana? Let them seek here and perhaps find a kind of beautiful death, a euthanasia, let them commit suicide on the path of pleasure).[30] This description mimics the trajectory of the cashier from his toil to ecstasy, a journey that, marked from the beginning by a warning of impending death, also ends in suicide. But if the cashier's journey mimics a larger culture of ecstasy, his experience is also at odds with his world.

Friction and Hubris

While there is a vitalistic over-excitement in the cashier's engagement with his surroundings, there is nevertheless also a sense of the foreignness of the modern world. Such an apparent alienation—not absent from village life either—is expressed in various ways in the drama and its adaptation to film. Most notably, as in *Malte Laurids Brigge*, alienation is expressed through objects and foreign language. In the film, the cashier's alienation from his environment is expressed by the repeated insertion of foreign text. The Bank has signs in English: "Safes" and "Change." The entrance to the bar is marked with the French "Entrée." And the German "Heilsarmee" becomes the English "Salvation Army."[31]

But the silent film also draws on possibilities more specific to this visual medium, such as being able to show (often humorous) friction between human bodies and objects, to show the foreignness of an environment. Thus such foreignness is expressed through the design of the décor, exemplified by the staircase leading to the Florentine woman's hotel room. Staircases seem to take an important place in German modernist concerns with human movement. In *The Haunted Screen*, Lotte Eisner discusses Weimar film's "obsession with staircases."[32] She writes that "flights of steps allow [the actor's body's] dynamism to assert

---

30 Schleich, "Kokainismus," 1314. Schleich, Cocainism, 723.
31 This may well have been done to appeal to a variety of foreign audiences. Yet the effect of the various languages remains that the city feels cosmopolitan and foreign.
32 Eisner, *Haunted Screen*, 123.

itself."[33] Beyond film, the most famous portrayal of a vitalist staircase is probably Marcel Duchamp's 1912 *Nu descendant un escalier no 2*. In this abstract painting, a (naked) figure descends a staircase. It shows the different steps or stages of movement in one image as if the various photos of an Eadweard Muybridge work were superimposed. Through this futurist abstraction, Duchamp highlights the motion of the body. In Martin's film, however, the vitalism of staircases is complicated by the apparent recalcitrance of this object.

The expressionist décor in the film, designed by Robert Neppach, looks like a black and white sketch. The "light" that shines onto clothes and decoration is represented by broad, white strokes of paint on the otherwise black or dark scenery and clothes. Surfaces, walls, and doors are crooked and seem to be made from cardboard. The stairs in the film—to the Italian lady's hotel room—has crooked slats and is covered in white brushstrokes to signify the light that shines on it from the—equally painted—bright light in the right-hand corner. When the décor first appears, it looks as if it is merely a background. The stairs look as if they are painted onto the back canvas. They look flat and fake; at best a cardboard construction that cannot support a human. If Heidegger discusses anxiety in terms of recalcitrance, then the film's décor equally expresses anxiety through objects that seem unable to sustain one's movements. Because the staircase looks flimsy, you expect the characters to skirt around it, or the scene to cut out before anyone ascends or descends it.[34] Instead, the Italian woman's son dynamically bounds up it as does the cashier. It is a moment in which audience's expectations might be thwarted. If the expressionist décor seems uninhabitable, seems an expression of anxious feelings of uninhabitability, the men deny it.[35] The seemingly recalcitrant

33 Eisner, *Haunted Screen*, 122.
34 As Siegfried Kracauer writes about *Das Cabinet des Dr. Caligari* (*The Cabinet of Dr. Caligari*; 1920), arguably the film most famous for its expressionist design: "the incorporation of human beings and their movements into the texture of the surroundings was tremendously difficult." Kracauer, *From Caligari to Hitler*, 69.
35 As Eisner points out, Austrian psychoanalyst Otto Rank argued that staircases stand in for the sexual act. Certainly, Martin's film allows for such an interpretation. Both the painting and the Florentine lady, which await the lady's son and the cashier at the top of the staircase, are erotically charged (*Haunted Screen*, 121). The movie turns the painting into an (art historically omnipresent) reclining female nude. This painting is linked to the clothed Florentine lady reclining on a sofa that turns into an image of her almost completely naked. In Kaiser's play, however, the painting is an erotic depiction of Adam and Eve—that is, Adam and Eve before the fall. The cashier recognizes himself in this biblical image, a recognition that corresponds with the final image of him as Christ. This biblical reference to Adam and Eve is lost in the film.

stairs are overcome. The stairs heighten the vitalism of both men, who are both driven by a sexual urge (one for the naked woman in the painting, the other for the Florentine lady).

A similar point must be made about barstools. In the silent film, the cashier, when he comes to the bar, struggles with the extremely high barstool, the seat of which reaches to about his sternum when he stands next to it. It is a sudden moment of exaggerated physical comedy, all but absent elsewhere in the film. The scene is framed by a wealthy-looking man with a monocle on the only other barstool and a broadly smiling black waiter behind the bar (which the cashier, his gestures suggest, has never seen the likes of).[36] The cashier repeatedly shifts his attention between the wealthy man atop the other barstool and his own stool and body. He then puts his leg on the lowest of the barstool's two footrests, repeatedly trying to lift himself up onto the seat. Finally, with a couple of movements gaining swing, he manages to get to the top. Once there, he orders the same drink as the wealthy man. The cashier not only dislikes the drink, but the ridiculously long straw with which it comes presents another hurdle and another moment of physical comedy. In these moments of exaggerated physical comedy, then, Martin's film adapts Kaiser's drama and the ways in which it portrays the foreignness of the big city by drawing on conventions from a popular part of silent film's recent history: that of slapstick.

The cashier's struggles to adapt to the habits of the wealthy anticipates the portrayal of Kringelein in Baum's *Menschen im Hotel*. Kringelein, too, comments on the barstools when he enters a Berlin bar. For both, it is presented as a moment of habituation. For the cashier, the barstool, phenomenologically if not *actually* higher than the one he is used to, comes to represent the hurdles of modernity and of social adaptation. As with the stairs, the barstool, as a tool for physically ascending, becomes a metaphor for social ascension. Eisner makes this link between stairs and stools when she reminds us that Paul Rotha and Siegfried Kracauer made a similar argument about "the unapproachable secretary perched on a tall stool in *Caligari*."[37] Nevertheless, the height of the stool as well as the length of the straw also signify how familiar objects become unfamiliar in new contexts. These familiar objects now need new physical approaches.

---

36 It is a stereotypical image of a black servant that should, it seems to me, be read as ironic in the context of the scene. Through physical comedy the scene takes aim at the habits and behaviors of the rich. The image of the subserviently smiling black man seems to fit into that scene because he illustrates, like the prostitutes in Williams's argument about *Von morgens bis mitternachts*, "that the life of luxury . . . depends on the exploitation of the weakest members of society." Williams, "Culture and Anarchy," 370.

37 Eisner, *Haunted Screen*, 122. See also Rotha, *Film Till Now*, 45; Kracauer, *From Caligari to Hitler*, 72.

The process of familiarizing unfamiliar environments, including social adaptation, are presented as moments in need of physical skill rather than conscious deliberation. While the film suggests a more general alienation from the world in the foreign language and the stairs in the small town, the city is the place where the cashier's unfamiliarity with the practices of the rich is pronounced.

In Kaiser's original drama, this unfamiliarity with the customs of the rich is also expressed in the bar scene. Yet here it is shown—unsurprisingly, perhaps, given the medium's usual foregrounding of speech—through a difficult conversation with the waiter. When the cashier is asked which brand he prefers, he says something about choosing the ladies himself. But the waiter was talking about champagne. When the cashier realizes this, he chooses Grand Marnier, which is a liquor that includes cognac:

> Kellner: Das ist Kognak nach dem Sekt.
> Kassierer: Also—darin richte ich mich entgegenkommend nach Ihnen.
> Kellner: Zwei Flaschen Pommery. Dry?
> Kassierer: Zwei, wie Sie sagten.
> Kellner: Extra Dry?
> Kassierer: Zwei decken den anfänglichen Bedarf. Oder für diskrete Bedienung drei Flaschen extra? Gewährt. (*MM*, 48)

> [Waiter: That's cognac after the champagne.
> Cashier: Well—I'll take your guidance on that obligingly.
> Waiter: Two bottles of Pommery. Dry?
> Cashier: Two, as you said.
> Waiter: Extra Dry?
> Cashier: Two should cover initial needs. Or for discreet service, three bottles extra? Granted.]

The cashier thus misunderstands the waiter's question about the dryness of the champagne, mistaking the English word "dry" for the German "drei." Subsequently, when the waiter asks him to choose between various dishes with French names, he ignores the question, instead calling them all excellent. Here, as also in the film, foreign language marks the fact that the cashier is in unfamiliar territory. But rather than asking for clarifications, he just keeps going, ignoring the friction. The vitalism of ecstatic behavior is thus complicated by a sense of friction between the cashier's behavior and his surroundings. As in the other text discussed in this monograph, the new environment of the city is also unfamiliar and recalcitrant to the cashier. The way in which he handles these situations, through an anarchic ecstasy, opens up the complexity within states of flow.

Control and Skill

Ultimately, the cashier's behavior complicates the seeming dichotomy between Csikszentmihalyi's skill and Evans's ecstasy, that is, between control and letting go. The cashier never masters the environments that he enters with skill, nor does he seem after it. Rather, his behavior is wild and lacks self-control, that is, it is anarchic. Moreover, he wants to whip the people he encounters into a similar frenzy. However, he does attempt to control the people around him. But this control is not due to skill, but rather through money. To the extent that he masters his environment, such mastery is due to his money. Money takes the place of skill. He does not attentively attune his action to objects and other people, but rather dominates and manipulates the people around him with money. Thus while his behavior is akin to Evans's ecstasy, losing himself, lacking self-control, he nevertheless manages to largely control the environment as in Csikszentmihalyi's "flow."

That is, his mastery is despite a lack of skill. Hence the effect is always partial and temporary. The frenzy at the cycling race is disturbed by the presence of the *Kaiser*, whose presence has an immediate calming effect on the spectators. The *Kaiser* clearly has more power than the cashier. The scene with the masked women also fails because the cashier does not pay attention to them. As Williams writes: "the first of the masked girls overindulges in the champagne and is incapable of supplying the sexual thrill which the Kassierer desires; the second is sober, but drops her mask to reveal a true face far less appetizing to him than the tinsel image; the third, who drives him to a pitch of excitement by her refusal to dance, turns out to have a wooden leg."[38] The hubris given to him by money means he dominates rather than learns and is thus not able to deal with the limits of what money can buy.

Here lies the difference between Csikszentmihalyi's concept of flow, in which mastery of the environment relies on skill, and the descriptions of ecstasy in *Von morgens bis mitternachts*, in which ecstasy relies on domination by the brute force of money. The necessity of skill for manipulation is replaced by money (and along with it, hubris and power). And although feelings of ecstasy, as Csikszentmihalyi points out, have always been important to get out of our all-too mundane lives, both Kaiser's text and its adaptation to film suggest that something else is needed for a life that is also sustainable beyond midnight.[39] If the cashier, as Schueler points out, is "guided by an all too unreflective and vitalistic response," then the question becomes what a more sustainable practice away from

---

38 Williams, "Culture and Anarchy," 370.
39 See Csikszentmihalyi, *Applications of Flow*, 134.

the boredom of everyday life might look like.[40] Both at the end of the drama and in a later essay, Kaiser suggests other ways forward. He suggests that a better way forward may indeed be achieved through skill and, as already indicated *ex negativo* by the cashier's lack of attention to the people around him, a responsiveness to others.

If human skill forms an important part of Csikszentmihalyi's argument but seems absent from the kind of ecstasy at play in *Von morgens bis mitternachts*, or rather replaced by money, Kaiser is nevertheless interested in it as the final achievement of humanity. In a short 1922 essay named "Der kommende Mensch" (The Future Human), he discusses "der gekonnte Mensch," that is, the skillful human, as the future of humanity. The essay is reminiscent of Nietzsche's *Zarathustra*, which Kaiser mentions in the text.[41] He writes that contemporary life turns against humanity's original totality "komponiert aus Kopf und Hirn und Herz und Blut" (composed of head and brain and heart and blood).[42] In what seems like a response to labor at the conveyer belt he argues that humans in the modern world are overspecialized and do not use the full breath of their possibilities. Nevertheless, mimicking Nietzsche's arguments in *Zarathustra* about the learned who should go out into the world, Kaiser does not limit his argument to manual labor alone: "Der Mensch, der nur Dichtung deutet und schreibt, vergreift sich an der Totalität genau so wie der Arbeiter, der nur mit eines Gliedes Druck sein Maschinenteil bewegt" (the person who only interprets and writes poetry violates totality in the same way as the worker who moves his part of the machine with only one limb's pressure).[43] Kaiser's argument here is a vitalist one, according to which body and mind will have to become balanced in the future human.[44] As Walter H. Sokel points out, in contrast to the vitalist, then, who "craves for spontaneity and impulsiveness to prove to

---

40 Schueler, "Symbolism of Paradise," 101. See also, Martens, *Vitalismus und Expressionismus*, 258–88.

41 Kaiser, "Kommende Mensch," 681. See also Hillebrand, *Nietzsche und die Deutsche Literatur*, 207–8. Landauer, too, was inspired by *Zarathustra* as attested from even his earliest writings. Landauer, "Twenty-Five Years Later," 64.

42 Kaiser, "Kommende Mensch," 682.

43 Kaiser, "Kommende Mensch," 682.

44 Kaiser's overall argument about using all of our capabilities mimics Landauer's arguments about how work should again be playful: "unsere Zeit hat den Sport, die unproduktive, spielerische Betätigung der Muskeln und Nerven zu einer Art Arbeit oder Beruf gemacht; in wirklicher Kultur wird die Arbeit selbst wieder ein spielendes Gehenlassen all unserer Kräfte sein" (our age has made sport, the unproductive, playful activity of muscles and nerves, into a sort of work or profession. In real culture work itself again becomes a playful unwinding of all our energies). Landauer, *Aufruf zum Sozialismus*, 89; Landauer, *Call to Socialism*, 120–21.

himself that he is a feeling human being," Kaiser's "new man wants action guided by reason in the pursuit of love."[45] In Kaiser's essay on the skillful human thus lies an inkling of an ecstatic engagement that seems closer to Csikszentmihalyi's "flow" and his emphasis on skill than on a hubristic ecstatic engagement. It is only a kernel, however, and Kaiser's concerns regarding a full cultivation of abilities seem far removed from the neo-liberal tendencies—with emphases on self-control and working hard, for example—that Evans has recognized in Csikszentmihalyi's flow.[46] In chapter 5, on Walter Benjamin's *Einbahnstraße*, we find a sense of what skill might look like beyond Csikszentmihalyi's approach.

But Kaiser's *Von morgens bis mitternachts* seems especially concerned about a lack of attention to other people. Only in the final scene in the meeting hall of the Salvation Army does the effect of the cashier's behavior become clear. A rider tells of how he got injured; a family man of his neglect of his family, and a prostitute tells her story. The ending suggests a concern for an attention to other people, a concern which we have seen is also present in Heidegger's concerns about authentic *Fürsorge*. As we will see in the next chapter, a similar concern also marks the end of *Berlin Alexanderplatz*. This value of community only becomes clear to the cashier at the very end of Kaiser's drama, when he reflects on the woman from the Salvation Army who he thinks stands by him, but then betrays him. Kaiser's own description of his drama affirms this reading: "Aufbruch des einzelnen in die Menschheit—Irrtum als Einzelner menschlich zu sein—ein Nein—gegen Betonmauer geführte Straßenkurve: das ist *Von morgens bis mitternachts*" (departure of the individual into humanity—the error of being human as an individual—a no—a road curve leading into a concrete wall: that is *From Morn to Midnight*).[47] The cashier's problem thus seems to be that in his all-too ecstatic engagement he ignores the relevant signals of his social environment. Indeed, this is exactly a mark of states of immersive experience. Csikszentmihalyi talks about the "one-pointedness of mind" and that "irrelevant stimuli are excluded from consciousness"; Evans about the danger of ego-inflation.[48] The danger is clear: that a one-track mind ignores stimuli that turn out to be relevant. Stimuli, for example, that are relevant to the lives of others. We are here back, then, to Landauer's understanding of "Geist," a more direct relation to other people, not mediated through the state or through money.

This is also the important point at which the film adaptation clearly parts ways with the original drama, and it does so by drawing on popular

---

45 Sokel, *Writer in Extremis*, 173.
46 Evans, "Mihaly Csikszentmihalyi on Flow and Ecstasy," n.p.
47 Kaiser, "Über mein Werk," 563.
48 Csikszentmihalyi, *Applications of Flow*, 134, 133; Evans, *Art of Losing Control*, xxiv.

film conventions. In the film, namely, the cashier's overly ecstatic behavior is a force that is not to be mediated through other people, but rather one to be controlled by the authorities. As Cynthia Walk has perceptively pointed out, the film, although certainly not devoid of experiment, takes the story of the cashier and maps it onto "the conventions of the detective film": "cross-cutting between the clerk on the run and the law on his trail, it recasts the narrative in subsequent acts as a sustained chase with action and suspense. Added scenes feature policemen, telegraphers and newspaper boys engaged in a manhunt across the city. The intertitles circulate news of the suspect's escape and the warrant for his arrest."[49] If in the drama the driving tension lies in an ecstatic engagement that ignores the social environment, in the film it lies between the cashier's engagement and state control. The film draws on the conventions of the detective film, thereby turning the cashier's anarchic, ecstatic behavior into a more ordinary story of the need for state control. Kaiser suggests rather that this ecstasy should be negotiated through other people.

Conclusion

Kaiser's *Von morgens bis mitternachts* and its adaptation to film complicate the developing picture of this book in two ways. First, while the emphasis in *Malte Laurids Brigge* is on the modern urban environment as overwhelming, especially when compared to the familiar environments that Malte comes from. The city in *Von morgens bis mitternachts* offers the cashier excitement. It brings into relief that familiarity can be rigid and boring (a picture further developed in chapter 5 through Benjamin), especially under modern conditions of labor, with its repetitive gestures. It gives a picture in which the city offers a way out of such repetition. Secondly, reading these texts in dialogue with Csikszentmihalyi's "flow" shows that another distinction needs to be made between the kind of ecstatic experience we find in mastering our environments through money, power, and hubris, and the kind of mastery that we achieve through skill. It is not that the cashier does not encounter unfamiliarity—both the drama and the film (in the latter by drawing on popular conventions of slapstick) emphasize moments of social not-knowing-how. But the cashier masters these situations through money or he walks away. That is, the cashier does not exactly habituate or attempt to habituate his new environment. The text shows that there are other ways to gain control than through skill.

Ultimately, the question becomes how we might retain some of the anarchic energy of the cashier within a more sustained and attentive practice of skill, a question to which we will return n chapter 5 on Benjamin's

---

49 Walk, "Cross-Media Exchange in Weimar Culture," 186.

Einbahnstraße. In the next chapter, however, we look harder at the question of the importance of attending to other people as itself a skill. If Kaiser hints at the importance of sociality and, as we saw in chapter 1, Heidegger describes the importance of attending to the gestures of others, then Döblin's text shows us that an attention to the gestures of other people takes an essential role in guiding us into unfamiliar environments. If Döblin's protagonist Franz Biberkopf for the most part, like the cashier, lacks the awareness of what is happening around him, his stubbornness marks again a different engagement with a recalcitrant environment.

4: Alfred Döblin's *Berlin Alexanderplatz*: The Affordances of Others

> *Die Welt ist nicht auf Anhieb neu zu erleben.*
> [The world cannot right away be sensed anew.]
> —Alfred Döblin[1]

ALFRED DÖBLIN'S EPIC NOVEL *Berlin Alexanderplatz: Die Geschichte vom Franz Biberkopf* opens, after parts of its epic framing, with its protagonist Franz Biberkopf standing anxiously with his back against a red brick wall: "Er ließ Elektrische auf Elektrische vorbeifahren, drückte den Rücken an die rote Mauer und ging nicht. Der Aufseher am Tor spazierte einige Male an ihm vorbei, zeigte ihm seine Bahn, er ging nicht" (*BA*, 13; he allowed one tram after another to pass, and he didn't take any of them. The guard on the gate strolled past him a few times, pointed to the tram, he didn't take it: *BA2*, 5). The red brick wall, which belongs to the jail Biberkopf has just been released from, as well as the trams that pass by, are recurrent objects in the novel. They seem to come to stand in for the contrast between the familiar jail Biberkopf has to leave and the unfamiliar city that is now his environment. The wall, suggestive of warmth in its red color and of stability in its structure, is opposed to the fast-moving and charged multiplicity of the trams passing by. Moreover, these objects get their affective strength particularly from Biberkopf's engagement with them: he seeks out the comfort of the wall, and lets tram after tram pass by, even if the warden is pointing him in the right direction.

Döblin's attention to the material and physical world, mirroring that of Rilke and Heidegger, is found throughout the novel, from his description of the dynamic city, to the bodies of animals, to the elements of montage, which not only literally bring worldly material into the novel but also emphasize, as Harald Jähner argues, the materiality of language.[2] Volker Klotz argues that in the end it is the materiality of the city that stays in readers' minds.[3] Döblin himself writes: "Die Fassade des Romans kann nicht anders sein als aus Stein oder Stahl" (the façade of the novel

---

1   Döblin, "Geist des naturalistischen Zeitalters," 83. All translations of this source by Chris Godwin: Döblin, "Spirit of a Naturalistic Age," here, 87.
2   Jähner, *Erzählter, montierter, souffliierter Text*, 132.
3   Klotz. *Erzählte Stadt*.

can be nothing other than stone or steel).[4] In opposition to this material world stands Biberkopf, whose physical engagement with the environment is emphasized. Not only is his story said to be a lesson for anyone in a "Menschenhaut" (human skin) but his relation to the environment is also described as a "fight": he is "pushed" and "beaten," "battered" and "torpedoed" (*BA*, 9; *BA2*, 1). His physicality is further emphasized by his losing his right arm—though this change rarely is shown to affect how he engages with the world—and a repeated comparison of him to animals, most notably in his name ("Biberkopf" means "beaver-head").[5]

This relation between the material world and Biberkopf's body plays out in different ways. On the one hand there is the anxious and overwhelmed response of the first pages that mirrors Malte's response to the recalcitrant environment in Rilke's text. The forces of the modern city seem to go right through Biberkopf. Most of the time, however, his engagement is antagonistic, aggressive, and close to that of a physical fight. Biberkopf's comportment is marked by what Baßler and Horn aptly call his "Zwangshandlungen" (compulsions): familiar behavior of aggressiveness and attempts at asserting control—a behavior Kiesel understands as representing modernity in its "Aggressivität und Herrschsucht" (aggression and imperiousness).[6] Döblin's repeated use of the imagery of the Book of Job reinforces this understanding of Biberkopf's interaction as violent and in terms of "blows" delivered to him (*BA*, 9; *BA2*, 1). But at times he manages to assert himself violently, such as when he rapes the sister of the woman whose rape and murder he went to prison for in the first place. He is called, by the narrator and the figure of death who appears near the end of the novel, in turns arrogant, stubborn, weak, and cowardly (*BA*, 9, 486; *BA2*, 1, 419). At the end of the novel, however, a different engagement is presented. A new Biberkopf, Franz *Karl*, is now standing, after a lesson dealt to him by the figure of death, on Alexanderplatz surrounded by other people from whom he learns and by whom he is supported. This ending as propagating learning from others

---

[4] Döblin, "An Romanautoren und ihre Kritiker," 17. All translations of this source by Chris Godwin: Döblin, "To Novelists and their Critics," here, 11.

[5] Throughout the text, the emphasis in Biberkopf's lack of an arm is on his social environment and the way in which people speak about disabled people as, for example, not deserving of welfare (often in front of Biberkopf). With the exception of a short scene in which Biberkopf, to the surprise of the men around him, ably helps rescue a horse from a shaft (*BA*, 269–70), the text does not explore how the loss of his arm affects what he can and cannot do or how this loss, and the way in which it is perceived socially, affects how he understands his own abilities.

[6] Baßler and Horn, afterword, 530; Kiesel, *Geschichte der literarischen Moderne*, 340. All translations of both these sources are mine.

is, however, as many critics have discussed, far from unambiguous.[7] The novel simultaneously ends with aggressively marching groups: "marschieren, marschieren, wir ziehen in den Krieg" (*BA*, 510; marching, marching, we're marching into war: *BA2*, 440). How are these aggressions of others to be squared with an otherwise positive treatment of community? Does it show the negative aspects of the new Biberkopf's choice for community, as for example Klotz argues, or is it merely another example of Döblin's general ambiguity as Muschg proposes?[8] Moreover, the lesson that Biberkopf gets taught by death raises, as Baßler and Horn point out, another question about his relationship to the environment. Was Biberkopf indeed at fault all this time, as death suggests, or was there at least a degree, as the actual *Schläge* (strikes) that befall Biberkopf suggest, of *Fremdbestimmung* (heteronomy)?[9]

Döblin's interest in the dynamic between body and material world, like the interests of Rilke and Heidegger, opens up a different way of investigating these questions by way of contemporary theories of embodied cognition and ecological psychology, in particular the so-called "theory of affordances" mentioned in chapter 2. As with the wall and the tram in *Berlin Alexanderplatz*, the theory of "affordances" focuses, as we have seen, on the ways in which the material environment is perceived as meaningful to an agent in terms of possible actions he, she, or it can undertake. A tree, for instance, affords humans shading and climbing, the woodpecker pecking, and the beaver building a dam. The way in which we perceive the environment, according to this theory, is not in terms of objective things, but as useful objects. Affordances are constituted between the materiality of an object and the bodily abilities of an animal or human being. They are therefore, as Gibson states, neither objective nor subjective.[10] Instead, affordances are shaped and reshaped in the dynamic between action and perception. Moreover, as Rietveld and Kiverstein recently developed, affordances are also contextual and normative.[11] A clock, for example, will afford gift-giving in most contexts, but not in the Chinese culture. Other people always already have shaped and continue to shape affordances, the way in which we see our environment. Affordances, thus, are on the one hand flexible, open to change and reshaping. As Terence Cave recently stated in his work on affordances for literary studies, to talk about affordances is

---

7   See, for example, Klotz, *Erzählte Stadt*; Bayerdorfer, "Wissende und die Gewalt"; Muschg, afterword; and more recently Jentsch, "Franz Karl Biberkopf als Sein-zum-Tode."
8   Klotz, *Erzählte Stadt*; Muschg, afterword.
9   Baßler and Horn, afterword, 532, 535.
10 Gibson, *Ecological Approach*, 129.
11 Rietveld and Kiverstein, "Rich Landscape," 330–35.

to talk of agency, purpose, contingency, and improvisation. In a sense, Cave states, they are "underspecified."[12] Yet affordances are also rigid, or over-specified. They imply norms and rules of engagement, a strong pull to do things a certain way, as well as (cultural) habits and skills that one might or might not possess.

Reading *Berlin Alexanderplatz*, therefore, through the theory of affordances, opens up a space from which to investigate the dynamic relation between action and perception as it plays out between Biberkopf and the materiality of the city in the novel. Moreover, it allows us to propose new answers to prominent questions surrounding both the novel's ending and Biberkopf's responsibility for what happens to him. This chapter will argue that the ending of the novel's emphasis on "seeing" and other people, should be read as an openness, or what Kiverstein has called a "responsiveness," to the (social) environment.[13] Other people can show us other ways of responding to the environment and teach ways of inhabiting new and unfamiliar environments. The novel, in turn, reminds us that this responsiveness should not be selective, that instead of learning just one way of engaging we should remain open to other (people's) ways of engaging. The responsibility of Biberkopf in the novel, this chapter will argue, lies not with the fact that what has happened was all his fault, but rather that he should have seen it coming by observing other people. The final lesson is thus not that community is necessarily *good*, but that other people can both show us what is going on in the world and help us reformulate new ways of engaging.

In what follows, I will attempt to draw out the dynamic between agent and environment through the theory of affordances in three sections. The first two sections focus on what objects afford and how these can change, be reshaped in a dynamic engagement. The third section focuses on what other people afford Biberkopf by showing what the environment affords *them*. In the end, there is a material reality constituted by objects, and there is human agency. Within this dynamic of action and perception *Berlin Alexanderplatz* is situated, and the novel's ending finds a stable and apt way of engaging that neither over- nor underspecifies the environment. That new way of engaging has new habits, a new body: Franz Karl Biberkopf. The experience of the modern environment is here thus not, as Simmel would have it, a place of shock, but rather a place that is underspecified. A place that points to habits that are not possessed but also to a variety of opportunities for action.

---

12   Cave, *Thinking with Literature*.
13   Kiverstein, "Empathy," 534.

What Objects Afford

Berlin Alexanderplatz was published in between Döblin's two works on natural philosophy. On the one hand there is *Das Ich über der Natur*, first published in 1927, and on the other his 1933 *Unser Dasein*.[14] Both books are reflections on especially the *human* organism's place in nature. Where the former is a relatively linear account of Döblin's monist ideas, *Unser Dasein* is a heterogeneous collection that veers between philosophical, anthropological, and biological thought and combines theoretical contemplation with, amongst other things, aphorisms, short stories, and medical records. Both works stand out, especially in relation to earlier non-fiction work in Döblin's professional field of psychiatry, by a move away from the mind toward the body. Both works investigate humans as organisms, as animals, and the way in which they are situated in their environments. Döblin is evidently engaging with philosophers, psychoanalysts, and biologists of the time.[15] Of these, the most important for the purpose of my developing argument is Uexküll. As we have seen, Uexküll's work is and was especially influential for his use of the word "Umwelt" to describe an animal's meaningful environment. To reiterate and elaborate, in this view, contrary to the Darwinian understanding, the animal is not engaged with an objective world to which it adapts, but instead perceives the environment in terms of its own possibilities for action. Every animal therefore has its own *Umwelt*. Döblin uses "Umwelt" (a term which, as Thomas Keil points out, did not have the common usage in the German language as it has today) repeatedly in both of his works.[16] What is relevant in Uexküll's work for our present discussion is his emphasis on the way in which action shapes perception. Particularly useful is Uexküll's programmatic sentence from 1922: "Merkwelt und Wirkungswelt bilden gemeinsam die Umwelt" (perception world and effect world together form the environment).[17] Our environments in Uexküll are dynamically shaped between what we take notice of and what we consequently take action upon. The idea that underlies this phrase returns in a different

---

14   In 1932, Döblin wrote that *Das Ich über der Natur* and *Berlin Alexanderplatz* were two different ways of exploring the same question about human existence. Döblin, "Mein Buch *Berlin Alexanderplatz*."

15   See also Keil, *Alfred Döblins "Unser Dasein."* For good overviews of both texts and their critical responses see Maillard, "Unser Dasein"; and Gelderloos, "Ich über der Natur."

16   Keil, *Alfred Döblins "Unser Dasein,"* 82. While Döblin thus seems influenced by Uexküll, I have not found any explicit reference to Uexküll in Döblin's writings.

17   Uexküll, "Wie sehen wir die Natur," 266. My translation.

guise in Döblin's *Unser Dasein* as an animal's "Fühl- und Aktionskörper" (feeling and acting body).[18]

This dynamic of action and perception returns in these two works in two passages that can be read as programmatic for a discussion of affordances in *Berlin Alexanderplatz*. In the first, Döblin writes about arriving at Berlin's Alexanderplatz, much like Biberkopf at the beginning of the novel, in a tramcar. When he suddenly "awakes" from daydreaming, he becomes aware of all the things that are happening around him and he starts to wonder how his surrounding world can be understood: "Man hat nicht zu denken, nicht so zu denken. Man hat zu denken, aber anders zu denken. Was sie [die Menschen auf dem Platz] tun—gehen, laufen, stehen, warten, um sich blicken, ausrufen—, so denkt man richtig. Nur so durchdringt man, was hier vorgeht" (one should not think, not like that. One must think, but differently. What they [the people in the square] do—walk, run, stand, wait, look around, shout out—that is how one thinks correctly. This is the only way in which one can penetrate what is going on here).[19] Understanding is not about sitting in an armchair thinking about the world, Döblin seems to say, but rather about acting in the world. In the second passage, in *Unser Dasein*, this idea of understanding in terms of action rather than contemplation returns. Knowledge becomes *praxis*:

> Die Welt ist erst real und konkret im handelnd vollzogenen Leben mit seiner Vieldimensionalität. Daher kann die bloße Optik, Akustik, die in Formen und Bewegungen stehende und ablaufende Welt nur eine unvollständige Welt sein. Sie ist eine Vorwissenschaft. Wo man Gefühle, Wollen, Denken—Lust und Schmerz—Anspruch und Abweichung—Werte und Sollen mit hinzunimmt, kommt man zur wirklichen vollständigen Wissenschaft. Aber ohne weiteres sieht man, daß es dann gar keine bloße Wissenschaft mehr ist, sondern, wie es sich gehört, eine Praxis.

> [The world is only real and concrete in the actively realized life with its multi-dimensionality. Mere optics, acoustics, the world standing and unfolding in forms and movements can therefore only be an incomplete world. It is a preliminary science. Wherever feelings, will, thinking—pleasure and pain—demand and deviance—values and duties are added, one comes to the actual, complete science. But it is easy to see that it is then no longer a mere science but, as it should be, a practice.][20]

18   Döblin, *Unser Dasein*, 86. All translations of this source are mine. See also Keil, *Alfred Döblins "Unser Dasein,"* 82.
19   Döblin, *Ich über der Natur*, 83. All translations of this source are mine.
20   Döblin, *Unser Dasein*, 86.

The "objective" world is not the real world for Döblin. Only the world as lived, as dynamically engaged with, and as fully affective, is a real world. It is between these two explorations of an active, embodied, affective approach to the environment that *Berlin Alexanderplatz* was written.

An important example of how in the novel the *material* environment is understood by Biberkopf in terms of action comes when the wall and the trams of the first scene return to his mind. When the objects return, they do so in a dynamic engagement of Biberkopf's with them that emphasizes the actions they solicit. After Biberkopf has made his "leap" into tram 41 to Alexanderplatz, still longingly looking backward at the wall, he is overwhelmed, in the novel's first pages, by the quickly succeeding impressions of Berlin. Biberkopf tries to find a dark and quiet place to rest, when a Jewish man invites him inside. Here, seated on a couch, the wall and the trams reappear as images to Biberkopf's mind:

> Der Entlassene saß allein. Es braust ein Ruf wie Donnerhall, wie Schwertgeklirr und Wogenprall. Er fuhr mit der Elektrischen, blickte seitlich hinaus, die roten Mauern waren sichtbar zwischen den Bäumen, es regnete buntes Laub. Die Mauern standen vor seinen Augen, sie betrachtete er auf dem Sofa, betrachtete sie unentwegt (BA, 17).[21]

> [The convict sat there all alone. "Es braust ein Ruf wie Donnerhall, wie Schwertgeklirr und Wogenprall." He took the tram, he looked out the side, the red walls were plainly visible between the trees, brightly coloured leaves were raining down. The walls were in front of his eyes, he was looking at them from the settee, looking at them incessantly. (*BA2*, 9)]

Not only do we get a situated account of the image of the wall here (as it includes the context of Biberkopf sitting in a tramcar driving away from these walls) but Biberkopf's own position on the couch in the here and now also mimics his position in the memory. Moreover, while in the first line we get his memory of looking at the wall from the tramcar *then* as if he were there now, in the second line this memory is enacted in the here and now: Biberkopf sits on the couch looking at an image of the

---

21 The lines that conjure up the walls "es braust ein Ruf wie Donnerhall, wie Schwertgeklirr und Wogenprall" (a roaring call like thunderstrike, like swords that clash, like waves that crash: my translation) come from a German nationalistic anthem called "Die Wacht am Rhein" based on a poem written by Max Schneckenburger in 1840 and set to music by Karl Wilhelm in 1854. Biberkopf sings the same anthem just before he gets invited in by the Jewish man, who has undoubtedly heard him sing it (*BA*, 17; *BA2*, 8), and later, naively, in a bar full of socialists (*BA*, 99; *BA2*, 81).

wall as he did in the tram-car. In other words, the imagery in his memory intertwines with his present position: his position *now* enacts the situation *then*.

This coupled physical movement between the here and now and memory becomes especially explicit when the image of the wall appears a second time in the same scene at the Jewish household. This second time, we get a similar enactment, although this time not of Biberkopf's drive away from the jail, but rather of him standing with his back against the red walls, hesitating to get into the tramcar and enter Berlin. Having sat back down on the sofa after wanting to leave the house of the Jewish man, the latter's question about where he came from, conjures up the walls again:

> Die roten Mauern, schöne Mauern, Zellen, er mußte sie sehnsüchtig betrachten, er klebte mit dem Rücken an der roten Mauer, ein kluger Man hat sie gebaut, er ging nicht weg. Und der Mann rutschte wie eine Puppe von dem Sofa herunter auf den Teppich, den Tisch schob er im Sinken beiseite. (*BA*, 20)

> [The red walls, the beautiful walls, the cells, he looked at them yearningly, his back was stuck to the red wall, a clever man had built them, he wasn't going anywhere. And the man slid down off the settee onto the floor, like a doll; as he went down, he pushed the table away. (*BA2*, 11)]

If in his first conjuring up of the wall Biberkopf's position on the couch matched his position in the tramcar, this time his sitting on the couch is linked with him standing with his back against that wall. This enaction of the wall is emphasized by the fact that the sentence where Biberkopf slides down the couch starts with the connective word "und" and therefore seems to refer to Biberkopf sliding down the wall in his memory. Only when the word "Sofa" (couch) appears, do we understand we are no longer in his memory. Again, the memory of the wall is linked to the here and now through coupled physical movements. We see Biberkopf lying on the carpet in front of the sofa, but at the same time we might also imagine him at the bottom of the wall. The repeated imagery of the wall is thus not just an image that comes to Biberkopf's mind but is a situation that is acted out. The objects are thus thoroughly embodied; they get their meaning from Biberkopf's interaction with them. Even something which at first seems so much like the realm of the mind like memory is here turned by Döblin into a thoroughly embodied experience (including its accompanying emotional resonance).

The way in which these objects thus become an embodied experience to Biberkopf places the scene in an understanding of the environment that is today fruitfully discussed in terms of affordances. The wall and the tram *afford* Biberkopf specific actions that he acts out both in his memory and in the here and now. Affordances, which are a development of Uexküll's *Umwelt*, were first conceived by Gibson as the actions that an environment affords a kind of animal.[22] They describe the way in which different animals perceive their environments differently according to the actions they can perform. Rietveld and Kiverstein importantly develop the theory in terms of "abilities" and, using a term borrowed from Wittgenstein, "forms of life" to replace "bodies" and "animals." This opens up the theory to wider application especially in the study of human behavior. The human form of life can still be differentiated from other animals, but within it, there are cultural ways of life and individual ways of life, all with their own sets of abilities. More so than in its initial iteration, in the theory of affordances as put forward by Rietveld and Kiverstein, perception is dynamic. While grounded in the material world, perception can, via a change in abilities, change too. A change in abilities comes to change the perception of the environment. Conversely, a new perception, a new view of the environment, is suggestive of different abilities.

The scene in the Jewish household implicitly raises an important question about affordances. Why, namely, does the wall suddenly appear again? Why does this particular object stand out for Biberkopf? In other words, how do some affordances, in certain circumstances, seem more salient than others? On the grain of analysis of the individual, Rietveld and Kiverstein make a helpful distinction between affordances and relevant affordances, or solicitations. The environment *affords* a large variety of actions but it only solicits so much for a given animal or human, in a given context. The world is not a homogeneous mass of affordances but has a certain depth. Some affordances come into the foreground while some recede into the background. The question of why and when affordances become solicitations, is, as Rietveld and Kiverstein point out, "an urgent open research question."[23] Like we have seen in Heidegger's account of a role as organizing authenticity, and in Rilke's emphasis on the task as the organizing center for writing, their proposal is that the individual's dynamic concerns in a situation are what turns affordances into solicitations.[24] Some affordances of an environment might not be relevant at all in a given situation and some might suddenly solicit us when our concerns ask for them. The heating in front of me, for example, has no use all summer until suddenly it becomes relevant when I get cold.

---

22 Yet see Barry Smith's article on the important differences between Uexküll's account of *Umwelt* and Gibson's affordances. Smith, "Toward a Realistic Science."
23 Rietveld and Kiverstein, "Rich Landscape," 340.
24 Rietveld and Kiverstein, "Rich Landscape," 341.

Döblin himself, too, explored the dynamic ways in which certain elements of the environment can come to stand out to someone. In 1909, when he was a psychiatrist at the institute called "Buch," the same that "cures" Biberkopf at the end of the novel, Döblin wrote an article called "Aufmerksamkeitsstörungen bei Hysterie." In this paper, about a case of hysteria he treated, he argues that attention is an important energy of the mind for understanding cognitive pathologies. If the mind functions well, Döblin argues, this energy of attention coordinates dynamically between "sense-impressions, thoughts, and affect" (Sinnesempfindung, Vorstellung, Affect).[25] But if it does not function well, as in the case of his hysteric patient, the patient may pay too much attention to the wrong things. He points out for example, that people might only pay attention to what fits in with their own concerns: "es kann vieles, was nicht dem eigenen Gedankengang entgegen kommt, nicht aufgefasst werden" (much that is not in line with one's thoughts cannot be taken in).[26] Moreover, Döblin points out that things, such as words, which are emphasized in the world, can come to be paid too much attention to. As Kiverstein and Rietveld do, then, he sees the importance of concerns for the shaping of our attention to certain objects. Yet he also reminds us that emphasis produced by the world itself grabs our attention. Importantly, what Döblin's article on attention shows is that he explores the way in which humans differentiate in the environment between objects.[27] Perception is not something passive, like a screen in front of a person, but something that is done actively, shaped by a meaningful engagement. Moreover, Döblin, when talking about how the energy of attention should work, emphasizes the importance of a more dynamic attention, which, as will be discussed below, is an important lesson presented at the end of *Berlin Alexanderplatz*. Yet whereas in his 1909 study of attention he is still very much interested in the mind's dynamic with the environment, in *Berlin Alexanderplatz* the body takes a central role.

In Biberkopf's attention to, and engagement with, the imaginary wall, his concerns play an important part in bringing the affordances of the wall and the tram forward. But Döblin also seems to play here with the way in which the same objects, the wall and the couch, can come to solicit different actions in accordance with Biberkopf's dynamic concerns. Döblin, after the times the wall comes back to Biberkopf's mind, always follows it with a discussion of Biberkopf's concerns. The concern that Biberkopf brings up the first time the wall appears to his imagination

25 Döblin, "Aufmerksamkeitsstörungen bei Hysterie," 488.
26 Döblin, "Aufmerksamkeitsstörungen bei Hysterie," 474. My translation.
27 The same kind of dynamic "attention" to the material environment, what Kleinschmidt calls an "Attraktionsmodell" (190), can also be found in Döblin's PhD thesis on the Korsakoff psychosis, presented in 1905. Döblin, *Gedächtnisstörungen*. See also Kleinschmidt, "Materielle und psychische Welt."

is the familiarity of the jail: "es ist ein großes Glück, in diesen Mauern zu wohnen, man weiß, wie der Tag anfängt und wie er weiter geht" (*BA*, 17; It's great good luck to live within these walls. You know how the day begins and how it continues: *BA2*, 9). Note that this is when he is imagining sitting in the tramcar moving away from the wall while he looks back at it. But while this enactment of the wall is thoroughly and literally backward looking, the second enactment, with his back against the wall, is forward looking, but also more desperate. Biberkopf says to himself: "es heißt sich entschließen, es muß ein Weg gegangen werden,— und du weißt keinen, Franze" (*BA*, 21; it's make up your mind time, you've got to choose a route, and you don't know any, Franz: *BA2*, 12). The affordance of the walls and the couch as well as Biberkopf's enactment of them thus change according to his concerns, from backward looking to forward looking. This becomes especially clear when in the subsequent paragraphs Biberkopf is increasingly encouraged to sit up straight against the couch until he finally sits normally on it. Because the wall and the couch were linked before—one might say, in the language of film, "superimposed"—we here get the feeling that Biberkopf is steadying himself against the wall too, ready to make the leap into the tramcar and into the city once again. The same wall thus comes to afford almost opposing movements in relation to Biberkopf's dynamic concerns. Far from being an objective environment, or a subjectively colored environment, the environment is differently *enacted*. The wall turns up in different constellations, in different relations to Biberkopf's body, and the couch is used to work through his concerns in terms of this wall. Biberkopf's perception of the environment and thus his actions in it are tied up in a dynamic constellation with his own concerns.

Changing Affordances

But how do Biberkopf's concerns change? If the way in which he perceives the environment dynamically changes in terms of his concerns, where does his "movement" originate? The answer is the environment. The dynamic between Biberkopf and Berlin works both ways. Indeed, in *Unser Dasein* he makes it clear that the world also shapes the agent. Having started off exploring the body's central position in experience, Döblin concludes, at the end of the first chapter:

> Es findet eine Hin- und Herbewegung zwischen Person und Welt statt, so kann sie stattfinden. In dieser Hin- und Herbewegung wird die Welt gebaut. . . . Das ist die ununterbrochene kämpferische, ringende Erschließung der "Welt" durch die "Person," den Fühl und Aktionskörper, und die ständige Durchtränkung der "Person" mit "Welt."

[A back-and-forth movement between person and world takes place, thus it can occur. In this back-and-forth movement the world is built. . . . This is the uninterruptedly combative, struggling exploration of the "world" by the "person," the feeling and active body, and the constant saturation of the "person" with "world."][28]

It is not just the concerns of an (independent) agent that dynamically shape the way in which the world is understood, but the agent herself is always shaped by this environment, too. In "Der Geist des naturalistischen Zeitalters" (The Spirit of a Naturalistic Age, 1924), Döblin argues not only that human beings are shaped by culture, but also that it is their bodies which are different depending on the culture: "Man bemerke, daß manche Kulturen einseitig bestimmte Organsystemen ausbilden, bestimmte Gehirnteile entwickeln, andere vernachlässigen" (we observe that some cultures develop lopsided organ systems, expand certain parts of the brain and neglect others).[29] Later in the same essay he writes "die Welt baut Gesellschaftswesen" (the world builds social beings).[30] And the same thought returns in *Das Ich über der Natur*: "Der Einzelmensch denkt und fühlt als Teil der Menschengruppe" (the individual human being thinks and feels as part of the group).[31] In other words, we are, in Döblin's view, socio-cultural beings who, because our brains and sense organs change, see the environment differently, as well.

The shaping of human behavior by its (social) environment is important for thinking about Biberkopf's entry into the unfamiliar city that is Berlin. If we zoom out from individual agents engaging with individual objects, the theory of affordances shows us two important aspect of affordances. First, affordances are situated, as we have seen before, in a context, or what Rietveld and Kiverstein, after Gibson, call an "ecological niche."[32] The "ecological niche" harks back to Uexküll's understanding of *Umwelt*, although it is more open to change. (Whereas Uexküll's *Umwelt* only opens up the possibility for a different view of the environment *between* species, the ecological niche as a set of affordances is more dynamic. Different people and different cultures also see the world differently.) Focusing on the ecological niche emphasizes that meaningful objects are not separate entities but are embedded in a meaningful context. Read in these terms, jail for Biberkopf was an ecological niche. The red-brick wall can only be understood in this larger picture of its meaning

---

28 Döblin, *Unser Dasein*, 31.

29 Döblin, "Geist des naturalistischen Zeitalters," 65; Döblin, "Spirit of a Naturalistic Age," 77.

30 Döblin, "Geist des naturalistischen Zeitalters," 83; Döblin, "Spirit of a Naturalistic Age," 87.

31 Döblin, *Ich über der Natur*, 159.

32 Gibson, *Ecological Approach*, 120.

as part of the jail with its daily routines. In fact, the wall comes to stand in for what jail afforded Biberkopf. Second, zooming out and away from the individual shows that affordances and ecological niches imply forms of life, or sets of abilities, also on cultural levels and on animal levels. There exist human forms of life as distinct from other animals, and specific cultural forms of life, as distinct from other cultures. Which implies that affordances are inherently normative. As Rietveld and Kiverstein write: "Exercising an ability can be better or worse, adequate or inadequate, correct or incorrect in the context of a particular situation, hence there is a normative dimension to the abilities for picking up affordances [. . .]."[33] Although Döblin does not explicitly link his understanding of socio-culturally shaped bodies to normativity, the picture is the same. Our bodies, our abilities and concerns, our perception of the world, are shaped by environments. Importantly, what a view of affordances in terms of normativity implies, and what makes thinking of objects in terms of affordances so fruitful as a tool of analysis for the present discussion is that affordances on the one hand can be, in Cave's words, "underspecified," open to agency, concerns, and experimentation, and on the other hand, due to their normative nature, "overspecified," demanding of a certain use, implying socio-cultural bodies.

Biberkopf's entry into the new environment of Berlin might be fruitfully read in terms of socio-cultural habits. As Fore points out, "Biberkopf is cast by Döblin into the transformed urban landscape of Berlin in media res, released from the prison that quarantined him from one of the most accelerated historical episodes of social upheaval and precipitous rationalization and modernization."[34] Even the *Schupos* have a different uniform than they did before Biberkopf went to jail (*BA*, 13). Eva Horn has described Biberkopf as an "experimental subject . . . released into a murky and inhospitable environment."[35] Moreover, just as Fore finds Biberkopf to have an "utter lack of inner psychic substance," so Horn argues that the experimental nature of Biberkopf attests to his "emptiness and indeterminacy."[36] However, while Biberkopf might be dropped into the city of Berlin like an experimental subject and without much of a backstory, to call him empty on the inside is to overlook Biberkopf's (cultural) habits from the ecological niche that is jail as well as his time in Berlin before, which, while perhaps rarely discussed in the novel explicitly, are played out in his interactions with the environment. The way in which the wall keeps coming back to Biberkopf's mind, and the way in which it is linked to the daily activities of the jail (*BA*, 18; *BA2*, 9), tells us something about Biberkopf's inner life. His looking for dark places

33 Rietveld and Kiverstein, "Rich Landscape," 326.
34 Fore, "Döblin's Epic," 200.
35 Horn, "Literary Research," 725.
36 Fore, "Döblin's Epic," 200; Horn, "Literary Research," 725.

that remind him of solitary confinement (*BA*, 15; *BA2*, 7) and his rape of the sister of the girlfriend whom he murdered are further examples of his habitual behavior (*BA*, 38–43; *BA2*, 27–32). What he responds to too, in the story told to him by the Jewish men, that the story's central character Zannowich was persecuted for his mistakes, is something that he links expressly to his own past: "Ja, sind wir denn nichts, weil wir mal was getan haben?" (*BA*, 30; is it that we're nothing once we've done something: *BA2*, 292). Indeed, in the main flashback we get from Biberkopf's time in jail, the rigid, regular, and communal practices of the inmates are emphasized (*BA*, 18; *BA2*, 9). Where Horn suggests, then, that the result of the experiment of placing Biberkopf in Berlin is a "successful normalization," I would suggest that instead of such a normalization, which suggests a universal behavior that could be deemed "normal," Biberkopf's adaptation constitutes a habituation into a particular, unfamiliar environment.[37] Jail, and his other past behavior, have shaped him, and the way in which he understands the environment is in terms of these old habits and concerns.

If we look at the way in which Biberkopf engages with his new environment, two distinct ways of doing so stand out. As Baßler and Horn write: "Zum einen geht die Urbanisierung offenkundig mitten durch Franz hindurch und macht ihn zum fremdbestimmten Charakter, zum anderen setzt er dem Kraftfeld des Milieus aber doch auch einen sehr eigenen Dickkopf, höchst individuelle Triebe, Vorlieben und Empfindlichkeiten entgegen" (on the one hand, the urbanization obviously runs right through Franz and makes him a character determined by others. On the other hand, however, he opposes the forces of his milieu with a very own stubbornness, with highly individual drives, preferences, and sensitivities).[38] These two ways of engaging, however, seem, with some exception, separated in time by the scene at the Jewish household. Having just come out of jail, he is mostly overwhelmed. The multifarious impressions of the city are listed one after another, and Biberkopf is looking for darker places to hide in. After the scene at the Jewish house, however, after the part of the Zannowich story that Baßler and Horn have called "einem Detail, auf das [die Geschichte] gar nicht abzielte" (a detail that [the story] was not aimed at), his behavior is best described in terms of stubbornness and arrogance.[39] On the one hand, there is an overwhelming environment of objects that Biberkopf does not know what to do with. Here everything and nothing seems to solicit actions. In other words, the world is underspecified: "es muß ein Weg gegangen werden,—und du weißt keinen, Franze" (*BA*, 21; you've got to choose a

---

37 Horn, "Literary Research," 725.
38 Baßler and Horn, afterword, 527.
39 Baßler and Horn, afterword, 527.

route, and you don't know any, Franz: *BA2*, 12). On the other hand, the world becomes over-specified. Biberkopf starts to have a very rigid view of the environment, where only very specific affordances, such as the rape of his ex-girlfriend's sister, stand out. The world only solicits, in relation to his bad habits, the repetition of the same mistakes. In the first instance, he all but ignores his environment because he is overwhelmed, and in the second he just goes at it with his old habits, still ignoring what happens around him.

It is important to acknowledge that Biberkopf is thoroughly affected, mentally and physically, by all of this, that his concerns throughout the novel cannot be separated from the feelings, the anxiety and aggression, that the world provokes in him, or from the physical hurt this engagement causes him and others. His engagement with the wall and the couch is just a small part of the many affective engagements he has in Berlin. The novel is gruesome in its depictions of aggressive acts such as rape and murder. The scene in the abattoir, in particular, in which human life is compared to the fate of cattle, implies the brittleness of human existence with an emphasis on its physicality (*BA*, 150–58). In theoretical discussions of affordances, however, affect is not always made explicit.[40] If the body is affected here, it is usually in neutral terms of habit and skill, not in the more harrowing details that the novel often confronts us with. Indeed, the complexities of human emotions are perhaps a prime place at which literature can help us, as Toril Moi points out about Stanley Cavell's criticism, "get clear on questions [we] couldn't get clear on in any other way."[41] What the novel shows, then, is that the way in which humans relate to their environment is never devoid of feelings and physical suffering, and that affordances thus need also to be further explored as "affectivities" (which I, in different terms, do in chapters 5 and 6).

For good reason, Döblin's narrator seems unsatisfied with either of the ways, either overwhelmed or aggressive, in which Biberkopf perceives and acts in the world around him. Instead, the text presents a middle way between being overwhelmed and not paying attention to the environment at all. At the end of the novel, after a lengthy "dance with death" at the psychiatric institute "Buch," a new Biberkopf appears. This Franz Karl has learned to "see," he is no longer blindly running against the world, but is standing amongst others, on Alexanderplatz. At first, this renewal of Biberkopf seems to be about passively observing only. The opening of eyes as a lesson to Biberkopf—"der Star gestochen" (*BA*, 9;

---

40 Yet see Heidegger's discussion of "moods" (*SZ*, §29), further discussed in chapter 6. And see Kiverstein's article on social affordances further discussed below. Kiverstein, "Empathy." See also, for example, Jensen and Pedersen, "Affect and Affordances"; Caravà and Scorolli, "When Affective Relation Weighs More."

41 Moi, "Adventure of Reading," 129.

his blindness is taken from him: *BA2*, 1)—or his blindness as his problem, is repeatedly brought up in the novel, and when the new Franz Karl enters Alexanderplatz for the second time, he is said to no longer run blindly into the world (*BA*, 508; *BA2*, 438). The figure of death also tells him that he sees nothing and hears nothing (*BA*, 487; *BA2*, 420) and, repeatedly, that he needs to "suffer [the world] to approach" (*BA2*, 421–26; herankommen lassen: *BA*, 491–93). However, this "herankommen lassen" is not passive at all. Instead it is, death tells him, about being alive: "Ich bin das Leben und die wahre Kraft, du willst dich endlich, endlich nicht mehr bewahren" (*BA*, 483; I am the life and the true strength, at last, at long last, you are no longer trying to preserve yourself from me: *BA2*, 416–17). It is about "erfahren" and "erproben" (*BA*, 484; experience, test: *BA2*, 417; translation altered). In other words, it is an active engagement, but with eyes wide open. It is a final *leitmotiv* that is already raised in the Zannowich story: "man muß die Welt sehen können und zu ihr hingehn" (*BA*, 24; you have to be able to see the world and direct your feet to it: *BA2*, 15). What Döblin seems to have in mind is a version of the dynamic he discusses in his essay on attention, but one that involves the body. Or what I would like to call, after Kiverstein, a "responsiveness" to the environment.[42] The new Biberkopf stands on the square watching but also walking along with others, doing his job, choosing what to do next. Attention not just as mere seeing, but attention to affordances, in other words: a responsiveness to the environment. Tim Ingold has developed an important account of the dynamic between attention and action that plays out when humans and animals explore environments:

> The abilities of the weaverbird, just like those of the human maker of string bags, are developed through an active exploration of the possibilities afforded by the environment, in the choice of materials and structural supports, and of bodily capacities of movement, posture, and prehension. Furthermore, the key to successful nest building lies not so much in the movements themselves as in the bird's ability to adjust its movements with exquisite precision in relation to the evolving form of its construction.[43]

Ingold calls this, after Gibson, an "education of attention." Such an education implies a dynamic between action and perception which attunes the animal to affordances in the environment. Döblin's focus on the environment in which Biberkopf is engaged, and the dynamics between the two, results in a lesson of a dynamic engagement with the environment that is responsive to affordances the environment has to offer. The

---

42 Kiverstein, "Empathy," 534.
43 Ingold, *Perception of the Environment*, 359.

way in which Biberkopf slowly changed his way of engagement with the couch and wall in the scene at the Jewish household was an example of this, albeit a deficient one. Biberkopf ruined it by ultimately paying attention to a part of the story that aligned with his own concerns. In the end, it seems to be the dynamic between seeing and doing that Döblin understands to be the solution for an unfamiliar Berlin. Time and time again, Biberkopf pays attention to the wrong things, or does not pay attention at all. As will be shown in the following, this is especially the case with other people.

Affording Others

It is not only *objects* as affordances and Biberkopf's dynamic responsiveness to them that *Berlin Alexanderplatz* seems to explore, but also how other people meaningfully shape, and are shaped by, these affordances. I have shown how Döblin seems to have been interested in the ways in which our understanding of objects as well as our habits are socioculturally shaped. But others, therefore, also become important affordances for understanding our environments, and vice versa. From its first lines, when the warden of the jail points a wall-ridden Biberkopf in the right direction, the novel shows how other people can help us understand our environments and shows us how the environment helps us understand other people. The former is also an important part of the lesson about "seeing" his environment that the novel gives Biberkopf at the end.

Döblin's interest in the materiality of the environment in literature extends to how he describes people in their active engagement in the world. In the 1913 essay on the epic, he states that he is more interested in describing the actions of characters than in describing their psychology.[44] To a large extent, this move towards the action of characters is how they are treated in the novel. Willy Haas states as much in a contemporaneous review of *Berlin Alexanderplatz*: "Der wirkliche Erzähler baut nicht Menschen auf. Er weiß, daß sie da sind. . . .Der Erzähler Döblin . . . weiß: ich nenne den Namen einer Person, mehr kann ich nicht tun. Der Name muß aufstehen und marschieren, von selbst. Ich sehe mir ihn an. Und jetzt los: erzählen!" (The real narrator does not build people up. He knows they're there. . . . The narrator Döblin knows: I mention the name of a person, that's all I can do. The name has to stand up and march by itself. I look at him. And now go on: narrate!).[45] The characters

---

44 Döblin, "An Romanautoren und ihre Kritiker"; Döblin, "To Novelists and Their Critics."
45 Haas, [N.t.], 222. My translation. See also Döblin's own words: "man erzählt nicht, sondern baut" (one does not narrate, one constructs). Döblin, "An Romanautoren und ihre Kritiker," 17; Döblin, "To Novelists and Their Critics," 11.

Herbert and Eva, for example, are introduced only by scant descriptions focused on outside appearance, the former "slim" the latter "black," but come immediately into action helping Biberkopf after his arm is amputated—this helpfulness is characteristic of their behavior throughout the novel. Anything we as readers become privy to about the characters, including Biberkopf, we predominantly get through their actions and dialogue. What we know about them we come to know through what they do and say, how they interact with their environments.

A good example of how Döblin describes the dynamic between the environment and other people, and how they come to shape Biberkopf's perception of others, can be found in the second scene in which Mieze, Biberkopf's new girlfriend in the final parts of the novel, appears. Biberkopf does not know Mieze is a prostitute when she comes too late for a date with him. Unbeknownst to Biberkopf, she is late because of a customer. Although he finds her tardiness strange, he does not pay further attention to it. Instead, Biberkopf is distracted by the personal environment she has created for herself and what this says about her:

> ... mittags trifft er sich mit Mieze. Da fällt ihm einmal auf, daß Mieze so sehr abgehetzt zu Aschinger am Alex kommt, wo sie essen. Sie sagt, sie hat sich verschlafen—aber irgend was stimmt ihm bei dem Mädel nicht. Er vergißt es auch wieder, das Mädel ist so zart, daß mans nicht glauben kann, und in ihrer Stube ist alles so sauber und manierlich mit Blumen und Läppchen und Bändern wie bei einem kleinen Mädchen. Und immer ist schön gelüftet und mit Lavendelwasser gespritzt, daß er eine ordentliche Freude hat, wenn sie abends zusammen nach Hause kommen. Und im Bett, da ist sie sanft wie eine Feder, jedesmal so ruhig und zart und glücklich wie zuerst. (*BA*, 287–88).
>
> ... at lunchtime he is seeing Mitzi. Then he suddenly notices how she is arriving at Aschinger's on the Alex, which is where they have lunch, steaming. She says she overslept—but something seems a bit off to him. He forgets about it by and by, the girl is tender like you wouldn't believe, everything in her room is so clean and tidy, with flowers and ribbons and knick-knacks, like with a little girl. And it's always so nicely aired, and sprayed with lavender water, that it's a proper delight for him when they arrive home together at night. And in bed she's as light as a feather, always so sweet and soft and happy, like the very first time. (*BA2*, 245; translation altered)]

What the environment affords Mieze, visible in her construction of a niche, cute, clean, and ordered, a counterpoint to the male-dominated, violent environment outside, shapes the way in which Biberkopf (as well as the reader) perceives her. Mieze has shaped her environment, and this environment shapes the way in which Biberkopf sees her. Biberkopf understands something about Mieze through the way in which she is engaged in her environment, including the way she has sex. It is not just Biberkopf who is meaningfully engaged in his environment in the novel, but also the other characters. How they are acting in this way affects the way in which Biberkopf perceives them.

This interest in how other people and their environments dynamically constitute their meanings to Biberkopf seems to correspond to how the theory of affordances thinks about the place of other people in affordances. The theory of affordances has implications for how we perceive other people in their environments. Kiverstein, in an article on what he calls "social affordances," argues that the necessarily selective responsiveness to affordances of *others*, or what solicits them, can be understood through their actions in the world. He writes: "Individuals differ in their concerns, needs and interests and thus differ in the possibilities for action that have affective significance for them. In perceiving the other's bodily orientation in the world, I can immediately grasp their selective responsiveness to the environment."[46] And through their selective responsiveness to affordances, what in the environment solicits them, Kiverstein continues, we also understand their "states of mind": "To the extent that I can determine which of the affordances in their surrounding environment are relevant, and have significance for the other person, this gives me a window through which I can gain access to their perspectives on the world."[47] It is thus through interactions of others with a material world, Kiverstein argues, that we understand them. Knowing that the environment solicited Mieze to make a cute, clean, and ordered home, tells us a lot about her state of mind.

The idea that we understand others not so much through a sort of mind-reading[48] but rather through their actions seems to bring a certain realism to Döblin's description of his characters. As we have already seen, it has been repeatedly suggested in criticism that Biberkopf in the novel does not have much of a personality or history. And I have already argued that we get to know much about Biberkopf through his habitual behavior in the environment. This is to say that critics are correct in observing

---

46 Kiverstein, "Empathy," 537.
47 Kiverstein, "Empathy," 537.
48 The other two theories of mind, take mind-reading as a central part of how we understand others. The so-called theory theory (TT) understands us to infer from someone's behavior what they might be thinking based on theories we have about how people behave in certain situations, simulation theory (ST) understands us to think about what we ourselves would be feeling or thinking if we acted like the other person in that situation. In comparison the direct perception theory does not believe we infer at all, but just "see" it directly in others' compartments. See also Kiverstein, "Empathy," 533.

that we know much less about Biberkopf than we might in more traditional narrative fiction; and that few words are wasted on his feelings, background, motivation. But I wish to add that there is a certain "realism" to the way in which we encounter Biberkopf and other characters in the novel. We encounter Döblin's characters as we encounter people on the street: before we engage in mind-reading, Kiverstein states, "we already have immediate experiential access to the minds of others . . . it is expressed in the way in which they comport themselves in the world."[49] This way of understanding others also seems to underlie the ending of the scene with Mieze. Having failed to contemplate her coming late, after sex, Biberkopf wonders what she is thinking: "Ob die was denkt, wenn sie so dasitzt und gar nichts tut, und was sie denkt. Fragt er sie, so sagt sie immer und lacht: sie denkt gar nichts. Man kann doch nicht den ganzen Tag was denken. Das findt er nu auch" (*BA*, 288; is there anything on her mind as she sits there, not doing anything, and if so, what. When he asks her that, she always replies with a laugh: nothing at all. You can't spend all day thinking. Which stands to reason: *BA2*, 245). There is a rich irony here to the fact that he is trying to find out what Mieze is thinking, when all he needed to know about Mieze's activities was right there, the novel seems to say, in her actions (her tardiness). Even if or because Biberkopf believes, too, that thinking is overrated, he does not pay attention to all relevant information.

This lack of attention of Biberkopf to other people around him is further explored in a scene with Biberkopf's neighbors. When the neighboring carpenter and his wife get arrested for having helped a band of criminals, the others in the house are gossiping but Biberkopf does not want to engage:

> An den Gesprächen im Hausflur, auf dem Hof hat Franz Biberkopf . . . nicht teilgenommen. Hat immer gehört bei der Gruppe und rumgehört bei der Gruppe. Nachher hat er zugesehen, und sie haben Spalier gebildet, wie der Zimmerer und sein dickes Frauchen über den Hausflur auf die Straße geführt wurden. Zoppen nu ab. Bin auch mal geloofen. War aber duster damals. Kuck einer, wie die gradeaus gaffen. Schämen sich. Ja, ja, ihr könnt hecheln. Ihr wißt, wie es in einem Menschen aussieht. Das sind die richtigen Spießer, hocken hinter dem Ofen, gaunern, aber die kriegt man nicht. (*BA*, 175)

> [Franz Biberkopf takes no part in any of the various conversations in hallway and staircase. Just listened to one group, picked up something from another. Afterwards watched as they formed a guard of honour as the carpenter and his fat little missus are taken down the

---

49   Kiverstein, "Empathy," 533.

passage onto the street. Now they're gone. Well, I was on the lam once meself. That was night-time, though. Look at them all staring. Should be ashamed of themselves. Yeah, yeah, I see the tongues hanging out. You know what a person's feeling inside. Those curtain-twitchers are the real miscreants, but of course nothing ever happens to them. (*BA2*, 147–48)]

The fate of the carpenter and his wife mimics Biberkopf's later fate when he helps Pums's band of criminals and loses an arm. Biberkopf chooses to pay attention to the carpenter and his wife rather than to listen to the "Spießer" (petit bourgeois) around him. Again, then, we learn something about Biberkopf's feelings. As with the objects, he pays attention to the things he knows, the things he is familiar with, rather than the unfamiliar opinions of the other neighbors. This failure of Biberkopf to pay attention to the people gossiping about, and staring at, the carpenter and his wife, is turned into an explicit statement by death in the psychiatric institute: "Ich sag, du hast die Augen nicht aufgemacht, du krummer Hund! Schimpfst über Gauner und Gaunerei und kuckst dir die Menschen nicht an und fragst nich, warum und wieso. Was bistu fürn Richter über die Menschen und hast keene Oogen" (*BA*, 486; And I say you never opened your eyes, you crooked hound. You wax indignant about thieves and rascals but you never look at people, and never ask how come and what. What sort of judge of people are you if you never open your eyes: *BA2*, 419).

Because Biberkopf does not pay attention to others he remains out of sync with other people. This being out of sync with other people, what the environment solicits them is not what it solicits Biberkopf, is a theme that runs through the novel. It is an important part of *Berlin Alexanderplatz* that Biberkopf makes his way through various different social *milieux* that are not necessarily his own: the Jewish home, the prostitutes, the communists, the Nazis, and the criminal gangs. A good example of this continuous discordance with other groups, even though they may play out in different ways, is his singing of "Die Wacht am Rhein," a German nationalistic anthem popular in the period amongst nationalsocialists. The Jewish man who hears Biberkopf sing it invites him in nonetheless, but the communists have no such patience and start a fight. Most interesting for the way in which the environment solicits differently for Biberkopf than for other people, however, is a scene at the beginning of the novel in which other people cause him much anxiety. Having just left jail, he sees two people eating and drinking in a restaurant:

> Schreck fuhr in ihn, als er die Rosenthaler Straße herunterging und in einer kleinen Kneipe ein Mann und eine Frau dicht am Fenster saßen: die gossen sich Bier aus Seideln in den Hals, ja was war dabei, sie tranken eben, sie hatten Gabeln und stachen sich damit Fleischstücke

in den Mund, dann zogen sie die Gabeln wieder heraus und bluteten nicht. Oh, krampfte sich sein Leib zusammen, ich kriege es nicht weg, wo soll ich hin? Es antwortete: Die Strafe. (*BA*, 14)

[He got a shock when he turned down Rosenthaler Strasse, and saw a man and a woman sitting together in the window, pouring beer down their necks from big steins, so, they were just having a drink, they had forks in their hands and they were jabbing at pieces of meat, and lifting them to their mouths, and pulling the forks out, and not bleeding. Oh, his body cramped, I can't get over it, what am I going to do with myself? The answer came: punishment. (*BA2*, 6)]

It is not that these practices are necessarily unfamiliar to Biberkopf—"ja was war dabei"—they just seem so far from his concerns in the world. In other words, the actions that the world solicits from these people are not the actions it solicits from Biberkopf. Döblin turns this into a physical metaphor; these people eating "normally" is for Biberkopf hard to swallow. It is thus not so much the objects in the world that are unfamiliar, but more so that there is a clear disconnect between what they solicit to other people and the actions they solicit from Biberkopf. Or rather, as the previous section has argued, they remain underspecified; they afford Biberkopf all and solicit nothing. What makes him anxious, therefore, does not only seem to be that he does not know how to deal with these objects, but that he does not understand why people are attracted by the world as they are. But as always, Biberkopf pays no further attention to others' practices.

The lack of "seeing," of being responsive to the environment, is thus extended to a lack of paying attention to others. Instead of interacting with others, Biberkopf turns away from other people—as death says, he is "frech" and "hochnäsig" (*BA*, 486; cheeky, stuck up: *BA2*, 419)—because their views do not fit his own. That they are bourgeois merely seems to be an excuse. Indeed, his own stubborn adherence to the bourgeois attitude of "anständig sein" (being decent) gets him into trouble. Biberkopf's refusal to ask his best friend Herbert Wischow for help, for example, after he gets out of jail, because Herbert is "ein Lude, und von dem wollte er nichts wissen, nee, nie mehr" (*BA*, 192; a ponce, and he was through with that, never again: *BA2*, 163), means that while trying to stay straight he first gets cheated and then he falls in with the wrong crowd. With people, as with objects then, Biberkopf pays attention to only what fits in with his own concerns; people whose practices are different are not of interest. The solution, again, is paying attention. Indeed, Biberkopf's version of "anständig sein," the figure of death says, is the opposite of paying attention to the environment: ". . . und er denkt, ist gut, wenn er anständig ist, was er anständig nennt, und sieht nichts und hört nichts und lebt druff los und merkt nichts . . ." (*BA*, 487; . . . and thinks it's enough if he's decent, or what he calls decent, and sees nothing and hears nothing and lives into the day and doesn't notice a thing: *BA2*, 420). Instead of learning from other people, then, about what *could* be done, Biberkopf is only interested in what he thinks *should* be done. A similar lack of a responsiveness underlies the scene with Mieze. He pays attention to what he likes about Mieze's engagement, the cute, clean, ordered room and her tender lovemaking, but not to her coming late. It consequently takes him much longer than needs be to find out she is still a prostitute.

Learning from other people, by being attentive and responsive to them, is also the final message of the novel, which seems to refer back to all the instances where Biberkopf did not listen to or accept help from the people around him. In the last chapter, a new Franz Biberkopf, now with the middle name "Karl," is back on Alexanderplatz, surrounded by other people. His old motto of "laß dich nicht mit die Menschen ein, geh deiner eigenen Wege" (*BA*, 69; do not get involved with people, go your own way: my translation) has been replaced by an understanding of the importance of other people: "Viel Unglück kommt davon, wenn man allein geht" (*BA*, 509; Much misfortune comes of walking alone: *BA2*, 438). Other people have several advantages for the new and improved Biberkopf. They, Döblin seems to say, help us, they are the support we need. We are "stronger," he writes, when we are a hundred people than when we are alone. And they offer emotional support: "es ist auch schöner und besser, mit andern zu sein. Da fühle ich und weiß ich alles noch einmal so gut" (*BA*, 509; also, it's nicer and better to be with others. Then I feel and know everything better: *BA2*, 439). They help us see the world better: "ein Mensch kann nicht sein ohne viele andere Menschen. Was wahr und falsch ist, werd ich jetzt besser wissen" (*BA*, 509; a man may not be without many other men. I know better now what is right and what is wrong: *BA2*, 439). An attention to other people's behavior shows us simply what the world has to offer: "Man muß sich gewöhnen, auf andere zu hören, denn was andere sagen, geht mich auch an. Da merke ich, wer ich bin und was ich mir vornehmen kann" (*BA*, 509; you have to get used to listening to other people, because what others say concerns me, too. Then I see who I am and what I can take on: *BA2*, 438). And they show us what is going on in the world: "Wach sein, wach sein, es geht was vor in der Welt" (*BA*, 510; be alert, be alert, things are happening in the world: *BA2*, 439; translation altered).

The theory of affordances proposed by Kiverstein and Rietveld similarly emphasizes the role of other people in shaping our attention to the environment. As we saw, skills and habits are acquired through an education of attention, and Döblin's "seeing" corresponds to such an education. Importantly, Kiverstein and Rietveld, following Ingold and

Zukow-Goldring in different disciplines, point out that this education involves other practitioners who help us guide our actions and attention dynamically onto a situation and show us what should solicit responses and what should not.[50]

Habit and skill, therefore, the ways in which we pay attention to the environment, are subject to normativity:

> As the novice engages with particular aspects of the environment, so his or her performance is subject to *normative* assessment as better or worse, as more or less correct given the specific demands of the situation. Think of a child learning to name colors: much of the child's learning happens unobtrusively and in an unnoticed way through the imitation of others. In this kind of situation the child learns to care about the right thing, that is, acquires the concerns of his or her community. Social feedback plays a central role: when children use a color term correctly they receive praise; when they use a term contrary to its normal usage they are corrected. As children become increasingly skilled in the color-naming game, they acquire a feel for which uses are acceptable and which are not. As they become increasingly fluent in the art of naming the color of things, they reach a point where they can simply perceive immediately which color term to apply in a given context.[51]

The normativity that comes from this education of attention, the normativity that applies to habits of engaging with affordances, Rietveld and Kiverstein name "situated normativity."[52] It is a concrete situation which shapes whether behavior is adequate or not. Because normativity is situated, it does not so much rely on opinions, they argue, but on how we do things.

The lesson shown by the new Biberkopf is an awareness of this kind of situated normativity. Indeed, the problem that Biberkopf, being "hochmütig" (*BA*, 9; arrogan[t]: *BA2*, 1), runs into repeatedly throughout the novel is that his own habits, as normatively situated abilities, are not adequate for his new situation. What the end of the novel seems to get at then, is that other people can help us become habituated to unfamiliar, normative environments. Hence Döblin writes that through others he knows "was ich mir vornehmen kann" (*BA*, 509; what I can take on: *BA2*, 438), and that "was wahr und falsch ist, werd ich jetzt besser wissen" (*BA*, 509; know better now what is right and what is wrong: *BA2*, 439). Norms and values, "correct" ways of acting, are not individual

---

50 Ingold, *Perception of the Environment*, 354; Zukow-Goldring, "Assisted Imitation."
51 Kiverstein and Rietveld, "Rich Landscape," 332.
52 Kiverstein and Rietveld, "Rich Landscape," 332.

propositions, such as "anständig sein," but situated in ways of life, in a culture, structured upon the environment in terms of affordances. By paying attention to other people's habitual performances in the environment, by being responsive to them, we can learn to be habituated performers in a culture, too. Franz Karl Biberkopf is finally able to find more adequate ways of acting in the normative situation of Berlin, by watching, and acting like, others.

Döblin is, however, doing something different than Rietveld and Kiverstein are. If they are trying to describe the way in which (blind) rule-following comes about, Döblin is giving a lesson about how other people can help us. This distinction is important for understanding the ambiguous position Döblin seems to take at the end of the novel toward other people. The new Biberkopf is not simply habituating himself by paying attention to the way in which others engage in the world. He is meant to take a critical distance to others, as well. What is insufficiently treated in the theory of affordances is that other people might not be good educators, and that we have to be critical as to whom we take our cues from. In *Berlin Alexanderplatz*, the new Biberkopf is standing in his doorway looking "coolly" at the groups marching by (*BA2*, 439; kühl: *BA*, 509). His demeanor is careful and composed from the moment he leaves jail; Döblin repeatedly uses words like "ruhig" and "langsam," "taktfest" and "fest auf den Beinen" (*BA*, 502, 504; quietly, slowly, keeping time, good on his pins: *BA2*, 432, 434, 435; translations altered). The way others see the world here is not just something to mimic, but more generally something to be open to, to learn from, about how the world works, and to take a critical stance on: "Wach sein, wach sein, man ist nicht allein" (*BA*, 510; be alert, be alert, you are not alone: *BA2*, 439; translation altered). We need to learn from others. But more so than what we *should* do, Döblin says, they teach us what we *can* do given our situation and circumstances.

This may also be an answer to the questions raised by the ambiguity of the end of the novel. The ending has been repeatedly discussed because it ends with marching groups. If the last pages, as shown, emphasize the positive aspects of others, and Biberkopf's aggression is repeatedly dismissed, why then, many critics ask, the return of these aggressive groups? The way in which Döblin thinks about the dynamic process between agent and environment, however, a dynamic responsiveness which this chapter has repeatedly thought of in terms of affordances helps us dissolve some of this ambiguity into productive complexity. Affordances, as combining both agency and material reality into a perception of the world, show that while the world might go a certain way, that is, that there are marching groups going to war, the way in which we respond to these groups can change. Other people, I understand Döblin to say, are affordances for good and bad. They are part of the world, and as such shape and reshape it, in ways we do not have control over. So if we pay attention to people we can also find new ways of engaging with them and with the rest of the world. The body as an open system, then, which Döblin borrows from Uexküll, allows us to think about this openness to others as an imperative. Be open to the practices of others and you will both understand better the world, and will gain ways of engaging in it differently. Being responsive to the actions of others needs to be dynamic, Döblin seems to say. It is not enough to get habituated into a culture. Instead Döblin's description of the different social *milieux*, as well as the different political factions in Germany at the time, is more interested in a dynamic responsiveness. He is not advocating just becoming habituated in the dominant culture, or being a person who is "anständig." Instead, he seems to be advocating keeping one's eyes open for as many human practices as possible, and learning from them.

Conclusion

In conclusion, what makes affordances particularly fruitful tools for thinking about perception in *Berlin Alexanderplatz* is their twofold structure. On the one hand, they are underspecified. They imply agency, intention, and improvisation. They show how objects can become dynamic. On the other hand, they can be over-specified. They are subject to socio-cultural norms; others constantly show us how we can use objects in more or less adequate ways, better and worse ways.

In Biberkopf's engagement, we see this dual structure of dynamicity and rigidity play out. On the one hand, the way in which he sees the environment in terms of his concerns changes, as is shown in the way in which he interacts with the wall in his mind and the couch in the actual world. Moreover, the way in which the environment is underspecified offers all kinds of actions and thus asks for agency and causes anxiety. On the other hand, he is aggressive and stubborn. In this mode of behavior, there is just one way of acting to him, and this way is how he has always acted. First, Biberkopf is overwhelmed by his environment, and does not know how to act, and after that he adheres only to his old habits (from jail and before), repeating his mistakes—with disastrous consequences for the women in his life.

Having been broken, it is a responsiveness to his environment which ultimately helps him to find a more apt engagement in the world. The new Franz Karl Biberkopf has his eyes opened and lets the environment "herankommen" (come to him). Far from a passive mode of engagement, this is described by death as "life," a responsiveness, an open exploration of the environment. He is also involved with other people. He is standing on Alexanderplatz, amongst other people, watching them. He no longer judges them. Instead, they become useful. He is stronger with them and understands the world better through them. Other people, Döblin seems to argue, show the way in which the world works, and can help us learn new ways of understanding and new ways of acting in the world. As in Malte's engagement with historical figures, then, Döblin's emphasis on paying attention to others ties into recent discussions of "relational authenticity" in the cognitive sciences by Shaun Gallagher, Ben Morgan, and Naomi Rokotnitz, whereby we find our "truest" way of life through a dynamic, critical engagement with the other people who have shaped and continue to shape our lives.[53]

The emphasis in affordances on the dynamic between the abilities and concerns of the animal on the one hand and material reality on the other, helps to rethink some recurring questions in scholarship on the novel. First, the question is whether Biberkopf bears responsibility for the strikes that befall him. The ending of the novel, in particular the lesson of death, seems to imply that Döblin understands Biberkopf to have been at fault. But, as Baßler and Horn, for example, argue, the bad things that happen to Biberkopf are not only his fault. Affordances, however, allow us to see the dynamic between agent and world differently. While there is a reality to the things that happen to Biberkopf, there is also an agency in how he deals with them, and how much he learns from them. Biberkopf is not dynamic in how he appraises his environment, and therefore keeps running into the same problems. The ending of the novel can be understood in the same way. Much has been made of how to square the importance of other people as advocated at the end of the novel with the negative overtones of the marching groups. Should we think of the end of advocating individuality after all? But to think of the environment in terms of affordances opens up a space from which to recognize both the material reality constituted by the (negative) movements of other people and the fact that other people can help us formulate new ways of engaging.

Reading *Berlin Alexanderplatz* through the theory of affordances also allows us to gain more insight into the nature of affordances. First, compared with how Ingold and Rietveld and Kiverstein talk about an education of attention, Döblin emphasizes not only the dynamic between action and perception that gets us habituated into certain environments, but also that we need to keep being continually responsive to new social circumstances.[54] We have to be dynamic, not only when we find ourselves in unfamiliar circumstances, but continually. Second, the story of

---

53 See Gallagher, Morgan, and Rokotnitz, "Relational Authenticity."

54 See, however, a recent essay by a group of researchers that includes Kiverstein and Rietveld, in which they discuss "metastable attunement" in which agents "are able to exploit affordances they are attuned to, while at the same time being ready to flexibly explore for other affordances." Bruineberg et al., "Metastable Attunement," 12819.

Franz Biberkopf reminds us that an unfamiliar environment feels a certain way. The red-brick wall returns as an image to his mind because it offers him a protection that he cannot find in his new environment. A thoroughly altered Berlin causes him anxiety, which turns into aggression. Much work can still be done in the exploration of affordances and in theories of embodied cognition more generally, on the place of affect within the dynamics between agents and their environments. In particular, more work is to be done, as *Die Geschichte vom Franz Biberkopf* points out, on the ways in which unfamiliar environments affect us. Much work can still be done in the exploration of affordances, and theories of embodied cognition more generally, on the place of affect within the dynamics of agent an environment, in particular, as *Die Geschichte vom Franz Biberkopf* points out, on the ways in which unfamiliar environments affect us. The next two chapters mark a beginning.

Ultimately, what this responsiveness to the environment seems to entail for Döblin is what he understands organisms always to already be: "open systems" connected to the world. The responsiveness he is advocating seems to be doing this basic disposition better. Hence he has death say to Biberkopf that it is as if he was never born at all (*BA*, 487). Humans are always already connected to the environment, open to it, and thus can connect anew to new environments. Biberkopf's entry into the unfamiliar city of Berlin, therefore, becomes a metaphor for the modern environment. As Döblin writes in his "Der Geist des naturalistischen Zeitalters": "Physiologisch werden in der neuen Epoche andere Organsysteme und Gehirnteile beschäftigt" (physiologically, in the new age other organ systems and brain components are put to work).[55] New environments need new abilities, and humans, unlike other animals, Döblin seems to say, are able to change: "Die Tierart Mensch will nicht stehen bleiben" (the animal species Homo will not stand still).[56] Döblin's comparison of the "beaver-headed" Biberkopf to other animals—as when he writes that Biberkopf would rather live as a mouse than a human being (*BA*, 481), or in the scene in the abattoir (*BA*, 150–58)—thus seems to come down to the fact that while animals cannot be responsive to new environments and learn new skills of engaging, or at least are understood to be unable to do so, humans can. Hence Biberkopf needs to be born again, this time with eyes wide open, not just attentive, but fully embodied and affectively responsive to the environment. The text emphasizes other people as well as dynamic contexts—mimicked in the dynamic structure constituted by the novel's montage form (discussed in detail in chapter 7)—as important

---

55 Döblin, "Geist des naturalistischen Zeitalters," 66; Döblin, "The Spirit of a Naturalistic Age," 77.

56 Döblin, "Geist des naturalistischen Zeitalters," 65; Döblin, "Spirit of a Naturalistic Age," 76.

ways to re-inhabit the modern urban world, for getting new abilities of action and perception, but only if we are responsive to them. If Döblin's text puts responsiveness forward as the way into unfamiliar environments, it does little to explore this embodied attitude. Benjamin, however, as we will see in the following chapter, explores exactly what an embodied responsiveness might look like.

5: Walter Benjamin's *Einbahnstraße* and Its *Nachtragsliste*: Critical Responsiveness

Ne jamais profiter de l'élan acquis.
[Never profit from an acquired élan.]
—André Gide[1]

IN A VIGNETTE CALLED "Chinawaren" in Benjamin's *Einbahnstraße* (One-Way Street, 1928), a collection of sixty of such "images," he writes: "In diesen Tagen darf sich niemand auf das versteifen, was er 'kann'. In der Improvisation liegt die Stärke. Alle entscheidende Schläge werden mit der linken Hand geführt werden" (*KGA* VIII, 16; these are days when no one should rely unduly on his "competence." Strength lies in improvisation. All the decisive blows are struck left-handed: *OWS*, 27). This rejection of the usefulness of a stiff know-how only, in favor of a more dynamic improvisation, is representative of Benjamin's concerns throughout *Einbahnstraße* as well as a series of subsequent vignettes, written between 1928 and 1934, known as the "Nachtragsliste zur Einbahnstraße." He is trying to find a way of acting that gets away from both debilitating contemplation and static, habitual behavior.[2]

Benjamin—like Rilke, Heidegger, and Döblin before him—crucially situates habit in the material environment. It is, as he suggests in "Spurlos wohnen" (To Live without Leaving Traces) the environment that prompts habitual action. The prime image of habit that he uses here is of the bourgeois *Interieur* of the 1880s, in which traces of (others') past use dominate behavior. For the agent in this vignette, this is a negative and disengaged experience: "Hier hast du nichts zu suchen" (*KGA* VIII, 111;

---

1 Gide, *Journal des faux-monnayeurs*, 89. The phrase is quoted by Benjamin in the vignette "Einmal ist Keinmal <II>" from the *Nachtragsliste* (*KGA* VIII, 90).
2 Benjamin wrote the manuscript list "Nachtragsliste zur Einbahnstraße" containing 43 titles around 1934. The text of 34 of those titles was published in newspapers and journals between 1928 and 1934. Eight others were unpublished in Benjamin's lifetime, but typescripts remain. The final title, Schöttker and Haug state, cannot securely be tied to a text. For more information see *KGA* VIII, 265–66; 292.

You've got no business here: *SW* II.2, 701). For Benjamin this seems to be the exemplary image of the experience of the modern environment at large. In a longer essay named "Erfahrung und Armut" (Experience and Poverty, 1933), in which he uses the same image of entering the *Interieur*, he suggests that for the generation who have experienced World War I, and the technological advances visible therein, this old material environment and the habits of its elders that sustain it are meaningless (*GS* II.1, 213–19; *SW* II.2, 731–36). It is meaningless to them, first, because this environment is obsolete as made visible by the technological warfare, and second, because it does not offer an outlet for the experiences of the war. Habit, for Benjamin, becomes shorthand for a behavior linked to a material environment that is in decline and meaningless.

Habit and other embodied practices have been widely discussed in scholarship on Benjamin's work.[3] In these discussions, habits and other actions are often conflated in an emphasis on Benjamin's movement away from contemplation as the dominant way of engaging with the modernist environment. Michael Taussig, for example, in an essay focusing on *Einbahnstraße* but here quoting from Benjamin's artwork essay (final version, 1939), writes:

> Benjamin wants to stress a barely conscious mode of apperception and a type of "physiological knowledge" built from habit. The claim is grand. "For the tasks which face the human apparatus of perception at the turning point of history cannot be solved," he writes, "by optical means, that is, by contemplation alone. They are mastered gradually by habit, under the guidance of tactile appropriation."[4]

What often gets lost in these treatments conflating habit and embodiment is Benjamin's ambiguous treatment of habit, at least in *Einbahnstraße*. Whereas embodiment seems to be an unequivocally positive response to modernity in this text, habit does not. What reading *Einbahnstraße* alongside contemporary cognitive science brings into relief is that while Benjamin reads habit as a predominantly restrictive force, there are more dynamic aspects to embodiment beyond habit. This space to think embodiment away from habit overcomes the difficulties arising from thinking embodiment as purely an automatic response to the environment. Miriam Hansen, namely, argues that because Benjamin could

---

3   See for example Taussig, "Physiognomic Aspects of Visual Worlds"; Hansen, *Embodying Technesis*; Hansen, "Of Mice and Ducks." For more recent treatments of the body in Benjamin see, for example, Barbisan, "Eccentric Bodies"; and Ruprecht, *Gestural Imaginaries*.

4   Taussig, "Physiognomic Aspects of Visual Worlds," 18. For the final and authorized version of *Das Kunstwerk im Zeitalter seiner technischen Reproduzierbarkeit*, see *GS* I.2, 471–508.

not be advocating for "a behaviorist adaptation to the present," as that would align him with fascism, he could not be arguing unequivocally for embodiment either.[5] Exploring embodiment away from behaviorism or habit gets us away from this pitfall, whereby the latter can be critiqued without losing the former.

This chapter starts with placing Benjamin's version of habit in *Einbahnstraße* alongside contemporary accounts of it, specifically as presented in a paper by John Sutton and colleagues.[6] Whereas Sutton et al. understand habit more in terms of skill, as dynamic, on-the-fly, and attuned to the needs of the moment, Benjamin here predominantly thinks of habit as rigid and unresponsive, stuck in everyday activities.[7] Benjamin is, nevertheless, after a similar kind of dynamic behavior as Sutton and colleagues describe in their useful account, but he refrains from muddying the waters by not calling such embodied engagements "habit" as well. Indeed, for Benjamin habit and the kind of engagement he is after are, at least ethically, profoundly distinct. Benjamin is concerned with overcoming both habit and debilitation through, as Ben Morgan has put it, a "revivification of the present."[8] Benjamin attempts a re-figuration of the relation between the body and its environment so that the latter draws us out of our habitual behavior and its meaning becomes flexible and vibrant. To achieve this, Benjamin argues for various kinds of immediate, pre-reflective, yet attentive action, which he explores through terms such as "embodied presence-of-mind," "innervation," and "ecstasy." In other words, he investigates in much detail the kind of responsiveness that Döblin's novel advocated in its final pages. Underpinning this

---

5   Hansen, "Mice and Ducks," 41. To distinguish between Miriam Hansen and Mark B. N. Hansen, I will refer to both by their first and last names throughout.

6   Sutton et al., "Applying Intelligence."

7   If my discussion focuses on Benjamin's *Einbahnstraße*, it should be noted that Benjamin's evaluation of habit is ambiguous between various of his texts as well as within them. Thus Scott McCracken explores the dynamics of habit in Benjamin's Arcades Project attending us to "the possibility of a dialectic between routine and creativity" therein. Tim Beasley-Murray, in his chapter on "Habit and Tradition" in his comparative monograph on Michail Bakhtin and Benjamin, explores habit through a variety of Benjamin's text. He, too, points out that "Benjamin's attitude to habit . . . contains a high degree of ambivalence." (24). For example, he directs our attention to "absolutely divergent evaluations of habit" in "The Storyteller" published in October 1936, and the second version of the artwork essay conceived between December 1935 and February 1936 (25). McCracken, *Completion of Old Work*; Beasley-Murray, *Mikhail Bakhtin and Walter Benjamin*.

8   Morgan, "Benjamin, Heidegger," 96. Morgan is referring here to a discussion by Detlev Schöttker and Erdmut Wizisla of Heidegger and Benjamin in Schöttker and Wizisla, eds., *Arendt und Benjamin*.

revivification of the environment in *Einbahnstraße* are repeated, affect-laden, images of excitement, passion, fire, and play which innervate the body. Both our practices and the meaning of the environment are loosened in such engagement. What Benjamin seems to be concerned with is what underlies habits, what Maxine Sheets-Johnstone describes in terms of "receptivity" and "responsivity," and Giovanna Colombetti calls "primordial affectivity": our innate propensity to be affected by and move towards our environment.[9] These "affective-kinetic coordination dynamics," as Sheets-Johnstone calls them, are what habits are grounded in.[10] It is such exploration grounded in the body, then, that (as Döblin's text already showed, but Benjamin explores in more detail) can take us out of static habits and away from debilitating contemplation. In other words, if Heidegger explored the ways in which our bodies are always already animated by a certain world in a certain way, Benjamin explores their reanimation.

Benjamin's exploration is also important for current debates in the cognitive science of embodiment because he helps us redirect its focus from individualism toward questions of social flourishing. The way in which, for example, skillful behavior, or expertise, is framed in such discussions by Sutton and his colleagues or Mihalyi Csikszentmihalyi shows an emphasis toward questions of personal growth, self-realization, and self-optimization.[11] Examples from (elite) sportsmanship are pervasive in such discussions. Our engagement with and for others is rarely used as an example of skillful behavior. While such individual approaches certainly are also ways of exploring human flourishing, Benjamin's ethical interest in the dynamic between habit and responsiveness focuses more deliberately on the possibility for a communal innervation and thus a communal flourishing.

In the final chapter, I also explore *Einbahnstraße*'s own possibilities of sharing the kind of reanimated, responsive, innervated engagement Benjamin is after, through its modernist form. A seemingly unknown contemporaneous Dutch review (it does not appear amongst the other reviews in the *Kritische Gesamtausgabe*) opens up important questions about the effectiveness of Benjamin's own style for sharing and motivating a revivification of the relation between its readers and their environments. In the current chapter, reading Benjamin's exploration of physicality

9   Sheets-Johnstone, *Primacy of Movement*, 501–10; Colombetti, *Feeling Body*, 19–24. See also Morgan's suggestion to look at Benjamin in light of Colombetti's work on primordial affectivity in Morgan, "Walter Benjamin Re-Situated."
10 Sheets-Johnstone, *Primacy of Movement*, 472.
11 Csikszentmihalyi's *Flow*, discussed in detail in chapter 3, is perhaps the best example because here his important academic work is marketed as a self-help book for self-optimization. Csikszentmihalyi, *Flow*.

alongside contemporary theories of embodiment in cognitive science thus helps bring into relief the ways in which a dynamically kinetic-affective body, that is, a responsive body, plays a fundamental role in Benjamin's investigations into the possible reanimation of human culture.

Rigid Habits in Overspecified Environments

In a vignette by the name of "Spurlos wohnen" in the *Nachtragsliste*, Benjamin explores habits and the ways in which they are sustained and shaped by our socio-material environments. He links habit to habitation, *Gewohnheit* to *wohnen*. Benjamin describes entering an 1880s, "bourgeois," "plush," "Interieur" (*KGA* VIII, 111). As Ursula Marx points out, the word "Interieur" for Benjamin is a synonym "der bürgerlichen Daseinsform des ausgehenden 19. Jahrhunderts" (of the bourgeois way of life at the end of the 19th century).[12] The *Interieur* as he describes it here is not only a space in which the inhabitant is invited to acquire "ein Höchstmaß von Gewohnheiten" (*KGA* VIII, 111; the greatest possible number of habits: *SW* II.2, 701) but also one in which the inhabitant reinforces these habits by leaving the same traces herself. In such rooms, freedom of movement is impeded by a material environment which calls out for a repetition of movement: "Das Wohnen war in diesen Plüschgelassen nichts andres als das Nachziehen einer Spur, die von Gewohnheiten gestiftet wurde" (*KGA* VIII, 111; living in these plush compartments was nothing other than following a trail created by habits: *SW* II.2, 701; translation altered). More generally, "das Wohnen," as Ursula Marx writes, "stellte für Benjamin seit Mitte der zwanziger Jahre ein Modell dar, das ins Zentrum seines Denkens zielte und an dem er grundlegende Ideen seiner materialistischen Geschichtsphilosophie entwickelte" (represented for Benjamin since the mid-twenties a model that was at the center of his thinking and from which he developed basic ideas of his materialist philosophy of history).[13] This kind of dynamic and mutually sustaining relation between environment and human practices is reminiscent of Gibson's theory of affordances, discussed in detail in the previous chapter. The environmental niche as a "set of affordances," in this theory, implies, shapes and sustains, a set of human practices, and such practices imply an environmental niche.[14] But whereas Gibson is especially interested in the ways in which we shape our environments to make things easier for us, Benjamin has an opposing interest.[15] He focuses on how these environ-

---

12 Marx, "Von Gästen und Vandalen," 54. All translations of this source are mine.
13 Marx, "Von Gästen und Vandalen," 48.
14 Gibson, *Ecological Approach*, 120.
15 Gibson, *Ecological Approach*, 122.

ments ultimately come to shape us more than we them. In a different version of the above passage in "Erfahrung und Armut," for example, he writes: "Und umgekehrt nötigt das 'Intérieur' den Bewohner, das Höchstmaß von Gewohnheiten anzunehmen, Gewohnheiten, die mehr dem Intérieur, in welchem er lebt, als ihm selber gerecht werden" (*GS* II.1, 217; And conversely, the *intérieur* forces the inhabitant to adopt the greatest possible number of habits—habits that do more justice to the interior he is living in than to himself: *SW* II.2, 734).

What is at stake in Benjamin is an overhaul of the environment. Benjamin contrasts the bourgeois rooms with modern architecture. He writes:

> Das haben nun die neuen Architekten mit ihrem Glas und ihrem Stahl erreicht: Sie schufen Räume, in denen es nicht leicht ist, eine Spur zu hinterlassen. "Nach dem Gesagten," schrieb bereits vor zwanzig Jahren Scheerbart, "können wir wohl von einer Glaskultur sprechen. Das neue Glasmilieu wird den Menschen vollkommen umwandeln. Und es ist nur zu wünschen, daß die neue Glaskultur nicht allzu viele Gegner findet." (*KGA* VIII, 112)

> [This is what has now been achieved by the new architects, with their glass and steel: they have created rooms in which it is hard to leave traces. "It follows from the foregoing," Scheerbart declared a good twenty years ago, "that we can surely talk about a 'culture of glass.' The new glass-milieu will transform humanity utterly. And now it remains only to be wished that the new glass-culture will not encounter too many enemies." (*SW* II.2, 701–2)]

Whereas the past for Benjamin is marked by a bourgeois inflexibility of habitual behavior, modern architecture of the kind he describes here is open to new forms of behavior. Moreover, whereas in the past the past played a significant role in living, living as a perpetuation of the past embodied by the material environment of the *Interieur* and its traces, in modern architecture, Benjamin hopes, living becomes less marked by the past. The last sentence quoted from Scheerbart reveals that this, for Benjamin, is a positive achievement of architecture. If the bourgeois *Interieur* is overspecified—to use the terms from the previous chapter—modern architecture, in its difficulty of having traces left on it, is for Benjamin underspecified, that is, marked by an ambiguity or openness of use, an ambiguity or openness, therefore, of meaning.

Such habits as shaped and sustained by, in this case, bourgeois interiors are problematic for Benjamin because they are not responsive to changes in the world, let alone that they offer tools to engage with these changes. The above image of a person entering a bourgeois 1880s living room also appears in "Erfahrung und Armut" in which the image stands in for how Benjamin understands his contemporary, post–World War I, environment (*GS* II.1, 217–18). Habit is here equated with relatable experiences (*Erfahrung*) which are of no use to a generation marked by the war, a generation that has no *relatable* experience of its own. What good is the experience of age, Benjamin asks, when faced with the new technological power of war: "Eine Generation, die noch mit der Pferdebahn zur Schule gefahren war, stand unter freiem Himmel in einer Landschaft, in der nichts unverändert geblieben war als die Wolken, und in der Mitte, in einem Kraftfeld zerstörender Ströme und Explosionen, der winzige gebrechliche Menschenkörper" (*GS* II.1, 214; A generation that had gone to school in horse-drawn streetcars now stood in the open air, amid a landscape in which nothing was the same except the clouds and, at its center, in a force field of destructive torrents and explosions, the tiny, fragile human body: *SW* II.2, 732).[16] Not unlike Döblin's Biberkopf, then, who comes out of jail to find people eating and drinking, an act he understands, yet which has no meaning for him, so Benjamin's subject of war seems to come into an environment to find that the traces of history that guide his elders have nothing to say to him: "Hier hast du nichts zu suchen" (*KGA* VIII, 111; you've got no business here: *SW* II.2, 701). On the one hand, there are those still holding onto old habits, safely, they believe, in their carefully constructed niches, not realizing that the world has changed, and on the other, those who *do* realize that the world has changed and to whom old habits and niches are therefore meaningless.

What is needed, Benjamin states, instead of the "galvanization" of practices such as yoga, astrology or "Christian Science," is "true revivification" (echte Wiederbelebung: *GS* II.1, 215). A fresh start is needed, a *tabula rasa*, from which to construct with only few materials. Art and architecture play important roles here, and have to become a "Veränderung der Wirklichkeit, nicht ihrer Beschreibung" (*GS* II.1, 217; changing reality instead of describing it: *SW* II.2, 733). Hence Benjamin's interest in Scheerbart's description of glass buildings: he believes habits cannot leave traces here. Of course, anyone who has ever washed a windowpane knows that traces can be left on glass and are more visible on it than on most materials. Nevertheless, if we move away from Benjamin's specific examples, we can see that certain environments and objects are more specified for use than others. A park with a path is more specified than a park without one. Benjamin, in his emphasis on the negative aspects of habit, also does not have an eye here for what Biberkopf has shown us, namely that an underspecified environment can

---

16 This passage also appears in "Der Erzähler" (*GS* II.1, 439).

be anxiety-inducing.[17] Today's society indeed seems to have moved in the opposite direction. The iPhone, despite its shiny surface, is understood exactly to be one of today's most successful tools, one which many of us are especially beholden to, because its use is intuitive, that is, clearly specified. It is, of course, exactly because of such a "beholdenness" that Benjamin hopes for a less specified world.

Habit is thus for Benjamin first and foremost a negative, conformist behavior entangled in a material environment. It is also something that is not open to changes in the larger environment and is based on the past rather than in contemporary events. Habitual practice is increasingly disconnected from the challenges of modernization. It has nothing to offer to the World War I generation, which has experienced the new technological possibilities to which the habits of the bourgeoisie, attuned to an old materiality, have no answer. What is at stake for Benjamin again becomes clear in a diary entry from June 8, 1931.[18] Here he writes about his day talking to Bertolt Brecht about the subject of *wohnen*, and summarizes his own position as having only two options when faced with a bourgeois interior. In the first option one does what the furniture wants. In the other, one takes on a behavior that "gewiss keine Gewohnheiten aufkommen lässt, weil es die Dinge, ihre Stützpunkte, fortschreitend wegräumt" (certainly does not give rise to habits, because it progressively removes things, their support).[19] The option against rigid, conformist behavior here for Benjamin is thus to do away with the material environment entirely.

Separating Habits from Responsiveness

Investigations of habit—as well as skills and other ways of embodied coping—are central to treatments of embodied cognition in contemporary discussions. These theories explicitly argue against, as Sutton

---

17 In "Gewohnheit und Aufmerksamkeit" (*GS* IV.1, 407–8) Benjamin does state we need habit to not be completely overwhelmed by the environment. This vignette was first published together with eight others, seven of which are on the *Nachtragsliste*, as the "Ibizenkische Folge." They were published in the *Frankfurter Zeitung* on June 4, 1932. See also *KGA* VIII, 297.

18 This meeting took place around the same time that he was writing "Spurlos Wohnen," an early draft of which appears in a diary entry on the May 5, 1931 (*GS* VI, 424–27). Benjamin was spending the summer with Brecht in the South of France. As Ursula Marx points out, it was not uncommon to talk about living situations in the beginning of the 1930s as migration to the city and the socioeconomic turmoil of the Weimar Republic required new ways of living for citizens of big cities. See Marx, "Von Gästen und Vandalen," 49.

19 Walter Benjamin, June 8, 1931, in Wizisla, *Benjamin und Brecht*, 47. My translation.

and colleagues write, the kind of "Cartesian" view of action based on "a deliberate, pre-planned, explicit blueprint which is merely executed in the expression of embodied action."[20] Instead, these discussions of habit and skill emphasize the pre-reflective, attuned kinds of behavior that make up a large part of our everyday engagements. In contrast to how Benjamin seems to think about habits, these discussions largely treat habit and skill positively. Habit is not only treated as a phenomenon worth emphasizing—because previously neglected—but Hubert L. Dreyfus, for example, goes as far as to write, counter to the idea that "mind at its best is detached from immersive action," that "human beings are at their best when involved in action."[21] This might well be true but, as Benjamin shows, the important difference is whether this action is responsive or not.

The difference becomes clear when we look at how Sutton and his colleagues theorize habits in relation to skills. They use the two terms almost interchangeably after arguing that habits should be seen as closer to skills than they often are. Both habit and skill, they argue, could usefully be seen as "the non-conscious and relational constitution and maintenance of agency."[22] Importantly, and against Ryle's view which positions habits, in their understanding, as statically automatic and reflexive, they argue that habits have a certain context-sensitivity which they share with skills: "Even in more frequently repeated everyday behavioral sequences, like brushing our teeth or gathering together our keys and belongings before leaving home in the morning, we can remain more or less open and responsive to any peculiarities of today's unique constellation of moods and events."[23] Habits can, thus, they argue, be helpfully seen as "flexible and adaptive" and thus as the more mundane versions of the "immersed embodied skills" of experts.[24] This flexibility and adaptivity is exactly what is at stake for Benjamin.

What the use of the word "habit" by Sutton and colleagues depreciates, and what Benjamin emphasizes in his use of the word, is that while perhaps in our habitual engagement we *might* be open and responsive, often we are not. It is hard to make sure when we brush our teeth to also brush the parts of our teeth that are hard to reach, and it is hard to remember to be careful grabbing our keys from glass surfaces as our partners ask us to do. And that is when we are actually somewhat impelled, by the outside world, to pay attention to our practices. Moreover, even if we are more responsive in our everyday habits, it is even harder to be

20   Sutton et al., "Applying Intelligence," 87.
21   Dreyfus, "Myth of the Mental," 372, 373.
22   Sutton et al., "Applying Intelligence," 81.
23   Sutton et al., "Applying Intelligence," 80; Ryle, *Concept of Mind*, 126–30.
24   Sutton et al., "Applying Intelligence," 81.

responsive to the realities that lie outside of our immediate environments and engagements and the changes therein, as Benjamin's bourgeois interiors suggest. Again, for Benjamin the word "habit" marks the exact opposite of being responsive to the environment. What I am suggesting in contrasting "habit" in these two uses is not that Sutton et al. are mistaken in their characterization of the phenomenon of embodied coping as more or less open to the environment, but rather that if we name all of this "habit" we lose the importance of the ethical difference between a responsive comportment and rigid, habitual use.

Responsiveness as Corporeal Attention

The kind of embodied, aware engagement that contemporary cognitive science explores in terms of habit and skill—"actions which are often sculpted on the fly, in response to the needs of the moment, and on the basis of a dynamic implicit repertoire of tendencies and potential responses"—are found repeatedly in Benjamin's *Einbahnstraße* and its *Nachtragsliste*.[25] In a vignette named "Madame Ariane zweiter Hof links," for example, one of the final vignettes of *Einbahnstraße*, Benjamin discusses the way in which one can engage productively with the jolts of the environment. Benjamin argues that faced with the information that comes at us at all times there are two ways of dealing with it, either interpreting it or using it: "Vorzeichen, Ahnungen, Signale gehen ja Tag und Nacht durch unsern Organismus wie Wellenstöße. Sie deuten oder sie nutzen, das ist die Frage" (*KGA* VIII, 70; omens, presentiments, signals pass day and night through our organism like wave impulses. To interpret them or to use them: that is the question: *OWS*, 87). They need to be used, Benjamin argues, because before they are contemplated to the point where they are a communicable word or image, they have lost all power. Immediacy of action is paramount. Interpretation or contemplation of *future* consequences—hence, the soothsayer in the vignette's title—is replaced by a "leibhafter Geistesgegenwart," an immediate and embodied presence-of-mind.

His use of the word "presence-of-mind," however, shows that Benjamin is not interested in mere habitual behavior here, but that he believes that an attention to the present moment is paramount. In "Der Weg zum Erfolg in dreizehn Thesen" (The Path to Success, in Thirteen Theses) of the *Nachtragsliste*, Benjamin defines presence-of-mind in similar terms to Heidegger's gesture (see chapter 2): "nicht das Daß und Wie—allein *das Wo des Geistes* entscheidet. Daß er [der Geist] im Augenblicke und im Raum zugegen sei, das schafft er nur, indem er in den Stimmfall, das Lächeln, das Verstummen, den Blick, die Geste eingeht. Denn Gegenwart

---

25 Sutton et al., "Applying Intelligence," 87.

des Geistes schafft allein der Leib" (*KGA* VIII, 107; The question is not whether mind is present, or what form it takes, but only *where* it is. That it happens to be present here, at this very moment, is possible only if it enters into a person's intonation, his smile, his conversational pauses, his gaze, or his gestures. For only the body can generate presence of mind: *SW* II.1, 147, emphasis original). What Benjamin seems to be describing is thus an attentive sensitivity to one's own physical presence in a particular moment in space, in other words, not just an attentiveness to a particular thing or thought but an acute awareness of one's surroundings and oneself in it.[26] This picture aligns with the kind of openness, responsivity, and "context-sensitivity," that Sutton and his colleagues are after in thinking habit and skill as "mindful." Discussing "practitioners in many skilled movement domains," they write:

> because they ... know that open-ended, flexible performance is context-sensitive and, in the ideal, exquisitely responsive to subtle changes in a situation, they also want to be able to bring all of their experience to bear in the moment, to bring memory and movement together, with thought and action cooperating instead of competing. ... An elite cricketer, for example, ... draws not only on smoothly-practised strokeplay, but somehow also on experience of playing *this* fast bowler in *these* conditions, and on dynamically updated awareness of the current state of the match and of the opposition's deployments.[27]

What Benjamin seems to get at in his images of *nutzen* or *leibliche Geistesgegenwart*, is this kind of context-sensitive, exquisitely responsive action. Although it is certainly not the only way in which skilled practitioners work—even the best violin players may get distracted, for example—it is the kind of engagement that Benjamin is interested in exploring.[28]

26 I realize that the use of the word "awareness" might be at odds with Benjamin's use of the word "distraction" in other texts for the kind of practice he is after. But, as Carolin Duttlinger states, such distraction is the opposite of *conscious* deliberation/attention, not the kind of embodied awareness to one's own presence in space I suggest he is after (on which more below). What I suggest, then, is that what Benjamin calls distraction is a distraction of the mind from such deliberation into nevertheless an awareness, but a kinesthetic or embodied one. Duttlinger, "Network – Figure – Labyrinth." See also Schwartz, *Blind Spots*, 73–86; and Duttlinger, *Attention and Distraction*.
27 Sutton et al., "Applying Intelligence," 80.
28 Shaun Gallagher, citing evidence from Simon Høffding, reminds us that experts, like musicians, might not always be fully attentive to their actions when performing. This may certainly be true, but that is not the same as to say that the kind of context-sensitive, responsive action that Benjamin is after here is not the ideal state for the skilled performer. A musician might be thinking about where

The description given by Sutton and his colleagues, and indeed their whole essay, is geared toward bringing mind and thought—separated from conscious deliberation—back into skilled practices. Benjamin similarly complicates the idea of the mind in habit and skill. Although he employs the word "Geistesgegenwart," he clearly wants to get away from such conscious thought. In the 34th vignette of the extra list named "Übung," for example, Benjamin discusses skills as coming about through endless physical practice whereby the will is only in the way. Starting off from Psalm 127:2 "For He gives to His beloved even in his sleep" and the German proverb which derives from it, Benjamin argues that such "luck" of a sudden ability arrives on the back of extensive practice, but does so exactly when the mind gives in to tiredness.[29] He writes, using the example of the skill of Enrico Rastelli, a famous Italian juggler:

> Die Uebung von Jahrzehnten die dem voranging, hat in Wahrheit weder den Körper noch den Ball "unter seine Gewalt," sondern dies zustande gebracht: daß beide hinter seinem Rücken sich verständigten. Den Meister durch Fleiß und Mühe bis zur Grenze der Erschöpfung zu ermüden, so daß endlich der Körper und ein jedes seiner Glieder nach ihrer eigenen Vernunft handeln können—das nennt man üben. (*KGA* VIII, 116)

> [The decades' worth of practice that came before does not mean that either his body or the ball is "in his power," but it enables the two to reach an understanding behind his back. To weary the master to the point of exhaustion through diligence and hard work, so that at long last his body and each of his limbs can act in accordance with their own rationality: this is what is called "practice." (*SW* II.2, 591)]

Through extensive training even the most difficult acts can become almost automatic. The use of the "will," Benjamin writes, is completely dismissed in favor of the use of the organs, in Rastelli's case his hands. Rather than the mind as conscious deliberation playing an active role here, the body and its environment become attuned only when the mind gives in, but with their own intelligence. Benjamin's *leibliche Geistesgegenwart* is thus

---

to have beers later while performing, and the performance might nevertheless go well, but that does not mean that she might not perform best when she is fully responsive throughout the performance. That said, knowing when to let go of concentration might also be an important part of a skilled performer's toolkit. Gallagher, "Mindful Performance," 49; Høffding, "Phenomenology of Expert Musicianship."

29 The proverb returns in a vignette called "Der Weg zum Erfolg in dreizehn Thesen" (*KGA* VIII, 103).

not a conscious embodiment but a corporeal cognition. Hence Miriam Hansen calls this "not self-reflection, but an integral 'actuality,' a 'bodily,' to some degree absent-minded 'presence of mind.'"[30] And Gerhard Richter states about this vignette, "[an autonomous gesture] is the enactment of the simultaneity of presence and absence of mind on the stage of the body."[31] However, we do not need such linguistically contradictory statements to describe something which is utterly natural to us.

As Sheets-Johnstone reminds us—and as Sutton et al. via the work of Elizabeth A. Behnke indeed also argue—conscious deliberation is not the only way of being attentive to our environments, nor are habits the only way to interact corporeally with our environments.[32] Our familiarity with the world, its "transparency," is grounded in responsivity:

> "Transparency" is not only not a ready-made but is grounded through and through in experience, which itself is grounded in both our evolutionary heritage to explore and make sense of the world and in the actual explorations and discoveries we all made as infants. . . . By failing to consider the basis of our developing familiarity with ourselves and the world, we fail to consider our inborn responsivity and those affective-kinetic coordination dynamics that are rooted in our being the animate organisms we are.[33]

An attentive engagement with the environment thus does not have to be consciously minded; animation is in and of itself attentive and responsive. How, then, can we "tap into" this innate corporeal dynamism? Benjamin suggests that it is exactly the impulses, or jolts, of a *terra incognita* that can elicit such a responsiveness. In the vignette about "nutzen," Benjamin states that the people of antiquity knew "true practice" (*OWS*, 88; wahre Praxis: *KGA* VIII, 71).[34] He uses the example of Scipio who stumbles into Cartage, and who, while falling, opens his arms and

---

30 Hansen, "Benjamin, Cinema and Experience," 200.
31 Richter, *Thought-Images*, 157. For more on the importance of gesture in Benjamin and early twentieth century German thought generally, see Ruprecht, *Gestural Imaginaries*.
32 Sutton et al., "Applying Intelligence," 92. See also Behnke, "Edmund Husserl's Contribution."
33 Sheets-Johnstone, *Primacy of Movement*, 472. While Sheets-Johnstone thus uses the word "responsivity," I will keep using "responsiveness" because while Sheets-Johnstone is interested in our innate propensity to be responsive, I am also interested in the degrees to which we can be responsive, which is better captured by "responsiveness."
34 In a later vignette he describes special abilities of antiquity's people in terms of ecstasy ("Rausch"; *KGA* VIII, 75).

cries out: "Teneo te, terra Africana!" (I hold you, Africa).[35] Benjamin writes: "Was Schreckenszeichen, Unglücksbild hat werden wollen, bindet er leibhaft an die Sekunde und macht sich selber zum Faktotum seines Leibes" (*KGA* VIII, 71; What would have become a portent of disaster he binds bodily to the moment, making himself the factotum of his body: *OWS*, 89). The image of falling captures intuitively the way in Benjamin brings together physical skill and attention in this embodied presence-of-mind. It suggests an innervation of the body, combining a heightened kinesthetic awareness, a sensitivity toward the environment, and an action-readiness.[36] In this particular image, the trip is a jolt which is productively and meaningfully dealt with immediately. The body might be lifted out of old, pre-reflective movements by the immediacy of the jolt, into a heightened state of awareness to both itself and its immediate environment. Importantly, having to react to the immediacy of the jolt, this "using" is thus both the opposite of contemplation and of pre-reflective, routine habits. Receptivity, awareness, and responsiveness come together here to respond sensitively to the immediate environment which is no longer transparent. Benjamin writes: "Der Tag liegt jeden Morgen wie ein frisches Hemd auf unserm Bett; dies unvergleichlich feine, unvergleichlich dichte Gewebe reinlicher Weissagung sitzt uns wie angegossen. Das Glück der nächsten vierundzwanzig Stunden hängt daran, daß wir es im Erwachen aufzugreifen wissen" (*KGA* VIII, 71; Each morning the day lies like a fresh shirt on our bed; this incomparably fine, incomparably tightly woven fabric of pure prediction fits us perfectly. The happiness of the next twenty-four hours depends on our ability, on waking, to pick it up: *OWS*, 89). Being able to seize the day, in all its fine detail, depends not on contemplation but on an aware, awake action-readiness, on what Lucia Ruprecht has called a "corporeal quick-wittedness."[37] Benjamin is investigating a dynamic picture of engagement, which, whatever the day brings, is sensitive, attentive, and ready for immediate action. What gets us into such an immediate, embodied responsiveness, Benjamin seems to

---

35 The phrase usually goes "teneo te Africa."

36 Carrie Noland, in reference to Theodor W. Adorno, writes that innervations stimulate "the nerves of a bodily part, and thus allow the body to achieve a certain awareness and knowledge of itself." Noland, introduction, ix. See also Ruprecht, "Gesture, Interruption, Vibration," 30.

37 Ruprecht, "Gesture, Interruption, Vibration," 31. The image of being awake and awakening in relation to a receptivity and responsivity to the environment is also famously employed by Husserl. See Husserl, *Experience and Judgement*, 78–79. See also Sheet-Johnstone's treatment of the subject in Sheets-Johnstone, *Primacy of Movement*, 501–10.

say, is precisely the jolts of unfamiliar environments; they are what can either demand reflection, or dynamic responses.[38]

But while in such unfamiliar situations like the one Scipio finds himself in we are more or less nudged into improvisation—unless, of course, we hesitate or ignore the situation completely—the question becomes how we can be responsive in more familiar situations. Benjamin also finds room for a dynamic responsiveness there and shows that habits have a role to play in responsiveness. The importance of the difference between habit and habituat*ing* comes into relief in a vignette that discusses the writing of André Gide as well as the manual labor of Leon Trotsky's father. This vignette, the second with the name "Einmal ist Keinmal," opposes the *Einmal-ist-Keinmal* (the "once-is-as-good-as-never") to the *Ein-für-Allemal* (the "once-and-for-all").[39] Benjamin states that writing "beautiful passages" (the *Ein-für-Allemal*) creates problematic successes as these works mark a standstill. To explain this, Benjamin uses Trotsky's description of his father's habitual, yet sensitive, practice in the field as an example. The father, in Trotsky's words, moves "gebräuchlich" (habitually), but also with "Probeschritte" (practice steps). It does not look as if

---

38 In one vignette, Benjamin describes how the unfamiliar (here a town) is both far and near, suggesting that the unknown (the far) is also what jolts us (the near) (*KGA* VIII, 47).

39 In the first "Einmal ist Keinmal," immediacy of action also plays an important role. Here Benjamin discusses Don Juan's erotic competence, his ability to think *during* the act of courtship. People who doubt their abilities, Benjamin argues, link their success to their initial doubt, whereby the first act of lovemaking is lost on them because it is only seen in the light of a successful courtship. "Im Don Juan, dem Glückskind der Liebe, ist es das Geheimnis, wie er blitzhaft in all seinen Abenteuern Entscheidung und süßestes Werben zugleich heraufführt, die Erwartung, im Rausche, nachholt und die Entscheidung, im Werben, vorwegnimmt" (*KGA* VIII, 89; In Don Juan, the lucky child of love, the secret is the way he simultaneously achieves—in a flash—resolution and the sweetest pursuit in all his adventures, the way he repeats the expectation in the midst of ecstasy and anticipates the resolution in the act of wooing: *SW* II.1, 269). In Don Juan, too, then, contemplation, and doubt, make place for a thinking in the act of wooing. But sex itself also becomes an ecstasy, it seems, which is not tainted by the initial doubt, contemplation, and excitement, but instead provides or hosts the excitement in the act itself. Indeed, it seems that it can only be ecstasy because it is not tainted by the past doubt; it can be the "ein-für-allemal" rather than *einmal ist keinmal*. Again, then, we find here an immediacy of action that is not absent of mindedness but is infused with an attention to the moment. By calling him the "Glückskind der Liebe," Benjamin here too almost seems to dismiss habit and skill as playing a part in Don Juan's ability to perform. However, his idea that this immediacy of action marks an "entanglement of the ages" (Verschränkung der Zeiten), suggests that it is a *historical* body that meets the immediate needs of the present.

he is doing his familiar job. In Trotsky's words: "eher könnte man denken, [seine Sichel] sei nicht ganz sicher; und doch schneidet sie scharf, hart am Boden und wirft in regelmäßigen Bändern nach links, was sie niedergelegt hat" (qtd. in *KGA* VIII, 90; You might be tempted to think he was not very sure of it [the sickle]—yet it cuts sharply and close to the ground, and throws off to the left in regular ribbons what it has cut down: *SW* II.2, 739). Benjamin then states:

> Da haben wir die Art und Weise des Erfahrenen, welcher es gelernt hat, mit jedem Tag, mit jedem Sensenschwung von neuem anzusetzen. Er hält sich beim Geleisteten nicht auf, ja, unter seinen Händen verflüchtigt sich das schon Geleistete und wird unspürbar. Nur solche Hände werden mit dem Schwersten spielend fertig, weil sie beim Leichtesten behutsam sind. "Ne jamais profiter de l'élan acquis," sagt Gide. Unter den Schriftstellern zählt er zu denen, bei welchen die "schönen Stellen" am rarsten sind. (*KGA* VIII, 90)

> [Here we have the work habits of the experienced man who has learned every day and with every swing of the scythe to make a fresh start. He does not pause to look at what he has achieved; indeed, what he has done seems to evaporate under his hands and to leave no trace. Only hands like those will succeed in difficult things as if they were child's play, because they are cautious when dealing with easy ones. "Never profit from an acquired élan," says Gide. He is one of the writers in whose works "purple passages" are extremely rare. (*SW* II.2, 739–40)]

Benjamin is thus looking for this kind of skilled work which at the same time never rests on what it can do, which is attentive and sensitive—see the "probing steps"—to the environment, and what might change in it. Again, Benjamin explores the kind of heightened state of awareness, the continuous sensitivity to the environment. Yet, this openness, treating the situation as new, is nevertheless decisively backed up by an embodied, skillful knowledge. Skill provides the ground for more responsive gestures in familiar environments. Elsewhere, mirroring Biberkopf's anxiety, Benjamin indeed states that we need at least some habit to not get completely overwhelmed by our environments.[40] Like Scipio's embodied

---

40 See *GS* IV.1, 407–8. This ties also into Mihalyi Csikszentmihalyi's study of states of flow, discussed in detail in chapter 3, or "the state in which people are so involved in an activity that nothing else seems to matter; the experience itself is so enjoyable that people will do it even at great cost, for the sheer sake of doing it" (4). The main characteristic of flow, he argues, is the right balance between skill and the challenges from the environment. Indeed, and this is where his treatment is especially relevant for Benjamin, he writes that when skills outmatch challenges

presence-of-mind, in Gide's writing, but more so in Trotsky's father, we find an engagement that is far from contemplative. Moreover, as Trotsky's description of his father's work shows, immediate action is based not only on a corporeal awareness of its situation but also on the body's habituated knowledge. But Scipio's successful improvisation, too, of course, when stumbling into Cartage, was not groundless, but was able to dynamically apply his experience to a new, sudden, and unexpected situation. What Benjamin puts in the place of rigid habits, then, is an embodied cognition that does not exclude habit but rather lets habit, in Taussig's words, "catch up with itself."[41] Habit is not done away with but becomes infused with a responsiveness to the present moment and one's corporeal position in it; this comportment treats even the most familiar situations as containing the unfamiliar. As such, it sensitively explores and is continuously trained and retrained in its relation to its environment; in its attentive action in the here and now it becomes *leibhafter Geistesgegenwart*. Opposed to rigid habit, we find in Benjamin a continuous habituat*ing*: an ever open and responsive, context-sensitive, kinesthetically informed engagement with the environment.

Realigning through Feeling

Important about Sheets-Johnstone's emphasis on affect in her account of responsivity is that such a corporeal attention is not merely sensitive to the environment but also to its own kinesthetics, that is, its own position as a body engaged with, and affected by, that space. This is important for Benjamin because such an affective responsiveness allows us to get away from an intellectualization of the situation, and thus of how we should behave, towards an attention to how we *feel* (about) a situation. A corporeal awareness is not an awareness of an objective outside world, but rather of the environment as *Umwelt*, as experienced through a body that is always already affected by it—the environment is part of what Heidegger calls *Leib*. Thus our responsiveness brings with it an awareness of *how* we are affected by *what* in the world and allows us to better align our practices with this revivified, affective space. Like a responsive batter minutely adjusting her hands when the balls flies faster than expected, or a dancer adjusting his foot when the floor feels uneven; if we zoom out a little, we can see how we can adjust our practices to a revivified environment. Responsiveness allows us to pay attention to what we often gloss

---

one gets bored, and more interestingly, when the challenges of the environment outmatch the skills one gets overwhelmed. Flow thus happens, he writes, when skills and challenges, or perceived challenges, are correctly matched. Csikszentmihalyi, *Flow*.
41 Taussig, "Physiognomic Aspects of Visual Worlds," 18.

over in our everyday habits, in the often-rigid execution of our tasks, namely how the things of our environment move us. And responsiveness thus allows us to redirect ourselves to what interests us and feels good, and away from what does not.[42] It allows us to resituate ourselves affectively in the world. We here thus get a clearer picture of what a critical responsiveness, which Döblin's text investigated at its end, might look like, thus getting us away from Miriam Hansen's fear, as quoted above, that an unequivocal argument for embodiment in Benjamin would align him with fascism.

Sheets-Johnstone's description of our innate responsiveness as an affective-kinetic coordination dynamic, connecting affect and response, therefore helps situate Benjamin's emphasis on an affective environment, and a passionate one more specifically, in *Einbahnstraße* within his concerns in the text, as discussed before, with corporeal dynamics. We can find Benjamin's interest in passion in the sexual imagery that he uses (for example, in the final vignette; *KGA* VIII, 75–6; *OWS*, 93–96), in his thinking about Don Juan (*KGA* VIII, 89), and in his vignette on Casanova (*KGA* VIII, 103). A famous passage concerning neon lights also ties into this turn to *feeling* (*KGA* VIII, 60; *OWS*, 77). Here the neon letters of a commercial message are reflected in a puddle on the street, turning them into a fire. A more primordial, immediate, and affective relation is suggested—it is preceded by Benjamin's statement that the reviewer who manually handles paintings knows more important things about them than the art lover merely viewing them (*KGA* VIII, 60; *OWS*, 77)—a relation that might innervate and revivify. The immediacy of fire, of *heat*, which comes to us not intellectually but corporeally, replaces language. The work itself, too, seems infused with a (sexual) excitement as it was, at least in part, realized within Benjamin's relationship with Asja Lācis (1891–1979), the Latvian actress and theatre director to whom the

---

42 In one of the vignettes of "Kaiserpanorama: Reise durch die deutsche Inflation" (A Tour through the German Inflation), in which Benjamin criticizes German society, he writes that Germans cling to their habits so much that they cannot even detect danger: "Wieder und wieder hat es sich gezeigt, daß ihr Hangen am gewohnheiten [*sic*], nun längst schon verlorenen Leben so starr ist, daß es die eigentlich menschliche Anwendung des Intellekts, Voraussicht, selbst in der drastischen Gefahr vereitelt. So daß in ihr das Bild der Dummheit sich vollendet: Unsicherheit, ja Perversion der lebenswichtigen Instinkte und Ohnmacht, ja Verfall des Intellekts. Dieses ist die Verfassung der Gesamtheit deutscher Bürger" (*KGA* VIII, 22–23; again and again it has been shown that society's attachment to its familiar and long-since-forfeited life is so rigid as to nullify the genuinely human application of intellect, forethought, even in dire peril. So that in this society the picture of imbecility is complete: uncertainty, indeed perversion, of vital instincts; and impotence, indeed decay, of the intellect. This is the condition of the entire German bourgeoisie: *OWS*, 34).

work is dedicated.[43] Benjamin writes that the one-way-street of the title is named after her because she is the one who has opened that street in/through him.[44] Can we read the one-way-street, then, as an image of the kind of innervating passion she instilled in him?[45] Susan Buck-Morss writes about Lācis' influence on him that "for anyone who has known the creative intensity of the erotic and the political as a double awakening, wherein work and passion are not separate corners of life but fused intensely into one, the decisive significance of their relationship will come as no surprise."[46] Read in light of Sheets-Johnstone's affective-kinetic dynamics, of the primordial responsiveness to the environment's impulses, the fire and passion of these images, like the sudden jolts of new environments, seem to mark another set of affective impulses allowing for corporeal innervation and realignment, and thus for a way out of static habit and debilitating contemplation.

Communal Innervation

Benjamin's description of Trotsky's father in *Einbahnstraße*, who combines action and awareness into the present moment of *leibhafter Geistesgegenwart*, importantly opens up an ethico-political perspective on art.[47] If for Malte—and perhaps for Rilke himself too—writing was a way of seeing the world afresh himself, for Benjamin art is a way of *sharing* such innervation. His description suggests that he finds art important for sharing this innervated engagement with a revivified world. Benjamin's reference in "Einmal ist Keinmal <II>" to Trotsky already brings Benjamin's political motives to the surface (as do many of the other vignettes that I do not cover here). Yet passages that only appear in an early manuscript of this vignette make it explicit that it is Trotsky's *description* of his father, rather than the expertise of the father, that marks the (truly) revolutionary. Moreover, these passages emphasize again the importance of an embodied engagement. In these extra lines introducing Trotsky's account, Benjamin states that Trotsky shows,

    43 Together they wrote "Neapel" about the Italian city Naples (*GS* IV.1, 307–16).

    44 "DIESE STRASSE HEISST / ASJA-LACIS-STRASSE / NACH DER DIE SIE / ALS INGENIEUR / IM AUTOR DURCHGEBROCHEN HAT" (*KGA* VIII, 9; This street is named / Asja Lacis Street / after her who / as an engineer / cut it through the author: *OWS*, 21).

    45 See also the vignette in which Benjamin describes going to Riga to visit "eine Freundin" (a woman friend). He describes the city as aflame (*KGA* VIII, 37; *OWS*, 52).

    46 Buck-Morss, *Dialectics of Seeing*, 21.

    47 For an argument how Benjamin can show us that ethics should be the fifth "E" of 4E cognition, see Morgan, "A 5th E."

through his description of his father, his "grasp" (Griff) of the depths of the "handling and manipulation" (Griffe und Verrichtungen) from which "practical, worldly wisdom" (praktische Lebensweisheit) arises (*KGA* VIII, 210).[48] It is this grasp, he states, that marks (true) revolutionaries—the "true" (*echten*) of "revolutionaries" has been crossed out in the manuscript (*KGA* VIII, 210). In similar ways, Benjamin says, Van Gogh shared the life of Belgian miners, and Adolf Loos tore apart the environment of the Viennese bourgeoisie (Spießer) (*KGA* VIII, 210). Trotsky's father as expert is thus, in this early manuscript, framed as the *object* of revolutionary artistry. Although the father is put on the same level as Gide as an expert, and although the manuscript, like the published version, ultimately centers its discussion on the expert and does not return to either Gide or Trotsky, this initial framing of the expert nevertheless suggests that it is not the expert who is truly revolutionary, but rather the artist who gets to the bottom of this physical expertise and turns it into art. Indeed, Benjamin explicitly states that this "grasp," which marks the revolutionary, is certainly not the privilege of the "grounded, folk-like" (Volkhaft-Bodenständigen) (*KGA* VIII, 210). The real revolutionary, Benjamin argues, is the one who is able to grasp, quite literally, an expertise like that of Trotsky's father and share its practical knowledge. Indeed, in the first vignette of *Einbahnstraße* Benjamin states: "Die bedeutende literarische Wirksamkeit kann nur im strengen Wechsel von Tun und Schreiben zustande kommen" (*KGA* VIII, 11; significant literary effectiveness can come into being only in a strict alternation between action and writing: *OWS*, 21).

Mark B. N. Hansen has, in similar terms, read embodied cognition, an ability to *grasp*, as what makes Charles Baudelaire important for Benjamin. Hansen argues that it is what he calls a "bodily attunement," which for Benjamin "differentiates Baudelaire from the poor wretch in the street." Baudelaire was able to bypass the shocks of the modern environment, Benjamin writes, "with his spiritual and physical self" (*GS* I.2, 616). According to Hansen, it is, for Benjamin, Baudelaire's "mind-body integration" that gets him away from psychological processing as a way out of the so-called shock experience (Chockerlebnis). Hansen writes: "Because [Baudelaire] parries shocks corporeally, rather than registering them in consciousness or letting them occasion a psychic defense against

---

48 I refer here to an extant manuscript version of the vignette printed in the *KGA*. The manuscript version can be found at Berlin, Akademie der Künste (AdK), Walter-Benjamin-Archiv (WBA), Nr. 698 (Ms 865). A similar typescript version can be found at AdK, WBA 699, fols 1–2 (Ts 1674–1675). The other typescripts are all close to the published version. For the different manuscript, typescript, and published versions, see *KGA* VIII, 309.

trauma, Baudelaire manages to *transform* their corporeal impact into the raw material for his poetry."[49]

It is important to share this experience, because Benjamin is ultimately after a communal innervation. While the above analysis focuses on a deleted passage, other vignettes from Benjamin's text repeat the imagery of the revolutionary potential of innervation but do so as a communal practice. At the very end of *Einbahnstraße*, in the vignette named "Zum Planetarium," Benjamin discusses the technology of World War I and how it allowed for communal innervation:

> In den Vernichtungsnächten des letzten Krieges erschütterte den Gliederbau der Menschheit ein Gefühl, das dem Glück der Epileptiker gleichsah. Und die Revolten, die ihm folgten, waren der erste Versuch, den neuen Leib in ihre Gewalt zu bringen. Die Macht des Proletariats ist der Gradmesser seiner Gesundung. Ergreift ihn dessen Disziplin nicht bis ins Mark, so wird kein pazifistisches Raisonnement ihn retten. Den Taumel der Vernichtung überwindet Lebendiges nur im Rausche der Zeugung. (*KGA* VIII, 76)

> [In the nights of annihilation of the last war, the frame of mankind was shaken by a feeling that resembled the bliss of the epileptic. And the revolts that followed it were the first attempt of mankind to bring the new body under its control. The power of the proletariat is the measure of its convalescence. If it is not gripped to the very marrow by the discipline of this power, no pacifist polemics will save it. Living substance conquers the frenzy of destruction only in the ecstasy of creation. (*OWS*, 95–96; translation altered)]

As elsewhere in Benjamin, the kind of wonder or excitement technology offers, in this case in World War I, is an opportunity for the kind of innervation he is after.[50] Technology (re)animates the people and therefore offers an experience of innervation. As the last word of *Einbahnstraße*, creation (Zeugung) is essential. Yet here it becomes clearer how the dynamic might work. The technology of the war made people feel the kind of innervation that itself is necessary for creation, the creation of art that in turn will allow the experience of innervation to be shared, etc.[51] In other words, through art especially, other people become part

49 Hansen, *Embodying Technesis*, 248.
50 E.g., in "Erfahrung und Armut." *GS* II.1, 217–18.
51 Benjamin's essay on surrealism shows a similar kind of dynamic between the body, environment, and art. He writes: "Erst wenn in ihr sich Leib und Bildraum so tief durchdringen, daß alle revolutionäre Spannung leibliche kollektive Innervation, alle leiblichen Innervationen des Kollektivs revolutionäre Entladung werden, hat die Wirklichkeit so sehr sich selbst übertroffen, wie das

of the dynamic of innervation and revivification between agent and environment; this dynamic is thought to be able to slowly change human engagement together with its media environment (hence, Benjamin's interest in film elsewhere).[52] The technology of the war thus offered, Benjamin thought, one way in which a new body, *Physis*, might be elicited, "in welcher ihr Kontakt [der der Menschheit] mit dem Kosmos sich neu und anders bildet als in Völkern und Familien" (*KGA* VIII, 76; in technology, a *physis* is being organized through which mankind's contact with the cosmos takes a new and different form from that which it had in nations and families: *OWS*, 95). Ultimately, then, what Benjamin is after is a communal version of Malte's lone attempt in his rewriting of the histories, namely, to ecstatically establish—without the debilitation of doubt or contemplation—a creative dynamic between bodies and environment in which manipulation of the environment establishes a structure for more of such output. What Benjamin hopes for is a change of environment in which art elicits innervation of others which, in turn, elicits more innervating art.

Conclusion

In a vignette called "Alte Landkarte" (Old Map), Benjamin writes that some lovers search for an "eternal homeland" (*OWS*, 59; ewige Heimat: *KGA* VIII, 44) in their partners, but some people, though only few, look for "eternal voyaging" (*OWS*, 59; das ewige Reisen: *KGA* VIII, 44). It is the latter that seems to underlie Benjamin's interest in embodiment in *Einbahnstraße*. What this chapter has brought into relief is the dynamic embodiment as presented by Benjamin in *Einbahnstraße* and its *Nachtragsliste*. In bringing these texts into contact with contemporary accounts of habit and skill in the cognitive sciences, my argument suggests the importance of divorcing the rigidity of habits, the "eternal home," from a dynamic and affective responsiveness, "eternal travel," which is nevertheless also grounded in corporeal experience. The

---

kommunistische Manifest es fordert. Für den Augenblick sind die Sürrealisten die einzigen, die seine heutige Order begriffen haben. Sie geben, Mann für Mann, ihr Mienenspiel in Tausch gegen das Zifferblatt eines Weckers, der jede Minute sechzig Sekunden lang anschlägt." (*GS* II.1, 310; Only when in technology body and image space so interpenetrate that all revolutionary tension becomes bodily collective innervation, and all the bodily innervations of the collective become revolutionary discharge, has reality transcended itself to the extent demanded by the Communist Manifesto. For the moment, only the Surrealists have understood its present commands. They exchange, to a man, the play of human features for the face of an alarm clock that in each minute rings for sixty seconds: *SW* II.1, 217–18).

52 E.g., his artwork essay (final version: *GS* I.2, 471–508).

opposite of conscious deliberation is thus multiform. It may be rigidly habitual, carefully sensitive, and/or dynamically proactive. It is not conscious deliberation that takes us out of rigid habits, nor is it for Benjamin a consciously aware embodiment. It is an immediate corporeal awareness, an innervation of the body, an action-readiness, attuned and responsive to the situation.

The question, however, is just how we can stop doubting ourselves and stop behaving rigidly to start acting dynamically instead. If our practices are entangled in the environment, how do we get into a more innervated engagement and thus a more revivified environment? How do we set life on fire? It might be the glass structures of modern architecture, which according to Benjamin are underspecified, not allowing for traces as much as the bourgeois environments do, and thus not eliciting habitual retracing but asking for dynamic agency. Or it may be the jolts of new environments that trigger immediate responses if we do not waste them with contemplation. Film—as shown both in a vignette in *Einbahnstraße* and, more famously, in Benjamin's artwork essay (*KGA* VIII, 60; *OWS*, 76–77)—and other changes in the environment—Benjamin describes how a friend moving into a new area of the city makes that part newly relevant (*KGA* VIII, 37–8; *OWS*, 52)—also elicit the possibility of more dynamic, affective engagements.[53] Or it might be love and/or sexual excitement, which do not merely provide an image for this kind of dynamic, aware, and excited or explorative engagement, but also exactly seem to make it happen, as Benjamin's dedication to Lācis suggests. And, as I will discuss in detail in chapter 7, Benjamin also attempts with the form of his own vignettes in *Einbahnstraße* to elicit open and affective responses by creating a more visceral linguistic space with concrete imagery. The goal, in the end, is to let our habitual body treat everything always as if it were new, to remove the traces that we have left on the material environment, and explore it again as if for the first time, paying attention to what objects and people affect us how and readjusting our practices accordingly: a critical responsiveness.

---

53 In another vignette, Benjamin describes a child's play as allowing new relations between objects to arise: "In Abfallprodukten erkennen sie das Gesicht, das die Dingwelt gerade ihnen, ihnen allein, zukehrt. In ihnen bilden sie die Werke der Erwachsenen weniger nach, als daß sie Stoffe sehr verschiedener Art durch das, was sie im Spiel daraus verfertigen, in eine neue, sprunghafte Beziehung zueinander setzen" (*KGA* VIII, 19; In waste products they recognize the face that the world of things turns directly and solely to them. In using these things, they do not so much imitate the works of adults as bring together, in the artifact produced in play, materials of widely differing kinds in a new, intuitive relationship: *OWS*, 31). See also Benjamin's artwork essay (first version, 1935: *GS* I.2, 431–469; second, extended version: *GS* VII.1, 350–84; third version *GS* I.2, 471–508).

The next chapter continues with asking just how we can become responsive. Baum's *Menschen im Hotel* proposes an answer, namely—counterintuitively—through the warmth and love of familiar others. If Benjamin separates the lover looking for the eternal home from the lover looking for eternal travel, Baum's text shows exactly how the home may sustain eternal travel.

6: Vicki Baum's *Menschen im Hotel*: Warmth

WHEN KRINGELEIN, one of the most engaging characters in Baum's *Menschen im Hotel*, enters the luxury hotel in Berlin, it appears to him like a different world.[1] The barstools are not quite as high as he had imagined from what he gathered from the media (*MH*, 47), and even the German language comes to feel strange. He attempts to speak as he feels he should in the most expensive hotel in the city, but it does not work: "Er kam mit den eleganten Sätzen, die er sich zurechtgelegt hatte, nicht aus. Seit er im Grand Hôtel wohnte, bewegte er sich wie in einem fremden Land. Er sprach die deutschen Worte wie eine fremde Sprache, die er aus Büchern und Journalen gelernt hatte" (*MH*, 51–52; The polished phrases he had prepared found no utterance. Since he had come to the Grand Hotel he felt that he was in a foreign land. He spoke his native tongue like a foreign language that he had learnt from books and newspapers: *GH*, 43). But Kringelein is trying to learn. He is incredibly receptive and responsive to the world around him. Partly, as Lynda J. King argues, this is an important move from Baum, aiding him to introduce the reader to the hotel in all its detail.[2] While the other characters are used to the splendor of the hotel, Kringelein's unfamiliarity allows Baum to give lengthy descriptions of it. Kringelein's receptivity and responsiveness also bring into relief ways in which other characters are not paying attention to their environment. The other characters seem indifferent. Kringelein's demeanor, however, is attractive and contagious to these characters. Dr. Otternschlag, the novel's most isolated and insulated character, for example, notes "seine hohe und angenehme Stimme, . . . eine Menschenstimme, eine klingende, suchende, tastende Stimme" (*MH*, 49; what a high, charming voice he had, a human, resonant, inquiring, tentative voice: *GH*, 41), and responds physically: "[Dr. Otternschlag] streckte seine kalten Finger vor sich hin auf die Tischplatte und nahm sie gleich wieder zurück" (*MH*, 49; [Dr. Otternschlag] put out his cold fingers in

---

[1] The initial subtitle to the novel, later removed, was *Ein Kolportageroman mit Hintergründen*. Like parts of Döblin's *Berlin Alexanderplatz*, Baum's novel was first serialized in a newspaper, but in its entirety in the *Berliner Illustrirte Zeitung*.

[2] King, *Best-Sellers by Design*, 179. See also Bettina Matthias's chapter on the novel in Matthias, *Hotel as Setting*, 182.

front of him on the table, and withdrew them again immediately: *GH*, 41). Kringelein's voice is thus inquisitive, and described as such in physical and spatial terms. Moroever, this "tactility" is noticed and (kinesthetically and emotionally) attractive; Kringelein moves Otternschlag physically and emotionally. Such moments of being animated by others run through the novel. Moreover, such initial movements often form the beginning of more sustained transformations in behavior. Thus, although the movements of many of the characters seem emotionally at odds with their immediate socio-material environments, meetings with Kringelein and others nevertheless pull them, almost automatically and even unwillingly, out of these fraught behaviors.

Menschen im Hotel is a mosaically constructed novel, following, in several shorter and larger episodes, six major characters and several minor ones. All its major characters seem, to lesser and greater degrees, at odds with their situation. Only Kringelein is unfamiliar with the hotel, however, but, both curious by nature and about to die, he has taken all his money to spend his last days in Berlin ready to explore it. The other characters' approaches are more negative. Grusinskaja, a famous and lonely Russian ballerina (modelled on Anna Pavlova) is still performing now out-of-fashion pieces to decreasing successes; Dr. Otternschlag, a medical doctor heavily wounded in the war with a *gueule cassée*, is an habitual and depressed guest of the hotel for whom the hotel surroundings seem all but meaningless; Baron Felix von Gaigern is a fallen, yet good-looking and alluring, aristocrat who makes his money through petty thieving; Preysing is the director of a textile company from the provinces and a family man, who seems to have a strong dislike for the ways in which business is conducted in the city and whose behavior cycles out of control when he forgets his familiar razor at home.[3] Flämmchen, a young, no-nonsense "new" woman, seems to be best adjusted to the new world, but she makes her money not only as a stenographer but also by selling herself.[4] Baum shows, however, how their interactions elicit immediate responses and they consequently become, for better and worse, increasingly responsive—engaging and inquisitive—to their environments at large. Grusinskaja, for example, as we shall see, during a particularly engaging interaction with Gaigern, "sees" new ways of performing; Preysing turns from a meek and honest director into the cunning and dishonest one he thinks his environment asks for.

The ways in which Baum describes her characters' initially rusty behavior as being physically and emotionally moved by others aligns with,

---

3 For Anna Pavlova being a model for Grusinskaja, see Baum, *Es war alles ganz anders*, 383–84; Nottelmann, *Karrieren der Vicki Baum*, 146–47.

4 For more on the so-called "new woman" in Weimar Germany, in general, as well as a great discussion of Flämmchen specifically, see Boa, "Women Writers."

and can be usefully investigated through, current philosophical explorations combining phenomenological and biological approaches. Sheets-Johnstone, as I have introduced in the previous chapter, importantly shows in *The Primacy of Movement* how movement and affect are intrinsically linked.[5] To recap, drawing heavily on Husserl, she uses the concepts of "receptivity" and "responsivity" to describe the grounds of human existence and meaning. Receptivity is the basic ability to be affected by the outside world and to direct attention to it. This goes together with the tendency to move toward the attraction: responsivity. In this view, affect is not passive, something that happens to us, but part of a dynamic engagement with the environment. Movement and affect are intrinsically and intricately linked. Affect and movement come together in the complements of receptivity as being affected and responsivity as moving towards. And, as we have seen, by focusing on receptivity/responsivity Sheets-Johnstone not only attempts to get away from theories of embodiment (and theories of cognition more generally) that neglect the foundational role that affect plays in cognition, but she also wants to get away from the primacy of habits in such views.

These considerations, then, open up a space from which to consider Baum's own foregrounding of levels of responsiveness in characters like Kringelein and others, as well as her perceptiveness in the novel to human movement. Baum does so in a framework of existential questions: How should we live? Yet such existential questions are not absent from Sheets-Johnstone's work either. The question of whether we take habit or responsivity as basic to human understanding is itself a question about *whose* behavior should be foregrounded. Sheets-Johnstone calls approaches focusing on familiar dealings with the world "adultist."[6] However, if Benjamin infused habit with responsiveness, Baum, as we will see, further explores and complicates the relation between the two. She shows the value of both, and shows how the familiar may be an important background for exploration, reminding us implicitly of the fact that children are not devoid of the familiar in their explorations, nor are their worlds devoid of other people. Indeed, Baum suggests that the "warmth" of familiar people might be what allows us to be inquisitive and engaging.[7] In other words, not only does becoming more responsive to what the environment has to offer potentially take us out of our all-too-rigid

5   Sheets-Johnstone, *Primacy of Movement*, 501–10.
6   Sheets-Johnstone, *Primacy of Movement*, 471.
7   One of the fascinating connections between Baum's text and the context of its serialization in the *Berliner Illustrirte Zeitung* in which it first appeared, is an article on the importance of parental love/warmth. This article by a Dr. Lily Wagner appears in the same issue as the fourth installment of *Menschen im Hotel* (April 21, 1929) and compares the child without parental warmth to a plant without sunlight (669).

habits, but habit also allows us to become more responsive. Responsivity to new environments becomes the answer for more emotionally positive engagements, and, most importantly for the developing argument of this study, Baum shows that familiar others may exactly elicit the beginning of such responses. If Benjamin explores the ways in which we can *be* responsive, Baum shows just how we can *become* responsive.

By bringing Baum's *Menschen im Hotel* in conversation with such theories of movement and affect, this chapter also reconsiders dominant readings of Baum's novel. The chapter challenges readings that put the text squarely within an understanding of human experience in modernism as alienated, isolated, fragmentary, and distant. Bettina Matthias, for example, in her chapter on Baum's novel in *The Hotel as Setting in Early Twentieth-Century German and Austrian Literature*, employs Simmel's *Reizschutz*, what she calls "modern man's necessary inner distance to the world and to each other to protect themselves from sensory and emotional overstimulation," to read Baum's portrayal of the hotel's guests as equally distant: "Life in modern times has erected invisible walls, Baum's closed doors, between people. The narrator who attempts to tell the full story of an individual's life runs the risk of being a fabricator."[8] Consequently, the hotel—although she states that its walls are at times transcended by such eternal themes as love and death—becomes the ultimate symbolic space of this version of modernism. However, in my reading, the hotel becomes a space in which people are thrown together and come, more and less positively, to interact. At the least, in these interactions they become more responsive to their environments. Baum's repeated use of the word "warmth" (e.g., *GH*, 103; Wärme: e.g., *MH*, 121) to describe the effect certain characters have on others, shows that any walls are already being pulled down in interactions. Baum's attention to the movement and touch of other people as fundamentally affecting us, as always eliciting responses from us, portrays a world in which the boundaries of our bodies are always already being crossed, and other bodies make us more responsive to the rest of our environments. *Menschen im Hotel*, although presenting physical comportments that are stiff, inflexible, blind, hard, and in control, also puts forward bodies that are not as unresponsive as they might initially seem. Instead of modern times in the novel causing unresponsive behavior, Baum's descriptions of the interactions in the hotel suggest that at least the hotel might have the very opposite effect, namely that of awakening her characters to the world around them.

8   Matthias, *Hotel as Setting*, 176, 177.

Historical Attitudes

Baum's characters are not in the first place receptive and responsive in the way Sheets-Johnstone characterizes them, in the sense of being exploratory rather than habitual. Baum clearly *situates* her characters' affective behavior historically. Indeed, with the exception of Kringelein and Flämmchen, the way in which her characters see and act in the world, what and how objects and other people are meaningful to them, is situated—most explicitly so, in the cases of Otternschlag, Grusinskaja, and Gaigern—in old, now defunct, environments. This is immediately suggested when Otternschlag is introduced. His listless, lonely, and slow movements, the way in which nothing seems to affect him, not even the naked women in the newspapers, are explained by Baum, it seems, with a description of his *gueule cassée*, which he calls his "Souvenir aus Flandern" (*MH*, 7; souvenir from Flanders: *GH*, 5). He seems physically and emotionally damaged by the First World War.

That the war caused Otternschlag's attitude towards life is expressed more clearly in an encounter near the end of the novel between him and Gaigern. The doctor tries to tell Gaigern why he carries a lethal dose of morphine around with him: to always have an exit. He calls himself "ein lebender Selbstmörder" (*MH*, 253; suicide before the event: *GH*, 215). When Gaigern in return calls life "großartig" (splendid), Otternschlag makes it clear where his depressed attitude derives from:

> "So. Großartig finden Sie es? Sie waren doch auch im Krieg. Und dann sind Sie heimgekommen, und dann finden Sie das Leben großartig? Ja, Mensch, wie existiert ihr den alle? Habt ihr denn alle vergessen? Gut, gut, wir wollen nicht davon sprechen, wie es draußen war, wir wissen es ja alle. Aber wie denn? Wie könnt ihr denn zurückkommen von dort und noch sagen: das Leben gefällt mir? Wo ist es denn, euer Leben? Ich habe es gesucht, ich habe es nicht gefunden. Manchmal denke ich mir: Ich bin schon tot, eine Granate hat mir den Kopf weggerissen, und ich sitze als Leiche verschüttet die ganze Zeit im Unterstand von Rouge-Croix. Da habense den Eindruck, wahr und wahrhaftig, den mir das Leben macht, seit ich von draußen zurückgekommen bin." (*MH*, 254)

> ["Indeed? You find it splendid? And yet you were in the war. And then you came home, and then you find life splendid? Good Lord, man, how do you all go on living? Have you all forgotten? All right, all right, we won't talk about what it was like out there. We all know it well enough. But how can you come back after that, and still say you're pleased with life? Where do you find it—this life of yours? I have looked for life, but I can't find it. I often think to myself: I'm dead already. A shell has torn my head from my shoulders, and

all this time I'm sitting as a corpse buried in that dugout at Rouge Croix. There you have the real and actual impression I have of life since I got back." (*GH*, 215)]

Since witnessing the horrors of war, life is thus devoid of all meaning for Otternschlag. His understanding of the present is clearly situated in his experiences of the war. What we get here then is a very different version of the link between affect and movement from the one presented by Sheets-Johnstone, one that is exactly not dynamically responsive, but statically habitual. Otternschlag seems to have learned in the war that the world is a bad place and has little to offer, and he responds to his current environment in this way. A discussion of affect that is particularly useful to enlighten Baum's attention to Otternschlag's attitude to his environment as well as such other such behaviors, one that can serve complementary to the description of responsivity given by Sheets-Johnstone as well as Kiverstein, and one which has shaped twentieth-century debates, is Heidegger's "Stimmung," most often translated as "mood" (*SZ*, §29).

Heidegger's treatment of our affective lives as moods, most prominently in *Sein und Zeit* and *Die Grundbegriffe der Metaphysik*, is important in the history of philosophy on emotions because it takes as central not the kind of sudden and directed emotional reactions that are "fear of x," or "love for y," but rather more fundamental moods. Moods are, in Heidegger's analysis, fundamental to human existence, our everyday pragmatic engagements in a meaningful environment. Such fundamental moods shape the way in which we approach the environment, the way in which it is meaningful for us. "Heidegger's proposal," as Matthew Ratcliffe writes, "is that moods constitute the various different ways in which we are able to experience things as *mattering*."[9] Hence, just as Sheets-Johnstone states that we are always receptive and responsive, affected and responding in some way, so Heidegger states that we are always already in a mood; there is no such thing as not having a mood. Yet Heidegger's attunements are more deep-seated, habitual, than Sheets-Johnstone's dynamic affective responses. Importantly, the way in which we are attuned does not just determine *how* we see things, according to Heidegger, but also *what* we see, what we engage with, what we pay attention to: "was man und wie man 'sieht'" (*SZ*, 170; what and how one "sees": *BT*, 159). Being-in-a-mood is thus not, Heidegger writes, a "Zustand drinnen, der dann auf rätselhafte Weise hinausgelangt und auf die Dinge und Personen abfärbt" (*SZ*, 137; it is itself not an inner condition which then in some mysterious way reaches out and leaves its mark on things and persons: *BT*, 129). A useful way of thinking about attunement is given by Julian Kiverstein's Heideggerian approach to affect,

---

9   Ratcliffe, "Phenomenology of Mood," 355.

when he states that it "makes some of the affordances of the environment inviting and enticing, and others threatening and repelling."[10]

Ratcliffe further explains Heidegger's position by making a clear distinction between moods as "pre-intentional moods," on the one hand, and "intentional emotions," on the other (in which "intentional" means the directedness of experience).[11] This also marks the difference, as I understand it, between Sheets-Johnstone's dynamic responsiveness of the body, and the deep-seated affectivity of Heidegger's attunement, by which responsiveness *is* perhaps the fundamental mood that shapes individual, dynamic responses. In Ratcliffe's view, pre-intentional moods are presupposed by intentional emotions; the possibility of having certain emotions supervenes on the actual fundamental mood someone is in. Using Heidegger's example of fear, Ratcliffe states: "In order to be afraid, one must already find oneself in the world in such a way that being *in danger or under threat* are possibilities. Some being, perhaps oneself, has to matter in a certain kind of way for fear to be possible."[12] Depression is a useful and intuitive example of a fundamental mood. In depression, namely, the intentional state of happiness, that something makes one happy, disappears. "It is not just," Ratcliffe writes, "that things no longer make one feel happy; a sense of their even having the potential to do so is gone."[13] It is also important to point out, as Ratcliffe does, that moods can be both relatively dynamic, "shift only momentarily" (although by no means as dynamic as Sheets-Johnstone's affective responses) or can be so long-lasting that we "refer to them as character or personality traits rather than moods."[14]

Baum's description of Otternschlag's comportment quite clearly shows how his deep-seated mood shapes his emotional understanding of the environment as well as what we could call his character. To him, almost everything in his current environment is repelling, his movements are slow and listless. Moreover, it is not just that Otternschlag sees it that way: as he states in the above quotation, he cannot even imagine anyone else not seeing the environment as repelling. As Ratcliffe points out in reference to Heidegger's elaboration on moods in *Die Grundbegriffe der Metaphysik*, in the deepest kind of mood "a sense of there being any alternative to this way of finding oneself in the world for *anyone* is absent from experience."[15] More importantly, Otternschlag's monologue shows that Baum envisages the doctor's mood as a learned one, garnered in the

10 Kiverstein, "Empathy," 536.
11 Ratcliffe, "Phenomenology of Mood," 354.
12 Ratcliffe, "Phenomenology of Mood," 355.
13 Ratcliffe, "Phenomenology of Mood," 360. See also Solomon, *Passions*.
14 Ratcliffe, "Phenomenology of Mood," 367.
15 Ratcliffe, "Phenomenology of Mood," 358.

horrible experiences of the war. These deep moods, Baum shows, do not so much "overcome" us, as that we come to inhabit a certain experience. Otternschlag's emotional understanding of his world is based on the war's horrors.

Heidegger, whose "being-in-the-world" emphasizes the shared, historical aspects of our existence, never quite extends this explicitly to his discussion of moods. Although in *Sein und Zeit* he alludes to moods of the public (*SZ*, 138–39; *BT*, 134–35), and in the later *Die Grundbegriffe der Metaphysik* to the sharing of moods in a group, his treatment of moods runs the risk of being interpreted as individual and closed-off.[16] Dreyfus goes as far as to comment that "affectedness, especially as manifested in individual moods, is [ ] dangerously close to Cartesianism."[17] Nevertheless, this does not seem to be Heidegger's intention. He does suggest, for example, that the way in which our shared, normative environment, what he calls *das Man*, determines the kind of moods we can have (*SZ*, 169–170; *BT*, 163–64). Dreyfus explains this in terms of cultural sensibility: "Shame over losing face, for example, is something one can only feel in Japan, while the exhilaration of romantic love was for a long time the exclusive property of the West."[18] Beside the point that shame over losing face might not be exclusive to Japanese culture, we also do not need to limit cultural sensibilities, as Heidegger himself hints at in *Grundfragen der Philosophie*, to the kind of emotions that certain cultures allow for or not. Indeed, this is where Baum situating Otternschlag's affective behavior in the war is a useful example. In *Grundfragen der Philosophie* Heidegger writes that the fundamental mood of Greek philosophy was wonder (*Erstaunen*) and that of his contemporaries alarm (*Erschrecken*).[19] Yet Baum showing how Otternschlag's behavior is attuned to the war helps us think about how such larger-scale cultural moods may come about (I will talk about smaller-scale intersubjective influences on moods below). It shows how certain massive events may fundamentally realign people's moods and thus behaviors, especially if they are as traumatic as Otternschlag's experience of the war seems to have been. It shows how a mood, as an emotional attunement to a common situation may be shared.

Interestingly, it is not only Otternschlag's comportment that is shaped by the war. Baron von Gaigern's seemingly vivacious and playful attitude also derives from his attunement to the war, complicating the idea of a shared mood through shared experiences. When addressing the war, Gaigern makes explicit that his attitude is habitual. Moreover,

16 Heidegger, *Grundbegriffe der Metaphysik*, 100.
17 Dreyfus, *Being-in-the-World*, 169.
18 Dreyfus, *Being-in-the-World*, 172.
19 Heidegger, *Grundfragen der Philosophie*, 196–97.

the fact that his attitude is equally a "souvenir from Flanders," suggests that the same experience can lead to wholly different moods in different people. Thinking he has understood Otternschlag's monologue, Gaigern responds with one of his own:

> "Ja, etwas davon ist wahr," sagte er leise. "Mit dem zurückkommen ist es nicht einfach gewesen. Wenn unsereiner sagt 'draußen', da meint er das so, wie 'in der Heimat'—beinahe so. Jetzt steckt man in Deutschland drin wie in einer ausgewachsenen Hose. Man ist unbändig geworden und hat keinen Platz. Was soll unsereiner mit sich anfangen? Reichswehr? Drill? Bei Wahlraufereien eingreifen? Danke. Flieger, Pilot? Ich habe es versucht. Täglich zweimal nach dem Fahrplan loszuckeln, Berlin—Köln—Berlin. Forschungsreisender, Expedition, das alles ist so abgekocht und ohne Gefahr. Sehen Sie, das ist es: Das Leben müßte ein bißchen gefährlicher sein, dann wäre es gut. Aber man nimmt's, wie's kommt. (*MH*, 254)
>
> ["Yes, there's some truth in that," he said in a low voice. "It wasn't easy coming back. When a man says 'out there,' he means something almost like 'back home.' Nowadays being in Germany is like being in outgrown clothes. We've become unruly and there's no place for us. What are we to do with ourselves? The army? Drill? Intervening in election scuffles? Thanks! Flying, pilot? I've tried it. Toddling off twice daily according to a timetable, Berlin—Cologne— Berlin. And as for voyages of discovery, adventure, that's all so stale and without danger. That's how it is, you see. Life ought to be a little more dangerous, and then it would be all right. But you have to take it as it comes." (*GH*, 215–16)]

Gaigern's lively and adventurous and, at times, risky attitude is thus linked to him being used to the excitement of war, an excitement that he cannot find in daily life in Germany, not even in a city such as Berlin. That Gaigern refers to the memory of war as close to a feeling of a memory of *home* confirms that life in the warzone has become his and others' habitual attitude. Situating Gaigern's adventurous attitude in the war in this way suggests that his behavior is much darker and more complex than it might initially seem on the surface, or than Gaigern lets on. It is hinted earlier in the novel that underlying Gaigern's vivaciousness is a certain blaséness about life (*MH*, 197), but here this becomes apparent in linking it to the excitement of war, which cannot be retained in normal life, wherever one looks. Unlike in Simmel's sociology in which blaséness is an adaptive attitude to the overwhelming city, here contemporary life is boring and bland to Gaigern. What once seemed like vivaciousness—such as when Gaigern is seen climbing the hotel façade—now seems like a desperate attempt at finding the excitement he has gotten used to in the war.

As it has for Otternschlag, the war has fundamentally shaped the way in which Gaigern emotionally appraises his environment; both men are out of tune with their everyday environments. Both are still attuned to the environment of war. Yet where Otternschlag's experience was one of horror, in light of which he cannot find meaning in everyday life, Gaigern's was one of excitement, one he cannot retain in everyday life. Their affective behavior is attuned to the war and that makes them out of tune with their current environment.

However, even if Baum situates both these characters' behavior in the war in very different ways, both characters are nevertheless shown to expect that shared situations lead to shared attitudes. In fact, their difference in attitude is what annoys and confuses Otternschlag. Gaigern's description of himself and other soldiers considering the war as home suggests that he also conceives of his mood as a shared one, if not with Otternschlag. In the above quotation, he talks of "unsereiner" to refer to a shared feeling after the war. Otternschlag is confused about the very fact that his mood is not shared by (more) people who went to war. In this light it seems significant that in the moment the two men might have shared in the war—it remains unclear whether Otternschlag treated Gaigern in the hospital, or just any number of similarly wounded men—Gaigern was unconscious. Had he seen what Otternschlag saw, it is suggested, their understanding of the war, and their concomitant emotional understandings of the world, might have been more similar.

Reading Historical Moods

Yet we do not merely know these characters' moods through these monologues. As I have argued in regard to Döblin's characters, we encounter Baum's characters, too, already in their selective responsiveness to the environment, in their meaningful comportment toward this world. We did not need Otternschlag's monologue about the war, nor any of the other more explicit comments he makes about the environment, to understand that the world has little meaning to him. Otternschlag's slow and listless movements, which Baum describes in much detail, already tell us he views the environment as having little to offer him in terms of meaningful actions. This is an important part of contemporary cognitive science about embodied minds, too. As I have discussed at length in chapter 2, such theories, often gathered under the label of "direct perception theory" (DPT), state that rather than that we mentalize the minds of other people, infer them in some way, we actually perceive much of other people's "inner lives" in their comportment. Understanding others hereby becomes a form of embodied practice.[20] Giovanna Colombetti

20 Gallagher, "Practice of Mind," 85.

writes that "experiencing others [as lived bodies] characteristically does not require any explicit process of reasoning or imagination; we usually just *perceive* life and subjectivity in the other's body."[21] Moreover, as Kiverstein argues—and as I have argued in chapter 1—such comportment does not happen in isolation.[22] Kiverstein's terminology of "selective responsiveness" is meant to convey that our comportment is selectively and affectively directed at objects and other people in the world. Our comportment tells something about what in the environment is meaningful to us and how so (or how we want it to be perceived as meaningful to us). The *how* of the mattering of the environment is also what Sheets-Johnstone emphasizes when she reminds us that movements have a dynamic, and these dynamics show the way in which things matter to us; there is a large difference, she says, between a violent and a quiet raising of the hand.[23]

In these ways the poetics of the meaningful comportment of characters allow us to understand much about the mood of a character and complicate our understanding of them. Baum seems especially perceptive to the way in which her characters carry themselves. The way in which the environment seems meaningless to Otternschlag, for example, is announced and pronounced in his movements. She introduces him in the following way: "In der Halle erhob sich ein Herr aus seinem Klubstuhl, ein langer Herr, dessen Beine wie ohne Gelenke waren, und kam gesenkten Kopfes zur Portierloge" (*MH*, 7; a tall gentleman in the Lounge, whose legs seemed to have no joints, got up stiffly out of an easy chair and came with bent head towards the porter's desk: *GH*, 4; translation altered). Otternschlag's limbs are stiff and his head down, suggesting that instead of facing the world head-on and dynamically, his body wants nothing, does not want to take on the world. A little later he returns to his chair "in den er sich steifbeinig niederließ, um dann mit blindem Gesicht in die Halle zu starren" (*MH*, 7; he sank down into [his chair] stiff-legged, and then stared blindly out into the Lounge: *GH*, 5). He is also said to have a "Marionettengang" (*MH*, 8; marionette gait: *GH*, 5). The *how* of the way in which the environment is meaningful to him, his lack of responsiveness to the world, is shown in his stiffness, blindness, and bent head.[24]

However, Baum's description of his comportment in the lobby of the hotel also suggests that there is more to his character than what this

21 Colombetti, *Feeling Body*, 173.
22 Kiverstein, "Empathy," 535.
23 Sheets-Johnstone, *Primacy of Movement*, 505.
24 While we might read this as just the physical results of the war, that would be to suggest that people with a handicap cannot be physically exuberant. Moreover, the fact that he looks "blindly into the Lounge" seems to me to be not a necessity of his one glass eye, but rather to signify the way in which the Lounge does not interest him much.

stiffness and his own story of the war put forward. Seemingly counter to the posture of "Erwartungslosigkeit und Langeweile" (*MH*, 7; listlessness and boredom: *GH*, 4) that he takes on—although this is a "betonte Haltung" (emphatic posture; my translation)—he seems restless and expectant (*MH*, 7; *GH*, 4). He is "loiter[ing]" (*GH*, 4; trödelte: *MH*, 7) in the hall. Moreover, he asks multiple times in a short amount of time whether there is any message, telegram, or letter for him. Although somewhat subtle, these movements do suggest that he is waiting for something or hoping for something; all is not completely meaningless. If his bodily comportment previously showed little responsiveness to the outside world, shown in his stiff muscles and slow gait, these movements suggest that he is at least somewhat awake to the outside world. Husserl's, and more recently Sheet-Johnstone's difference between *being awake* and *to be awakened*, is useful here. If Otternschlag does not seem responsive, awakened by the environment, moving actively toward it, he does at least seem to be receptive, or awake, to the outside world. Quoting from Husserl, Sheets-Johnstone writes: "the primary '*tendency to give way*,' to be affected by that which comes to our awareness in pure attraction, is grounded in awakeness, an awakeness that carries with it not just the tendency, but the very possibility of giving oneself over to it."[25] It seems that Otternschlag, though not finding anything to awaken him, is at least somewhat awake to the possibility. Indeed, his loitering and his restlessness announce a responsiveness in him to other people that is made explicit when he meets Kringelein later, the meeting that I started this chapter with, in which he is somewhat emotionally and physically swayed by Kringelein's energy and enthusiasm for life. Thus assuming a reader who can read uninterested behavior, Kringelein's meaningful comportment in his environment as portrayed by Baum shows and complicates his moods without making an explanation immediately necessary.

It is important to note that we can be mistaken in reading other people's affective lives in their comportments. Baum's portrayal of Gaigern shows us this, while nevertheless complicating the relation between his movements, other characters' interpretation thereof, and what he says he feels. While he comes across, and is presented, as vivacious and joyful, his description of his experience of the war suggests that rather than enjoying himself he is instead desperately looking for excitement. In this way it seems that the dynamics of his behavior are just interpreted badly. After a drive together in a sports car, for example, Gaigern makes a comment about Kringelein's excitement, to which the latter responds that Gaigern does not quite seem blasé about the

---

25 Sheets-Johnstone, *Primacy of Movement*, 504. Quoting from Husserl, *Experience and Judgement*, 78–79.

drive himself either (*MH*, 197).[26] Like Biberkopf's partial misreading of Mieze, Kringelein seems to be misreading Gaigern's behavior here. But Gaigern is also putting on a deliberate show. He is trying to show bonhomie to ultimately steal Kringelein's money. The comment about Kringelein's excitement seems a mere slip which might have betrayed his own feelings of boredom. Indeed, it is when he ultimately hands over Kringelein's wallet to Dr. Otternschlag that he drops his facade. In that moment, the doctor sees past Gaigern's excited engagements: "Ihm kam Gaigerns Gesicht, dieses besonders schöne und lebensvolle Gesicht, so sandbleich vor, so gezeichnet, so ausgeleert und gestorben, daß er sich fürchtete. Gibt es denn nur Gespenster auf der Welt? sagte er zu sich selber . . ." (*MH*, 258–59; instead of Gaigern's particularly handsome and lively face he saw a mask so blanched, drawn, vacant, and dead, that he was frightened. Are there nothing but ghosts in this world then?: *GH*, 219). This is not a counterargument to the idea that we can read affect in other people's comportments. In fact, that Gaigern can fool his surroundings in the novel by—consciously or unconsciously—moving differently, exactly suggests that Baum can draw on the reader's familiarity with such performed emotions and their mistaken interpretations.

All in all, Baum's interest in these war-situated attitudes is important, because it shows the way in which she thought of the war as reverberating long after its end. This reading of her characters' moods as shaped by the war thereby reworks a reading of the text that understands her characters as having no past or future and as only "encountered" in their relevance to the particular hotel situation. Matthias writes that Baum "resist[s] the temptation to delve into . . . psychological depth or complexity" and that "the lives and fates of characters are limited to the part they spend as guests in the hotel, and their experiences are only told as long as they can be told as hotel experiences."[27] However, Baum situating her characters' attitudes in the past in this way shows that history does matter in the novel. History reverberates in complex ways in her characters' attitudes toward the hotel environment, in their meaningful comportment toward their environments. The way in which the environment, in this case the hotel, is meaningful to people, is shaped by historically situated moods. Moreover, these characters' histories do not only surface in the text because we are directly told about these experiences. These explicit

---

26 Gaigern says: "Sie erleben das zum erstenmal. Man findet so selten Menschen, die etwas zum erstenmal erleben" (it was your first time and it's so seldom you find anyone who is experiencing something for the first time). To which Kringelein responds: "Sie selber machen aber gar keinen blasierten Eindruck, wenn ich mir gestatten darf—" (*MH*, 197; But you do not give one the impression of being blasé yourself, if I may say so: *GH*, 167).

27 Matthias, *Hotel as Setting*, 175, 177.

statements might help us situate these characters better, but I argue that we already share in this information, because we read these attitudes in their meaningful comportments toward the world. Baum's characters are already motivated, moved, animated, by their historical environments, and we read this in their comportment. Indeed, the interesting thing about the novel is the way in which these different historical attitudes come together dynamically and come to be influenced and transformed.

Pre-Reflective Responses

Through their encounters in the hotel, the characters of the novel become more responsive to the world. An important example of such an encounter, one that I wish to explore at length, is the one between Gaigern and the famous ballerina Grusinskaja. The two characters have in common that they are both representatives of a now-defunct old-world order: she is a famous ballerina struggling to get audiences in light of new developments in dance; he is a bankrupt aristocrat in a newly democratic society. In other words, their practices as representatives of this old-world order, their comportments, fall flat on their new environments. One might suggest that at least Gaigern has adapted to the new environment somewhat by using his aristocratic flair to come close to and steal from the rich, and the novel does suggest this, but the text neither endorses this unethical solution—Gaigern is killed *in flagrante delicto*—nor does it show Gaigern to be happy with this situation. Instead, Gaigern is ultimately, in Otternschlag's words, "ausgeleert und gestorben" (*MH*, 258; vacant and dead: *GH*, 219). This is most obvious in the changes that happen to him in his interaction with Grusinskaja. At the time, she, in their meeting, escapes her skeptical and cold attitude to the world, as well.

The two meet unexpectedly in Grusinskaja's hotel room. Gaigern, having got hold of Grusinskaja's pearls from her hotel room, is stuck, pearls in pocket, on her balcony. In a modern twist the electric lighting, which has been blinding everyone's view of the hotel's façade, has stopped working. Gaigern can no longer climb back to his own room. Grusinskaja, meanwhile, is at the end of her wits, has left her performance early, and has cancelled her attendance at a party at the French ambassador's house later in the evening. She thus enters the room earlier than Gaigern expected while he is still on the balcony.

Their interaction starts when he is watching her from the balcony and she elicits immediate responses in him. In the hotel room, Grusinskaja is looking with horror in the mirror at a reflection of her face; she considers herself old, ugly, and flabby. Her cold attitude towards her reflection is mirrored in her own shivering and the cold overhead lighting that she turns on to find warmth, but which brings no such thing. Impatiently, she takes off the costume in which she fled the theatre, and, naked but for her tights, presses herself against the radiator. Baum writes: "sie dachte wenig dabei, sie suchte nur Wärme" (*MH*, 121; she scarcely thought at all as she did so. She only desired warmth: *GH*, 103). Her cold, rational attitude toward her own face is thus reflected in the physical feeling of coldness. The immediate and frantic search for a source of warmth shows how this feeling of coldness takes over. After having put her wrists under scalding hot water and having ordered tea, her attitude changes quite suddenly. She returns to the mirror, now completely naked, to look at her full body: "Plötzlich schlug der Haß," Baum writes, ". . . in Zärtlichkeit um" (*MH*, 121; suddenly the hatred she felt for herself changed into tenderness: *GH*, 103). Seeing "the body of a sixteen-year-old ballet student," she starts to caress and kiss different parts of her body. She tells it: "Bjednajaja, malenjkaja": you poor one, you little one (*MH*, 121; 103).[28] But if her own face seems to elicit a cold response and consequently an immediate search for warmth, in Gaigern her comportment elicits a stronger response.

Gaigern's response to this scene is as corporeal and immediate as Grusinskaja's search for warmth. Her beautiful and delicate body is almost irrelevant to Gaigern. What affects him is her helplessness, her shaking, and her desperate confusion and misery. Although he is a criminal, "entgleist" (crook), Baum writes, he is still far from being an "Unmensch" (*MH*, 122; inhuman: *GH*, 104). His humanity manifests itself, unbeknownst to him, in his body: "Gaigern, zwischen den Vorhängen, machte ein achtungsvolles und mitleidiges Gesicht, ohne es zu wissen" (*MH*, 122; unconsciously Gaigern, between the curtains, showed pity and admiration in his face: *GH*, 103). He physically loses attention to his job and the pearls; he lets go of them and takes his hands out of his pockets. Instead of holding on to the pearls, his body wants to support her:

> Er spürte in seinen Handflächen, in seinen Armen eine ziehende Lust, diese kleine, einsame Frau aufzuheben, sie wegzutragen, sie zu trösten, sie zu wärmen, damit in Gottes Namen dieser abscheuliche Schüttelfrost und ihr fast irrsinniges Flüstern aufhören könne . . . (*MH*, 122)

> [He felt in his hands and in his arms a compelling desire to support this poor lonely woman, to take her away and console her—to do anything to put a stop to that terrible shuddering and almost crazed, despairing whispering. (*GH*, 104)]

Gaigern is thus animated for the better. His cynical attitude changes to one of care in a pre-reflective, corporeal response. Indeed, at the end of

---

28 This is both incorrect Russian and an unorthodox transcription. In German it would usually read: "bednaja, malen'kaja" (Бедная, маленькая).

the long scene between the two he has forgotten all about the pearls, a thought that is replaced by a pressing feeling of wanting to be good to Grusinskaja: "Er hatte jetzt völlig, bis zur gänzlichen Ausgelöschtheit, die Perlen vergessen. Er spürte nur ein klammerndes und pressendes Gefühl für die Frau, einen unabmeßbaren Wunsch, gut zu ihr zu sein, gut, gut, gut" (*MH*, 160; [the pearls] were actually and utterly erased from his memory. He was conscious of nothing but the grip and the stress of his feelings for this woman, and the infinite desire to be good to her, good, good, good: *GH*, 135). Counter to his negative impulses, then, his embodied attitude is changed by this woman's naked, vulnerable body. The response that her comportment in this moment elicits is one of care and support. These pre-reflective responses point to the idea in DPT that we do not just take other people's meaningful comportment indifferently. We do not just *read* other people's comportments, we are engaged with other people in an unfolding pragmatic process: other people's actions matter to us, they are affordances for our own comportments, for further action. Gallagher writes: "I see the other's actions as an affordance for my own possible responsive action (which may be very different from hers); I see the other's action as inter-actionable or as calling forth a response on my part."[29] But as Baum suggests, such unexpected, but immediate, responses elicited by people *outside* of our everyday lives may pry us loose from our current rigid ways of being.

Becoming Responsive through Social Warmth

In addition, the novel also suggests a more fundamental way in which at least Grusinskaja gets out of her habitual ways through this meeting, namely through Baum's emphasis on "warmth." Baum repeatedly uses the word "warmth" for positive encounters in the novel, a use which again intimates the continuity between physical and emotional feeling as well as the immediacy with which we can respond to other people. We have already seen that when Gaigern is spying on Grusinskaja from the balcony, she is looking for physical warmth: in the lighting, from the radiator, the scalding hot water, and the tea. But she is also said to miss the warmth of people, and Baum explicitly links the two. Thinking about the people in her entourage, Grusinskaja states: "Der alte Pimenoff. Der alte Witte. Die alte Suzette. Sonst kein Mensch, nie ein Mensch, nie eine Wärme. Man legte die Hände auf die Heizkörper fremder Hotels, das war alles" (*MH*, 128; old Pimenov. Old Witte. Old Suzette and not another soul, never any warmth. You held your hands to hotel radiators and that was all; *GH*, 109). She thus links the emotional warmth that other people bring with the physical warmth of a radiator. Baum does the same when

---

29 Gallagher, *Enactivist Interventions*, 80.

Grusinskaja finds Gaigern on her balcony: "Sie fror," Baum writes, "und zugleich spürte sie, wie der Mensch neben ihr auf dem kleinen Balkon Wärme ausstrahlte" (*MH*, 127; the air was cold and she felt at once that the man beside her on the little balcony radiated warmth: *GH*, 108). The warmth Grusinskaja is looking for is thus not merely either a physical or an emotional warmth, but rather both at the same time. Baum clearly entangles the affective life in the physical life of the body. This entanglement also emphasizes that Gaigern's immediate, gallant response is not something that is registered in Grusinskaja mentally first, or something that in any case seems to be able to be held off. In Baum's phenomenologically attentive account, it is something that assails Grusinskaja. The warmth seems to be something she immediately shares in. The scene thus presents us with a positive, affective-kinetic dynamic between the two characters. She is looking for such affective and corporeal warmth. He responds, in turn, "automatically" with a gallant gesture. And she, again, responds to this warm comportment towards her positively, as well. A positive kinetic-affective dynamic unfolds between these two characters.

We can take this reading of their dynamic further, however, through approaches to human warmth in the cognitive sciences. Physical warmth is an important part of humans' fundamental responses to each other. Our endothermic regulation, the way in which the human body regulates its temperature, is one way in which the body is thought to incorporate parts of its environment into its system. India Morrison, who has worked extensively on human touch in the cognitive sciences, hypothesizes that human touch (she focuses on being touched) may be an important part of the human system to make sure that a source of warmth is close by.[30] She traces this in humans and mammals, as well as other animals. She believes that over time the neural paths of the sensation of touch and warmth may have come to be connected, by which touch became related to warmth. "This possibility also," she writes, "carries an important implication that such temporal and contextual shorthand may manifest in regulatory neural short*cuts* in which 'warm and close' states can be instigated by social touch alone, rather than requiring a cycle of behaviorally mediated physical warmth restoration following actual temperature decreases."[31] But this connection is not just "encoded," as per Cecilia Heyes's metaphor, in our brains, but also in our socio-cultural environment.[32] As Hans Rocha IJzerman writes, "it appears that the biological links between physical temperature and psychological temperature become activated only if we have experienced early in life that physical warmth and caring for others go hand in hand—and if we are securely

---

30 Morrison, "Keep Calm."
31 Morrison, "Keep Calm," 349.
32 Heyes, *Cognitive Gadgets*.

attached."[33] If this is the case, being close to someone may thus immediately give us a feeling of warmth regardless of whether that person is actually making us warmer. Indeed, as IJzerman writes, even positive *virtual* social encounters can make you not only *feel* warmer but actually raise your body temperature.[34] Thermoregulation is one way in which Morrison suggests that "social attachment represents a form of flexible, context-dependent physiological regulation."[35] Other people, in other words, are already taken as part of our basic regulatory system. Baum's portrayal of Grusinskaja and Gaigern's interaction thus hints at a more fundamental role of other people. They are not only there to interact with, to elicit certain responses we may like or not, but also to fulfil one of the most fundamental parts of human existence, namely providing us with ways of regulating our warmth. They are already part of our core system of regulating heat. Gaigern's proximity provides a direct solution to Grusinskaja's feeling cold, whether he actually brings heat or not. The cold situation with a warm Gaigern in it drives Grusinskaja into his arms. What Baum importantly shows, however, and what Morrison only hints at, is that other people are not just a source of warmth for the body to regulate its own warmth, but that through such warmth we can also become more responsive to the environment.

The warmth that assails Grusinskaja in her meeting with Gaigern, sharing in his warm composure toward her, does not just change how she appears to him, but importantly changes the way in which her environment seems meaningful to her. Grusinskaja is about to kill herself, tired as she is from a tour ever decreasing in success, when she goes to the balcony for some fresh air and discovers Gaigern there. He tells her a lie about why he is on the balcony, which she accepts. She almost immediately finds the warmth she has been looking for in him. They first kiss and then sleep together. What is particularly interesting, however, is that in his arms she finds, even if only temporarily, a new way of approaching her performances. Using derogatory language, she blames Berlin audiences, their love for, it seems, *Ausdruckstanz* and the work of black revue dancers such as Josephine Baker, for her lack of success the previous nights (*MH*, 140; *GH*, 119).[36] But, lying in bed after their sexual intercourse, she is suddenly revitalized: "'Aber ich lebe ja,' denkt sie erschüttert, 'ich

33 IJzerman, *Heartwarming*, 15.
34 IJzerman et al., "Cold-blooded Loneliness." See also IJzerman, *Heartwarming*, 9.
35 Morrison, "Keep Calm," 355.
36 She tells Gaigern as part of a long monologue about her fame: "Nun versuche das doch, wenn du berühmt bist, verschwinde aus der Welt, ruh dich aus, laß andere tanzen, diese häßlichen, verrenkten Deutschen, diese Negerinnen, diese Nichtskönner alle, laß sie doch tanzen, ruh dich aus!" (*MH*, 140; well, try it, when you are famous, disappear from the world and take your rest, let others

lebe, ich werde neue Tänze tanzen, ich werde Erfolge haben'" (*MH*, 138; but I am alive, I am alive, she thought with a shock. I shall dance new dances and I shall have success: *GH*, 117). She even contemplates not dancing the new program on pointe shoes, which suggests that she might leave ballet for something more "contemporary" (*MH*, 138; *GH*, 117). Yet when she talks to Gaigern after that, she seems to slip back into negative thinking. She talks to him about the burden of responsibility she feels for her audiences, the burden of always travelling and needing to have success. She cannot, she says, be like the people in small villages who just sit there outside their homes completely stiff; she cannot escape from the world like them. Gaigern, however, who has seen her performances and was bored by them, nudges her thinking in a different direction. He says he likes her description of these people "mit den steifen Händen" (*MH*, 142; stiff hands: *GH*, 120); she should dance that. Grusinskaja responds:

> "Das? Aber das kann man nicht tanzen, Monsieur. Oder will man mich sehen als eine alte Frau mit einem Tuch um den Kopf und Gicht in den Fingern und nur aus Holz sein und ausruhen—?"
>
> Sie brach mitten im Satze ab. Schon während sie sprach, hatte ihr Körper sich der Vorstellung bemächtigt, er zog sich zusammen und steifte sich. Sie sah schon die Dekoration, sie wußte schon einen jungen, verrückten Maler in Paris, der so etwas malen konnte, sie sah schon den Tanz, sie spürte ihn schon in ihren Händen und in den gebückten Halswirbeln. (*MH*, 142)

> ["That? But one can't dance that, Monsieur. Do you think they'd want to see me as an old woman with a shawl over her head and gout in her fingers, sitting like a block of wood and resting—?"
>
> She broke off in the middle of her sentence. Even while she spoke her body took hold of the idea and grew tense. She saw the scene and she knew a crazy young painter in Paris who could paint it. She saw the dance, she felt it in her hands and in the bent vertebrae of her neck. (*GH*, 120)]

Against her own judgement, then, her body is already animated by this suggestion and she starts to imagine all the things she could dance. But they are far from the kind of usual figures of ballet—not a bird, for example, as she danced that night, nor a butterfly, as her ballet master would certainly, she thinks, tell her to dance (*MH*, 143; *GH*, 121). Rather, she imagines a beggar, a farmer, and a prostitute (*MH*, 142; *GH*, 120); the

---

dance, leave it to those ugly, clumsy Germans and black women, and all the other incompetents, let them dance and take your rest: *GH*, 119).

kind of portrayals *Ausdruckstanz* was known for.[37] Furthermore, it is suggested that she starts to imagine scenes from her own life: a naked girl forced to dance in front of a Grand Duke—whom she had mentioned previously as being part of her ballet education—as well as her own possible suicide—in the middle of which Gaigern catches her (*MH*, 142–43; *GH*, 121). Gaigern's presence thus animates her in such a way as to make her engage with the new age with its new audiences. Having previously characterized herself as from a different age, the possibility opens up that she might be able to adjust to this new one (*MH*, 140; *GH*, 118). Moreover, the physicality of this change in attitude is emphasized in her embodied practice as a dancer. Her turn from ballet to *Ausdruckstanz* makes visible the way in which her attitude is not so much a "state-of-mind" as it is a different way of approaching or appraising our environment; she "enacts" the world differently. Grusinskaja's physical and pre-reflective attitude, like Gaigern's, is changed through this encounter. They do not just elicit immediate responses in each other, but, at least in the case of Grusinskaja, also different comportments toward their environments.

In her discussion of "social touch" and the importance of other people to our physical systems, Morrison also hints at the possibility that the presence of other people can change our understanding of the environment. Social touch, as indicating the presence of others, is not only a part of thermoregulation, but also of stress regulation. Morrison argues that social touch "can 'buffer' disadvantageous physiological effects of potentially inefficient and maladaptive responses [to stressors]."[38] Stress responses are usually adaptive, only used when really necessary and returning to normal states quickly when not needed, among other characteristics. Stress responses have what scientists call an "efficiency zone," within which the benefits outweigh the costs.[39] An interesting effect of stress responses being outside of this "zone" is that they might come to stunt learning and blunt our responsiveness to the environment. A "buffer," per Morrison's definition, is "*any mechanism or process that mitigates, attenuates, offsets, or prevents energy efficiency losses among regulatory systems, while remaining adequately responsive to external challenges.*"[40] Social touch is, Morrison suggests, exactly such a mechanism for our stress-response system. Social touch, as the knowledge that

---

37 Most famous are Mary Wigman's *Hexentanz* (1914), literally a witch's dance, and Kurt Jooss's *Der Grüne Tisch* (1931), a political *danse macabre*. For a recent text on German dance in the early twentieth century see Ruprecht, *Gestural Imaginaries*. For more on German dance in the period, see Brandstetter, *Tanz-Lektüren*.
38 Morrison, "Keep Calm," 344.
39 Morrison, "Keep Calm," 346.
40 Morrison, "Keep Calm," 348.

others are near, regulates the stress system; it aids in the "manifestation of adaptive responses to stress challenges."[41] It does so in part by stimulating oxytocin and opioid release, leading, amongst other things, to hedonic feelings, mild painkilling, and, interestingly, to "fine-tuned context-sensitivity."[42] In other words, there is evidence that suggests that other people are part of our extended system of stress regulation, part of a self-regulatory "device" modulating stress, which not only makes us feel better and more enthusiastic, but also regulates our dynamic responsiveness to our environments. In short, "stress or anxiety could trigger a motivation to *seek* proximity in order to dampen [stress-response systems'] arousal, just as being cold can drive behavior to huddle close to others in order to restore warmth."[43]

Reading Grusinskaja's immediate responses after her clearly stress-induced episode in these terms makes visible not only the way in which her search for warmth in other people is connected to a sense of safety, but also an increased responsiveness to the environment. At one point a kiss from Gaigern almost literally seems to reawaken her (*MH*, 133; *GH*, 114). But it also makes it clear how Gaigern can be read as a completion of her "system" (and *vice versa*). Baum's description of Grusinskaja's increased responsiveness, the way in which her career becomes one of possibilities rather than difficulties, emphasizes the extent to which Morrison's empirical considerations could become important to human flourishing. Baum shows that other people are not only important extensions of our stress-regulation system but also that they are therefore important contributors to the ways in which we can comport ourselves more dynamically in a world that might be unfamiliar, hostile, stressful. Yet what seems to make their pull on one another especially strong, the text suggests, is what seems the exact opposite of responsive: namely, recognition and shared habitual practices.

Familiar Movements

Both their immediate, embodied responses to each other and the increased responsiveness through warmth are underpinned by a familiarity between them. The point on which their pull on one another rests seems to be a recognition of their own past lives in the other. Grusinskaja, when she first meets Gaigern, recognizes something in him from her past. When she catches him on the balcony, he makes the excuse that he was

41 Morrison, "Keep Calm," 357.
42 Morrison, "Keep Calm," 352.
43 Morrison, "Keep Calm," 351. For an interesting account of how touch and proximal others may shape so-called "minimal selfhood," see Ciaunica and Fotopoulou, "Touched Self."

there because he is an admirer. This takes her back to an earlier episode in her life and career. While she was staying as a young dancer in a castle per the Grand Duke Sergei's invitation, a young officer had, like Gaigern now, sneaked into her room. "Sie erinnerte sich an seine Augen und an ein paar Küsse" (*MH*, 127; she remembered his eyes and one or two kisses too: *GH*, 108). This young officer had soon afterwards been killed in a suspicious hunting accident (prefiguring Gaigern's demise at the end of the novel). It is at that moment that she realizes how lonely she is now and that she feels Gaigern's warmth. Moreover, Gaigern's warm response, which reminds her of being loved before, also directly motivates her different stance toward her performances. She states that someone who is loved cannot *not* have success (*MH*, 138; *GH*, 117).

In Gaigern, too, there seems to arise a feeling of recognition when Grusinskaja calls him "Du—Mensch" (*MH*, 130; you—kind man: *GH*, 110). After consoling her when she is crying over her loneliness, these "zärtliche Worte" (endearments) strike him; the words "prallte . . . an sein Herz" (*MH*, 130; hit his heart: *GH*, 110).[44] Baum writes that he "horchte auf den Seelenklang, es rief ihn etwas an wie aus der Kindheit, wie aus einer Sphäre, die er verlassen hatte" (*MH*, 130; he heard an echo in his soul as though from his childhood, from a world he had left behind: *GH*, 110). Even if he wishes to close himself off to this feeling by having a cigarette, the word clearly elicits a side of him, indeed a whole situation, that previously remained hidden. What Malte could not find but in his memory and some heroic stories he read as a child comes to Gaigern in the form of Grusinskaja, whose words elicit feelings from his childhood home.

Their immediate responses that remind them of their previous lives is couched by Baum in the fact that they recognize each other's backgrounds as familiar. This familiarity is announced in the novel through moments of "mimicry" before they even meet. The encounter between Gaigern and Grusinskaja starts, at least for the reader, before they meet. Baum sets up their connection in moments of what I will call "mimicry," moments in which their comportments match. They both perform difficult balancing acts. While Grusinskaja is in full control of her own body on stage, balancing on her pointe shoes, Gaigern is performing equally difficult physical movements climbing along the façade of the hotel to try and steal her jewels. They both talk to their own bodies and do so in similar ways: They praise and scold their bodies. They are both observed (almost) naked: Grusinskaja is observed by Gaigern, as we have seen,

---

44 The word "Mensch" is not usually used in German as an evaluative term. Baum might be using the word as the Yiddish "Mentsch," "Mensch," or "Mensh" which also found its way into English in Jewish usage as "a person of integrity or rectitude; a person who is morally just, honest, or honourable" (OED).

walking around in her hotel room with initially only her stockings on and then fully naked, Gaigern is observed by his chauffeur with only his socks on. Thus, when Gaigern reflects on why Grusinskaja appeals to all his best instincts he thinks: "Sie war so zerbrechlich, so gefährdet, so schutzbedürftig—und so stark dabei. Aus seiner Existenz heraus, die immer wie über einen Grat balancierte, verstand er die ihre" (*MH*, 155; she was so fragile, exposed to such dangers and so much in need of protection—and at the same time so strong. His own existence, always trembling on the edge of a precipice, taught him to understand hers: *GH*, 131). Gaigern recognizes her existence as similar to his. It is not a revelation, something new, that he finds in her, but rather a familiarity. The physical imagery of the balancing act that alludes to their earlier acts couches this familiarity in a shared affective-kinetic dynamic. The recognition thus seems to be also a kinesthetic recognition; what is recognized is not merely her "inner feeling" but her *comportment*. In the terms that I laid out in the Heidegger chapter, what he finds in her is a body similarly animated by the world.

Current empirical research in the cognitive sciences is very interested in mimicry. In recent years, ample evidence has been gathered in the cognitive sciences, that humans immediately and unconsciously mimic other people.[45] We copy facial expressions, postures, movements, and voice, and do so unconsciously. Such copying is mediated, it is now believed, by so-called mirror neurons, neurons that fire significantly when we perform a specific object-oriented action *as well as* when we watch someone else perform that action. In other words, other people always already move us in some way. The mirror neurons are a sign that we share another person's comportment.[46] But why do we mimic? Importantly for our present discussion, Gallagher has suggested that the mirror neuron system might be employed precisely for aiding our responsiveness to other people. In line with suggestions made by Newman-Norlund and colleagues, he argues that instead of the activation of mirror neurons preparing us for matching another person's action, it might rather attune us to their gestures in order to be able to smoothly come up with congruent responses.[47] Citing a variety of empirical evidence, he thus argues that mimicry aids the way

---

45 E.g., Meltzoff and Moore, "Imitation, Memory, and the Representation of Persons"; Gallagher and Meltzoff, "The Earliest Sense."

46 Cecilia Heyes has importantly argued that the discovery of the mirror neuron has only shifted the question from "how do people imitate?" to "how do mirror neurons imitate?" Her answer is "sociocultural experience," in other words, by learning with and through others. Heyes, "Imitation," 121, 124. See also Heyes, "Where Do Mirror Neurons Come From?"

47 Gallagher, *Enactivist Interventions*, 77; Newman-Norlund, Noordzij, Meulenbroek, and Bekkering, "Exploring the Brain."

in which we perceive others' meaningful actions in the world as affordances for our own responses to, or interaction with, these gestures.[48]

What I want to suggest about the mimicry-at-a-distance between Grusinskaja and Gaigern, then, is that their matched actions not only point to the intimacy and pre-reflective gestures that are to come when they meet, but also that it shows that they are especially well prepared to respond reciprocally and dynamically to one another. One might say that they are particularly attuned to another, but that would overlook the fact that at the moment of "mimicry" they have never met. Rather, I would argue, Baum shows how they are attuned to similar social environments, and similar people. The matched comportment seems to come from a similar background or education. They both represent a now-defunct, (Prussian) world order which is acted out physically: beautiful, elegant, and in full control of their bodies. He is an aristocrat with military training; she is a ballerina trained in Imperial Russia. This reading of control as a shared comportment is thematized later when Grusinskaja tells him that she belongs to a different century, and then states that she and the dancers were trained "wie kleine Soldaten" for sex with the Grand Dukes of Russia (*MH*, 140; like little soldiers: *GH*, 118).[49] She was, she says "hart wie ein Diamant" (*MH*, 140; hard as a diamond: *GH*, 118). Moreover, when Grusinskaja first sees Gaigern on the balcony he bows to her; a sign, perhaps, of a shared culture. It is this cultural background, then—emphasized in their matched movements—that seems to form the background for an attunement of their bodies, which allows for the fine-tuned, immediate physical responses they produce when they meet. The fact that it is the shared history that aids their helpful, if temporary, interaction is evident in their recurring comments about recognizing something in each other, as well as in the fact that they return to older ways of behaving. Yet what is important about Gallagher's emphasis on the difference between

---

48 Gallagher, *Enactivist Interventions*, 78. He cites, e.g., Trevarthen, "Communication and Cooperation"; Goodwin, "Action and Embodiment"; Bayliss, Paul, Cannon, and Tipper, "Gaze Cueing"; Bayliss, Frischen, Fenske, and Tipper, "Affective Evaluations."

49 It seems that Baum is deliberately referring to Grand Duke Sergei Mikhailovich (1869–1918), who famously had a long affair with the ballerina Mathilde Kschessinska (1872–1971). Grusinskaja also mentions Kschessinska together with Kschessinska's rival Vera Trefilova in a monologue about her life, as the dancers she learned from when she was little (*MH*, 140; *GH*, 118). I here use the Russian names of these historical figures as they are usually transcribed into, or used in, English and not as how they appear in the novel. While I recognize that this contrasts with "Grusinskaja," which I have left as it is written in the novel, I do so because the latter is not a historical figure but a character. Transcribing the names of the historical figures as they are known in German and not as they are in English, I believe, would look strange in an English text.

thinking about mimicry as for matching movements or as a preparation for congruent responses, is that what Gaigern and Grusinskaja recognize in one another is not so much their own behavior copied, but rather, they recognize their own responses to the other. Gaigern does not only recognize Grusinskaja's predicament but more importantly recognizes, through her, the responses his aristocratic upbringing has instilled in him. She, through him, recognizes the responses elicited by a loved, successful ballerina. Crucially, they like their own responses in this interaction. It is not just that the elicited responses are old habits resurfacing, but these are habits that they feel good about. In other words, they like what the other person affords and elicits: she wants to be an adored ballerina, he seems to want to be a gallant man rather than a criminal. They elicit precisely those parts of each other. The same can be viewed in Dr. Otternschlag's response to Kringelein. The sick Kringelein elicits a meaningful response from Otternschlag exactly because the doctor gets to feel useful.

Importantly, the meeting between Gaigern and Grusinskaja also challenges readings of modernist culture as responding to an "existential homelessness."[50] Gaigern explicitly calls this meeting a "homecoming" (*MH*, 135; *GH*, 115). It is their mutual fine-grained responsiveness to one another—announced in their mimicry-at-a-distance—that provides them, even if only temporarily, with what explicitly was not available to Rilke's Malte: a home away from home. The comportment of the other affords them positive, habitual ways of responding and interacting. This home away from home is perhaps best metaphorized in Gaigern's repeated reference to growing up amongst gypsies (e.g., *MH*, 139). He feels most at home, it seems, with those who do not necessarily have a stable material environment. These immediate responses between Grusinskaja and Gaigern thus give us a version of home that is not focused on the material environment, a *place*, but rather on other people's behaviors that elicit familiar movements. Baum puts forward a version of authenticity that relies on others eliciting positively familiar behaviors.

We might be worried that Baum takes a reactionary stance here. We might be worried that, ultimately, a homecoming in the familiar comportments of others, although one that gets rid of the necessity of a particular *space*, still marks a turn backwards to old, rigid habits. In fact, not only Grusinskaja and Gaigern are most at home with one another, as representatives of the aristocracy, but Kringelein, an office clerk, also ends up with someone from *his* social class, namely the typist and occasional prostitute

---

50 Matthias, *Hotel as Setting*, 8. Although Matthias recognizes that some modernist texts she discusses respond more positively to modernity, they do so in her reading by freeing the individual from socio-cultural constraints rather than by finding their way in them as I suggest. For more on existential homelessness and modernity see, e.g., Adorno, *Minima Moralia*.

Flämmchen. Thus it is crucial that Baum does not make these moments of homecoming merely regressive. It is important that through the meeting Grusinskaja sees precisely a way forward in a *new* environment, with its new demands. It shows that this homecoming is a dynamic one. Gaigern and Dr. Otternschlag, too, are able to get out from their pasts by finding positively habitual movements precisely within the dynamics of the big city hotel.[51]

Baum is thus able to imagine mobilizing the past for a new situation. While Malte had no recourse to the past but for a few heroic tales from his childhood, and indeed seems to believe his background is constraining, Baum's characters recollect the past through others and show how our historical backgrounds might be enabling. And whereas Benjamin and Döblin do not fully explore—only hint at—the ways in which Asja Lācis may have influenced Benjamin's own responsiveness, or Biberkopf's friends, and the "tenderness" of the Jewish men (*BA*, 99; *BA2*, 81), could have had a positive influence on him, Baum *does* explore enabling love and familiarity fully.

In part it is exactly the familiar form of the popular novel that helps Baum explore these themes. Its familiar topos of a love story as well as the myths of a gallant aristocrat, an adored ballerina, and a good doctor, amongst other characters, seem to aid Baum in exploring the possibility of an enabling familiarity, where the more experimental forms used by Rilke, Döblin, and Benjamin could not. Nevertheless, the kind of employment of familiar topoi of Baum can also be detected in Döblin and Rilke's work. As we have seen, Malte rewrites stories from the past for his new situation, including the parable of the prodigal son. There is, however, no way of telling whether that fictional space has any influence on Malte's real-world engagements, as the novel ends within the former. Within the narrative of Döblin's novel, the story of Zannowich as told by the Jewish men suggests a similarly possibility, but the story is ambiguously told and not properly paid attention to by Biberkopf.

Baum's gender, and the expectations that come with it, will have also enabled her to explore more fully the stereotypically feminine aspects of affect and warmth. Her sustained attention to female characters is absent in the other texts, and it is on Grusinskaja that her text's exploration of enabling love focuses. Yet Baum complicates the gender dynamics by ascribing aspects of care predominantly to her male characters. It is Gaigern who comforts Grusinskaja, the isolated and alienated figure. And other roles of care in the novel are especially taken on by

---

51 Gaigern's ultimate downfall seems to come about because he falls back into his criminal ways rather than sustaining his gallantry through Grusinskaja in this modern city (even if it is supposed to be one last heist to be able to follow Grusinskaja on her next stop in Vienna).

Kringelein and Dr. Otternschlag.[52] But rather than reading Baum's text as an anomaly compared to the previous texts discussed, I want to read her emphasis on "warmth" as an extension of those texts. My argument has been to move away from the masculinist "cool conduct" that Helmut Lethen has explored in his book about New Objectivity in particular, to show that these male authors too, albeit in less pronounced ways, explore enabling sociality, reaching out to other people. If Lethen discusses men between the wars turning away from the "sources of heat" of, for example, working-class culture or of women, Kaiser, Döblin, and Benjamin do (eventually) turn to, or speak from within, such warmth.[53] That is, Baum's position as a female popular author in a society that was more open to female voices than it used to be—even if they "continued to be muted"—and in which women are becoming more economically emancipated, would have allowed her to turn to and reach large audiences with a sustained treatment of warmth and affect, the kernels of which we find in the writings of her male counterparts.[54]

Conclusion

In sum, what I aim to show in this chapter is the dynamism of the Grand Hotel presented by Baum. This dynamism brings people together and allows their interactions to elicit behaviors that pry the characters loose from their everyday habits. Positively or negatively, human interaction in the novel never leaves its characters unmoved. Baum does this by paying attention to the minute details of movements, movements that are shown in their full affective-kinetic dimension portraying these characters' emotional attunement to the world. In her repeated use of the word "warmth," Baum captures this affective-kinetic dimension of other people, and the ways in which these elicit our "automatic" embodied responses. We do not first consciously register warmth: it assails us. The novel presents us with a dynamic of characters being moved physically and emotionally. Although Preysing's life spins out of control when he lets his sexual desire take over, this dynamic is mostly presented as a positive thing. As Otternschlag states: "Tanzen muß man können. Dieses Aneinanderklammern im gleichen Takt, dieses schwindlige Drehen und Sichhalten zu zweit" (*MH*, 53; one must know how to dance. The mutual embrace in time with the music, the dizzy turning and twirling of two as one, eh? *GH*, 44).

---

52   Although, as Elizabeth Boa argues, it is Flämmchen who ultimately takes on the most maternal role at the end of the novel in her relationship with Kringelein. Boa, "Women Writers," 127.
53   Lethen, *Verhaltenslehre der Kälte*, 171, 43; Lethen, *Cool Conduct*, 133, 25.
54   Boa, "Women Writers," 123.

The habits from which the novel's characters are pried loose are situated not in modern city life but in old, defunct situations. Gaigern and Otternschlag are still attuned to the war. Grusinskaja is stuck in the movements of ballet in a city that has moved on to other forms of dancing. Interactions allow for more responsiveness, in part by no more than giving positive feedback, by giving warmth. But these interactions mostly show that the practices they had before things started to go wrong—doctors, aristocrats, artists—have a place in their new environments, too. Grusinskaja elicits in Gaigern the gallant gestures of his aristocratic education; and he helps her show that her feelings, and her past experience, can be used for new dance pieces. The critically ill Kringelein provokes the doctor in Otternschlag. These moments may not last, but they do show the possibilities of a more dynamic engagement and the ways in which other people, if we are able to pay attention to them, might show us ways of re-inhabiting. They find meaning, in other words, in and through each other.

This dynamic also shows that the familiar, the habitual, and the homely are not precluded from the responsive features of inquisitiveness and engagement embodied in the character of Kringelein. If Sheets-Johnstone argues that we need to move away from an "adultist" view of embodiment focused on the transparency of familiarity, Baum suggests not only that responsiveness is essential to human flourishing, but also the ways in which familiarity might play an essential role in our ability to be responsive. *Menschen im Hotel* should remind us then that not only children are responsive, or adults familiarized, but that we are always already attuned to another body and have a home somewhere with other people. In other words, what I have tried to argue in this chapter is not only that Baum shows that the uncertainty of exploration can be alleviated by the certainty of familiar and safe, warm others, but also that this very dynamic between habit and exploration may be fundamental to human flourishing. Or, as Marcel Proust writes in *Le temps retrouvé* (Finding Time Again; 1927): "In society (and this social phenomenon is merely one application of a much more general psychological law), novelties, blameworthy or not, arouse horror only if they have not been assimilated and surrounded by reassuring elements."[55]

The novel ends with the most habitual inhabitant of the hotel, Otternschlag, returning from tiny bouts of animation at the hand of Kringelein, to his depressive routine in the lobby. However, his mood is

---

55 Proust, *In Search of Lost Time*, 33. "Dans le monde (et ce phénomène social n'est d'ailleurs qu'une application d'une loi psychologique bien plus générale) les nouveautés, coupable ou non, n'excitent l'horreur que tant qu'elles ne sont pas assimilées et entourées d'éléments rassurants." Proust, Le temps retrouvé, 51.

relativized by the appearance of the sunlit street, which is only just out of reach for Otternschlag:

> Doktor Otternschlag sitzt mitten in der Halle, eine versteinerte Statue der Einsamkeit und des Abgestorbenseins. Er hat seinen Stammplatz, er bleibt. Die gelben Hände aus Blei hängen ihm herunter, und mit dem Glasauge starrt er auf die Straße hinaus, die voll ist von Sonne, die er nicht sehen kann.
> Die Drehtür dreht sich, schwingt, schwingt, schwingt . . . (*MH*, 319)

> [Doctor Otternschlag sat in the middle of the Lounge, a fossilized image of Loneliness and Death. He has his regular place, and so he stays on. His yellow hands hang down like lead, and with his glass eye he stares out into the street, which is full of sunshine that he cannot see . . .
> The revolving door turns and turns and turns. (*GH*, 270)]

Thus before we conclude that the doctor's mood is the one we should take away from the novel, the light and warmth of the sun breaks through. The stiffness in his hands and the mention of his regular place where he will stay are the exact opposites of the revolving doors that Baum uses to represent the dynamism of the hotel. He remains fixed in a place meant to be dynamic, unable to see or feel the warmth that lies just on the other side of the revolving doors.

7: Evolving Form

> *An unfamiliar genre of music sounds perplexing, grating, discordant; yet, if I hear it over and over, it may start to resonate, to echo insistently on my mind. Moving to a big city, I am dazzled by the confusion of gaudy neon signs, flashing lights, video advertising screens; as days pass by, this confusion slowly dissipates and the kaleidoscope of color comes to seem comforting rather than confusing.*
>
> —Rita Felski[1]

IN CHAPTER 2, I ARGUED that Malte is constructing a niche from literary material to support his attempts at "freedom." I return now to the concept of the ecological niche to discuss modernist form. Remember Ingold's description of the weaverbird building its nest:

> The abilities of the weaverbird, just like those of the human maker of string bags, are developed through an active exploration of the possibilities afforded by the environment, in the choice of materials and structural supports, and of bodily capacities of movement, posture, and prehension. Furthermore, the key to successful nest building lies not so much in the movements themselves as in the bird's ability to adjust its movements with exquisite precision in relation to the evolving form of its construction.[2]

This is not only a useful description of how weaverbirds adjust to the evolving form of the nest, but also a useful model for how we as humans actively build our worlds. Animals, including humans, build ecological niches, sets of affordances, such as houses, nests, burrows, webs, "altering the material environment so that it offers possibilities for action that may improve the animal's situation."[3] Humans equally build houses and cities, and on smaller scales we also put together work stations, living rooms, and fitness centers, to support the ways in which we want to live our lives. Such building is an ongoing process in which we, on different timescales, adjust our actions to the evolving form.

---

1   Felski, *Hooked*, 72.
2   Ingold, *Perception of the Environment*, 359.
3   Rietveld and Kiverstein, "Rich Landscape," 328.

This image of the weaverbird building his nest is also useful to discuss modernist form. My argument is that the German modernist authors discussed in this monograph present us with texts that are like ecological niches. They construct texts in which narratives are dynamically mediated through spaces of (linguistic) "objects": montage (Döblin), "stations" (Kaiser), "thought-images" (Benjamin), or magazine serialization (Baum). Texts that highlight the visual and visceral, open-ended and dynamic natures of our ecologies; that conjure a world that is itself subject to construction, familiarization, and enaction. Modernist texts are constructed as weaverbirds construct their nests and as humans "[tailor] the places they inhabit."[4] The emphasis is on creativity and exploration, on the dynamic meaning of material, on spatiality, and on an open-ended, evolving form. That is, modernist form does not just present a lived experience of this world (showing what is attended to how, for example) but also emphasizes the dynamic evolvement of our environments through human practice.

At the same time, just as the evolving ecological niche, in particular that of the fast-changing city, demands its inhabitants to keep adjusting, so modernist form elicits in its reader the formulation of a new or dynamic engagement with the text, asks for new skills of reading. Modernist form is also an evolving form, because it changes under readers' familiarization and active participation. In general, reading literature, too, is a matter of experience and skill. It takes knowing a language as well as an alphabet.[5] Reading literature takes the kind of body that can handle the medium in which literature comes. Material books need to be held and pages need to be turned; letters on the page need to be discerned. And this body is supported by all kinds of aids: reading glasses, magnifying glasses, or reading lights, for example. Audiobooks and (other) digital devices have made texts more accessible. It also takes a recognition, on the basis of experience and knowledge, of at least parts of what is going on in the text.[6] To read about a body navigating a world, it is helpful to have such a body, or to have seen such a body in action. It is also helpful to have familiarity with literary forms, to be able "to distinguish or discriminate among . . . features."[7] In fact, an anthropological study of a group of people with little experience of film showed that they came up with "standard interpretations" of film clips 36–41 percent of the time, compared to 90 percent

---

4   Rietveld and Kiverstein, "Rich Landscape," 328.

5   In the German modernist space, one could also think here of the debates, often heated, about Fraktur versus Antiqua script, which included the question of which script was more readable.

6   In Marco Caracciolo's words, "stories offer themselves as imaginative experiences because of the way they draw on and restructure readers' familiarity with experience itself." Caracciolo, *Experientiality of Narrative*, 4.

7   Hubbs, *Rednecks, Queers, and Country Music*, 97.

of the time for experienced viewers.[8] Thus while, as Paul B. Armstrong points out, "narrative understanding is to some extent natural," much of our comprehension when reading texts also relies on a familiarity with form.[9] And reading relies on a responsiveness to the text. As Joe Moran writes at the end of his book on sentences: "When I am coming out of a dispiriting mood, and feeling rejoined to the world, I don't start worrying about whether the swifts will ever return. I start thinking in sentences again. I notice the ones printed on railway platform signs, or the walls of train carriages, or bottles of pills, and roll them silently around my head."[10] While we often think of literary form as static, it is in fact subject to all kinds of dynamic processes.[11] Like unfamiliar places, literary forms are subject to familiarization, and this changes how it appears to us. That is, literary form, too, is to be understood as an affordance; it exists in the relationship between body and material and changes through context, relevance, skill, habits, culture, and mood. Modernist form especially, as often particularly underspecified and (historically at least) unfamiliar, is subject to shape-shifting under our various evolving experiences and knowledges.[12]

To open up these questions about evolving modernist form, I also return to the concept of "affordances," as the constituents of the ecological niche. "Affordance" is not only a concept frequently employed in discussion of embodied cognition, but also one employed in literary studies. I already discussed, in chapter 4, Cave's use of the term as connoting "agency, intention, purpose," but other literary scholars, working in and beyond cognitive approaches, such as Karin Kukkonen, Rita Felski, and, most extensively, Caroline Levine, have used the term to their advantage as well.[13] Yet while Levine's *Forms* offers insightful analyses on the connections between social and literary forms, as well as their uses, my approach here is different. I use the term "affordance" to explore how modernist form as a set of affordances is a dynamically meaningful space, with an emphasis on affordances as subject to skill, context, and social processes. My aim is to show how modernist literature, like the city,

---

8 Schwan and Ildirar, "Watching Film," 974–75. See also Shimamura, "Psychocinematics," 19; and Armstrong, *Stories and the Brain*, 47–9.

9 Armstrong, *Stories and the Brain*, 49.

10 Moran, *First You Write a Sentence*, 209. See also Felski's chapter on attunement in *Hooked*, ch. 2.

11 For a recent treatment of modernist form as dynamic, with a focus on intermedial experiments in the English-language context, see Lewis, *Dynamic Form*.

12 See also Michaela Bronstein's *Out of Context*, in which she discusses modernist authors as especially interested in imagining a reception by future audiences.

13 Cave, *Thinking with Literature*, 51; Kukkonen, *Probability Designs*; Felski, *Hooked*; Levine, *Forms*.

consists of various elements that are arranged into surprising or unfamiliar constellations, inviting and shedding light on (often social) processes of familiarization and the (re)formulation of practices of reading. I draw a parallel between modernist form and modernist content in that they both highlight how humans familiarize the new and/or unfamiliar, whether it is literary form or the shapes and practices of the city. But I also argue that by being in direct engagement with their extratextual environments, modernist texts do not only reflect on, but also intervene in the evolving form of the city. Far from thinking about modernist forms as representing the modern experience of the environment in Georg Simmel's terms as shock, this chapter explores how modernist form allows for the "agency, intention, purpose" that Cave recognizes as important elements of affordances and extends the parallel that Felski draws out in the motto of this chapter between familiarizing cities and familiarizing artistic forms.

Making Form

German modernist form is often in close contact with real-world materials. Döblin takes elements directly from modern life and pastes them into the text in *Berlin Alexanderplatz*. Baum's story first appears serialized in a city newspaper surrounded by advertisements—for shaving creams, perfumes, shampoos, clothes, and shoes—and news articles. Benjamin's *Einbahnstraße* is built like a city, the individual vignettes standing on the page like shops on a street. In *Malte Laurids Brigge*, Rilke uses (parts of) his own letters to his wife Clara Rilke-Westhoff. The use of these elements of the world shows that they are "affordances," not static documentary objects, but dynamic pieces that can be, and are, re-arranged into new constellations of meaning.

In Döblin's description of his creative process, it is evident how the form of *Berlin Alexanderplatz* is the result of a dynamic, kinetic-affective exploration of the city. If the montage elements of *Berlin Alexanderplatz* are indeed "documentary," as Benjamin has called them, then how can we square these elements of montage with an interest of Döblin in the environment perceived through a purposeful and affected body (*GS* III, 232)? That is, how do we square the objectivity of documentary with the subject/object negotiation of an embodied experience? Devin Fore does away with part of this problem of squaring embodiment with documentary realism by showing the evolution in Döblin's documentary method between his 1924 *Die beiden Freundinnen und ihr Giftmord*, based on a sensational homicide in Berlin that became a large media event, and the 1929 *Berlin Alexanderplatz*. *Die beiden Freundinnen* was an attempt at depicting real events through realist literature, though one that Döblin immediately questioned in the novel's epilogue. *Berlin Alexanderplatz*, however, "collapsed," Fore argues, "the distance between artistic work and extratextual experience."[14] Rather than documents, Döblin's montage in *Berlin Alexanderplatz* offers us an experience. Fore argues that by its use of montage, the novel "transform[s] language from a specular medium into a productive force that actively constitutes the parameters of lived, embodied experience."[15] Through a reading of the language philosopher Fritz Mauthner, Fore argues that in Döblin's montage technique language becomes "a sense organ that is as vital and inalienable to the organism as the eye or the ear."[16] However, while Fore's account of montage in Döblin as presenting rather than *re*presenting is helpful and convincing, montage does not so much become a sense-organ as that it constitutes a niche of individual materials that together form what Heidegger has called a "totality of references," that is a web in which individual affordances of objects become specified toward a certain purpose. Of course, the difference between our arguments is small. My argument is indeed that tools can be like sense-organs in many ways—a microscope enhances eyesight; a walking stick enhances the senses of touch and equilibrium. It is just to say that we do not have to refer to the senses, to say that tools and niches "actively [constitute] the parameters of lived, embodied experience." As Gibson says about niches (see also chapter 2): "why has man changed the shapes and substances of his environment? To change what it affords him. He has made more available what benefits him and less pressing what injures him."[17]

Jähner, in his famous study of montage in *Berlin Alexanderplatz*, indeed discusses its elements, and Döblin's language in general, as possessing a "Materialität."[18] On the one hand, he emphasizes this materiality of language. The sounds and rhythms of its words and sentences offer Döblin an intrinsic logic that he can follow by, for example, stringing them together. On the other hand, Jähner views the individual pieces of montage as materials that Döblin puts together and builds a fictional world with. "Er klebt, versetzt und montiert seinen Zettelkosmos aus vorgefundenen Bruchstücken—aus Sprachfragmenten, deren Dinglichkeit sich der immateriellen Transparenz der Sprache in der herkömmlichen Fiktion widersetzt" (he glues, shifts, and assembles his cosmos of notes from found fragments—fragments of language whose materiality opposes the immaterial transparency of language in conventional fiction.).[19] Like Ingold's description of the weaverbird and its "active exploration of the

---

14 Fore, "Döblin's Epic," 175.
15 Fore, "Döblin's Epic," 175.
16 Fore, "Döblin's Epic," 180.
17 Gibson, *Ecological Approach*, 122.
18 Jähner, *Erzählter, montierter, soufflierter Text*, 132.
19 Jähner, *Erzählter, montierter, soufflierter Text*, 132. My translation.

possibilities afforded by the environment,"[20] Jähner describes Döblin as actively exploring, choosing, and rearranging pieces of "language" from which he builds his own world, which is attested by the manuscripts of the novel, full of clippings, in the German Literature Archive in Marbach.[21]

Döblin himself emphasized the dynamic and processual nature of his writing in "Der Bau des epischen Werks" (Construction of an Epic Work, 1928).[22] In the second stage of writing, after the incubation period, "ringerder Kollektivarbeit" (collective struggle) takes place, Döblin states, between the poet and the "Dinge, Gedanken, Werte" (things, thoughts, values) of his environment, through which the work is created.[23] He found it essential for authors to immerse themselves in their environments—"sie anzufassen" (to grapple with it)—including in the various everyday languages used by people belonging to different social strata, professions, and provinces, and for them to incorporate the found elements into their process.[24] The author partly loses conscious control here, Döblin states, and is, like Biberkopf in the whirlwind that is the city, drawn into an external process, the process of the creation of his work. Indeed, language, according to Döblin possesses a certain "Zwangscharakter" (coercive character), forcing one to use it in a certain way. Mimicking Malte's statement in *Die Aufzeichnungen*, Döblin writes: "man glaubt zu schreiben und man wird geschrieben" (you think you are writing and you are written).[25] Again, not unlike the weaverbird, the process of writing the epic is dynamic and contingent, and has no preconceived plot; it is immersed in a "Spielsituation" (game-situation) but with elements that have strong solicitations.[26] Hence, like the dynamic between action and perception that underlies Biberkopf's engagement in Berlin, so Döblin describes his own engagement as such a dynamic

---

20 Ingold, *Perception of the Environment*, 359.

21 See also Maskarinec, "Rethinking Montage." In recent years, work has been done in general on manuscript genetics read through hypotheses of the "extended mind," that is exploring what manuscripts can tell us about how we use the materials at our disposal to help creative cognition. See, e.g., Bernini, "Supersizing Narrative Theory"; Van Hulle, *Modern Manuscripts*; Kukkonen, *4E Cognition and Eighteenth-Century Fiction*.

22 Döblin, "Bau des epischen Werks." All translations of this source by C. D. Godwin: Döblin, "The Construction of the Epic Work." While Godwin's work translating many of Döblin's essays into German, and making them freely available online, is invaluable, I have changed his translation of the title of Döblin's essay here. His "The Construction of the Epic Work" sounds unnecessarily clunky to me.

23 Döblin, "Bau des epischen Werks," 121.
24 Döblin, "Bau des epischen Werks," 107.
25 Döblin, "Bau des epischen Werks," 131.
26 Döblin, "Bau des epischen Werks," 121.

process: "das Ding hat sich im Sprechen, im Schreiben verändert" (in the speaking, in the writing, the thing has changed).[27] From Döblin's reflections on his process of writing emerges the kind of purposeful, kinetic-affective dynamic with his environment that describes the weaverbird's engagement with the evolving form of his nest.

My argument here aligns with Stephen D. Dowden's recent argument that mimesis is central to modernist form. He opposes the mimetic principle to the intention to realistically represent the world as well as to the so-called novels of ideas.[28] For Dowden, mimesis "emerged from a search for a mode of artistic creativity imbedded in natural process, a practice by which to relate to the world naïvely . . ."[29] Drawing on Benjamin's discussion of mimesis, he likens it to (child's) play, "which is not so much an act of representation as it is an act of empathy and transformation. It emphasizes the porous border between us and the world."[30] Ingold's weaverbird thus provides the kind of natural image that connects Döblin's montage with Dowden's arguments about mimesis. Like the weaverbird building its nest out of twigs, like Mieze building her own niche away from the violence of the city outside, the montage of *Berlin Alexanderplatz* is the result of a dynamic process of involvement in his surroundings, which creates a niche of material that gains new meaning in a new constellation. As Michael Hofmann writes: "The work-in-progress of the book matched the work-in-progress of the city—one can imagine the former, too, with its own duckboards and drillings and tunnellings and detours and demolitions and temporary closures and promised improvements."[31] That is, Döblin's montage highlights the dynamism of the objects in our worlds, and their subjection to processes of meaning-making, as well as the possibility of re-making their meaning.

Reading Affordances

But modernist form is also an evolving form because the *reader* is especially involved in the active process of meaning-making. One could read, as Moritz Baßler and Melanie Horn point out, the montage technique in light of Georg Simmel's *Die Großstädte und das Geistesleben* (The Metropolis and Mental Life, 1903) as creating a "Fülle von Material"

---

27 Döblin, "Bau des epischen Werks," 128.
28 Dowden, *Modernism and Mimesis*, 23; 83. That is to say that he contrasts "breakthrough figures" like Kafka and Beckett to "transitional figure[s]" such as James Joyce and Thomas Mann (23).
29 Dowden, *Modernism and Mimesis*, 25.
30 Dowden, *Modernism and Mimesis*, 26.
31 Hofmann, afterword, 449.

(abundance of material) requiring a stimulus shield.[32] Such a reading, however, emphasizes an aggressive and antagonistic approach to the environment, one that Döblin, at least on the intra-fictional level, in the end tries to get away from by proposing a more responsive engagement with the social environment. What happens if instead we read the elements of montage as affordances for readers, with an emphasis, in Cave's terms, on agency, intentions, and also underspecification? As Jähner points out, montage is a process that engages the reader to create the meaning. Like a pointillist painting that only comes together in the eye of the viewer, the gaps between the separate elements of montage, he argues, are only bridged by the reader.[33] Baßler and Horn, as well as Stijn De Cauwer, similarly emphasize the process of engagement that montage asks for. But in contrast to Jähner, who suggests that the reader *concludes* the gaps created by montage, they show that this process never ends. As Baßler and Horn write about the references that can endlessly be explored: "Von jeder Stelle des Textes . . . geht es ins Unbegrenzte, in die Weite des kulturellen Netzes der Zeit ebenso wie in die Tiefe der poetischen Struktur des Romans" (at every point in the text . . . the reader is taken into the infinite, into the vastness of the cultural web of time as well as into the depth of the poetic structure of the novel).[34] De Cauwer, citing Georges Didi-Huberman's work on montage in Brecht, highlights the open structure of the elements of montage and thereby the connections and possibilities that arise from them.[35] To him, the world of *Berlin Alexanderplatz* in its presentation of singular elements "allows [Döblin's] construction to retain an openness to new, fleeting and unexpected experience."[36] Fore, too, speaks of the novel's "open and contingent montage structure."[37]

The same question arises as Döblin seems to ask throughout the novel: how do we as readers, new and old, make sure that we are not overwhelmed by the contingency of meaning, and how do we make sure we avoid forcing a fixed meaning onto the text, over-specifying its affordances? How do we follow David R. Midgley when he writes that "our response as readers needs to acquire something of that dynamism which we have seen to characterize the text, neither succumbing to what Döblin calls the 'passive' and implicitly 'tragic' aspect of human affairs as depicted in the novel, nor yet seeking, in a form of hubris, to subordinate the material reality of its language to our interpretative schemes"?[38] In

32 Baßler and Horn, afterword, 538.
33 Jähner, *Erzählter, montierter, soufflierter Text*, 152–53.
34 Baßler and Horn, afterword, 544. My translation.
35 De Cauwer, "Beyond the Stimulus Shield."
36 De Cauwer, "Beyond the Stimulus Shield," 111.
37 Fore, "Döblin's Epic," 197.
38 Midgley, *German Novel*, 108.

part the answer seems to lie in the structure of montage itself. Just as the affordances of objects in the real world gain specification in a given context (see chapter 4), so too the elements of montage gain specification through the other elements they are put into contact with. Despite the spatial metaphors that are often used to think through montage (as montage found its zenith in the visual arts), in *Berlin Alexanderplatz* it is a process that happens over time. It is an accumulation, but one that both complicates *and* specifies what has come before. Just as "unexpected connections and affinities light up" in montage, so also other meanings withdraw.[39] The elements do not need to become so underspecified as to become overwhelming, nor so specific, in its open and contingent structure, as not to challenge straightforward interpretation. The structure solicits us to make more of a weather report, a line of a song, or a list of tram stops, but it does so in the context of a built fictional environment and a character's engagement, which nevertheless give us some clues as to how to interpret it. Thus, as De Cauwer points out, montage allows for the opposite experience of the one put forward by Simmel: "in this new experience, a person is no longer a distinct entity which is separated from his or her surroundings, but part of a constantly evolving and changing world."[40]

Eliciting Responsiveness

The form of Benjamin's *Einbahnstraße* equally emphasizes the material world as a constructed, meaningful ecology, but Benjamin is especially interested in revivifying our relation to the environment. If, as we have seen in chapter 5, Benjamin's interest lies in making the (potentially revolutionary) dynamic between an innervated agent and her revivified environment communicable, then how does his own work attempt such a communication? *Einbahnstraße* conjures up a lived material space. Its sixty aphorisms, varying in size between half a page and multiple pages, stand in the text as shops on a road: "Ihre Form," Ernst Bloch writes at the time, "ist die einer Straße, eines Nebeneinander von Häusern und Geschäften, worin Einfälle ausliegen" (is that of a street, a side-by-side of houses and shops in which ideas are on display).[41] Their titles and subtitles refer to shops (e.g., Optiker, Spielwaren), slogans (e.g., "diese Flächen sind zu vermieten"), or objects (e.g., Torso, Stereoskop) and their distinct typography, too, adds a sense of materiality to the work's language.

39 De Cauwer, "Beyond the Stimulus Shield," 110.
40 De Cauwer, "Beyond the Stimulus Shield," 111.
41 Bloch, "Revueform," 276. My translation. This sense of the text as different houses, or stops on one's way through the city, resonates with the various "stations" in Kaiser's *Von morgens bis mitternachts*.

Benjamin's turn to imagery in the content of these vignettes, turning to so-called "thought-images," to ideas entangled in concrete images, rather than to abstract philosophical deliberation, most importantly allows the visceral to penetrate the linguistic realm. As Benjamin's friend Franz Hessel writes in a 1928 review of the text, approaching objects in this way means talking in a language that has "handles like a door."[42] Considering Benjamin's interest in bringing the material world into his text, it is no wonder that the work's distinct form is highly indebted, as different recent critics have pointed out, to modernist artists such as Louis Aragon and constructivists such as László Moholy-Nagy.[43] Benjamin constructs the text materially and spatially, as a city to walk through and to be engaged with physically and affectively. As Tyrus Miller points out, it is a space that is lit with affective meaning. He calls it "a *psychogeographical* mapping of urban space, in which place, movement, and affectivity are bound together in a topological braid, in which inner and outer, subjective and objective elements become indiscernible."[44] Benjamin's focus in *Einbahnstraße* on text as image inspired, as he writes himself, by leaflets and advertisements (*KGA* VIII, 11), his extensive use of imagery, his use of plastic language, attempts to bring the semiotic realm into a more visceral realm. If Benjamin believes that the purely semiotic has lost its power, images, like film, might be better at still touching and moving us. The form itself, then, might make us more responsive.

A Dutch reviewer of *Einbahnstraße* shows how the form of Benjamin's work registered with a contemporaneous reader. Chris de Graaff (1890–1955), a Dutch poet and journalist who would become a Nazi collaborator, wrote a thorough review of *Einbahnstraße*. The review sheds (further) light on the reception of the work, while not in Germany, at least in a country that Benjamin was clearly interested in involving himself with, as attested by the fact that a longer version of the vignette "Kaiserpanorama" (Imperial Panorama) was first published there.[45] This heretofore unknown review of *Einbahnstraße* was published on May 18, 1929, in the Amsterdam-based, liberal newspaper *Algemeen Handelsblad*.[46] It might be the "Feuilleton-length" Dutch review that Benjamin mentions in his letter to Gershom Scholem dated July 24, 1929.

42 Hessel, "Walter Benjamin," in *KGA* VIII, 511; my translation.
43 On Aragon, see Miller, *Modernism*, 43–44. On avant-garde constructivism see Schöttker, *Konstruktiver Fragmentarismus*; and also, concentrating on Moholy-Nagy's work: Schwartz, *Blind Spots*. For more on the distinctive genre of the thought-image see Richter, *Thought-Images*.
44 Miller, *Modernism*, 44.
45 De Graaff, "Duitsche Literatuur." See the appendix for an English translation of the piece. See also Peters, "Benjamin in *i10*."
46 The review does not appear in the section of German and international contemporaneous reviews in the *Kritische Gesamtausgabe* (*KGA* VIII, 500–538).

Indeed, while the title of the newspaper for which De Graaff wrote his article does not match the one given by Benjamin in his letter, the article is one *unter den Strich*, that is, an entire Feuilleton.[47] De Graaff clearly appreciates the work; he ends the review by saying that at least some pages "may be counted among the rare precious possessions of contemporary literature, even if the work is 'merely essayistic.'"[48] More relevant is his view on how it might appear to the reader. Describing Benjamin's style as "free journalism," he argues that the danger is clear: "anyone who can causate to his heart's content about God and about merry-go-rounds, about Shakespeare and neon signs, is sometimes seduced to rattle, with so much freedom, the judgmental and prejudiced bourgeoisie [*burger*]."[49] Indeed, in the next sentence he clearly refers to the French Decadent poets' rallying cry of "épater la bourgeoisie": "Benjamin does not always get away from that tendency to shock [*epateeren*]."[50] It might, of course, have been Benjamin's purpose to shock, but it is nevertheless interesting to see the extent to which this shock registered as such with a Dutch author, who also uses quite strong language to describe it.[51] In other words, bourgeois habits are under attack and are forced into the spotlight. At the same time, however, and this is where De Graaff finds Benjamin's strength, a new, sensitive, loving, intuitive, way of observing

---

47 Benjamin writes to Scholem: "A titre de curiosité erwähne ich, daß ich im Rotterdamschen Courant ein ganzes Feuilleton ausschließlich über die 'Einbahnstraße' gefunden habe" (as a curiosity I mention that I found in the Rotterdam Courant a whole feuilleton exclusively on "Einbahnstraße"). I, just as the editors of the *Kritische Gesamtausgabe*, have not been able to retrieve any review matching Benjamin's description. But, the *Algemeen Handelsblad*, in which De Graaff's review was published a month before Benjamin's letter (earlier non-German reviews had been published in Polish and French as early as March 1928), had the surtitle *Nieuwe Amsterdamsche Courant*, with which it had merged in 1831. Might Benjamin have been mistaken about which newspaper the review was published in? Benjamin, *Gesammelte Briefe*, 469; my translation. Howard Eiland and Michael W. Jennings explain what the feuilleton looked like in Benjamin's time: "the feuilleton appeared on the bottom third of most pages of the paper, demarcated by a printed line." Eiland and Jennings, *Walter Benjamin*, 258.

48 "Wie gevoel heeft voor . . . dit proza, . . . zal erkennen, dat zulk een bladzijde tot de zeldzame kostbaarheden der nieuwe literatuur mag worden gerekend, al is dit werk dan 'maar essayistisch.'"

49 "Wie naar hartelust kan causeeren over God en over draaimolens, over Shakespeare en lichtreclame komt wel eens in de verleiding met zooveel vrijheid den aan ontelbare oordeelen en vooroordeelen gebonden burger te overbluffen."

50 "Benjamin ontkomt niet altijd aan die zucht tot epateeren."

51 He says: "Hij . . . bekogelt graag, naar de mode der salon-bolsjewieken glazen huisjes, zonder te bedenken dat hij zelf allerminst in een burcht woont" (He . . . likes to throw, in the manner of champagne socialists, stones at glass houses without realizing that he himself far from lives in a fortress).

and describing the world is presented by Benjamin. *Einbahnstraße* does not present us with new wisdoms, he states. "Besides," De Graaff writes beautifully, "how could the new ever be *wise*?"[52] Herein De Graaff seems to sum up the *clou* of Benjamin's argument in *Einbahnstraße*. The work is not trying to bring forth new information, but rather attempts to shed a new light on old objects. What is new for De Graaff is first the form—he mentions the "visual" titles especially—which seems to capture new ways of seeing the old. And this new way of seeing is not intellectual but visceral and affective; he uses terms such as "animating," "intuitive," "spiritual," "personal," "secretive," "tender," "vital" when describing the ways in which Benjamin presents objects. For De Graaff, the way in which Benjamin captures the child-like view is the biggest accomplishment of *Einbahnstraße*. He quotes "Karussellfahrendes Kind" in whole and talks about this "simple and yet so profound children's adventure" as "brought to the surface, shining delicately and mysteriously."[53] For this Dutch reviewer, in other words, Benjamin not only shocks the bourgeoisie but also revivifies old objects into new images, as if viewed through the eyes of a child. Benjamin not only brings the reader's attention to his or her own habits and norms, but also attempts—and succeeds in De Graaff's view—to revivify the environment and remind the reader of a more visceral, responsive, affective engagement, thereby hinting at, if not achieving, new ways for us to act toward familiar objects. Indeed, Hessel writes that from Benjamin's words "spricht dauernde Einladung, mitzutun, mitzumachen" (comes a constant invitation to join in, to participate).[54] What is thus renewed here is not the object but our response to it.

Nevertheless, De Graaff raises an important question when he wonders whether Benjamin's images would ever appeal to a "level-headed grown-up."[55] In his opinion, it takes a certain predisposition to recognize their beauty; others would just shrug their shoulders. Indeed, if Benjamin believes that new environments and art might make us more responsive, there is nevertheless no reason to believe that people will engage rather than keep living their habitual lives. If art and the new are meant to make us responsive, we already need to be responsive to art and new environments to become even more responsive through them; the choice to ignore is always there. As Felski writes: "the possibility of gaining any kind of knowledge through literature requires a prior acknowledging, a

---

52   "Nieuwe wijsheid moet men in dit boekje niet zoeken. Trouwens, hoe zou het nieuwe ooit *wijs* kunnen zijn?"

53   In the original: "eenvoudige en toch zoo diepgaande kinderavontuur" and "teeder en geheimzinnig glanzend."

54   Hessel, "Walter Benjamin," in *KGA* VIII, 512; my translation.

55   "Groote menschen die alleen nog maar met hun nuchter verstand kunnen denken. . . ."

willingness to be perceptive."[56] Yet, as I explored earlier in this section, it was certainly Benjamin's intention to construct a text that could invoke such an engagement. He was not just attempting to give a more responsive view of real-world objects: he was also attempting to turn bourgeois readers into innervated agents through literary form. Benjamin's form is designed to elicit responsiveness by creating a more visceral linguistic realm. Successful or not, Benjamin attempted to revivify the relationship between the reader and the text with the hope that her innervation may carry over into her relationship with the environment at large.[57]

Scaffolding the Novel

Other people take an important part in keeping literary forms dynamic. The guiding hand of a teacher or another experienced reader helps turn unfamiliar forms into more negotiable texts. They can either teach us ways to read a particular text, or teach us critical faculties that can be applied to a range of texts.[58] But a particular guidance into singular texts is often also part of the text we hold in our hands. The early reception of Franz Kafka's novels, if you will allow me the detour, offers a good illustration. It is not novel to point to the influence Max Brod had on Kafka's early reception. Had Brod not acted counter to Kafka's instructions to burn his manuscripts, had he not edited, published, and publicized Kafka's novels as he did, often improving their readability (and thereby acting counter to current standards of editorial practice), Kafka would most probably not have found fame as quickly as he did, if at all. However, another aspect of Brod's influence is less frequently commented on, namely that his interpretative paratexts would have helped readers struggling with Kafka's novels. This is clear in an early review of *Das Schloss* (The Castle, 1926). In 1927, the Dutch and Jewish literary critic Siegfried van Praag published a curious review of *Das Schloss*. In this review he states that the novel itself is not fascinating; the only fascinating thing about the novel for the critic is *why* someone would write it. Thus Van Praag writes that before even finishing the novel he turns to Brod's interpretation, ultimately repeating it

---

56 Felski, *Hooked*, 153.

57 Of course, the move from text to environment, as Alfred North Whitehead has noted with "inert knowledge," is a whole problem in its own. Whitehead, *Aims of Education*. See also Auyoung, "Becoming Sensitive," 162.

58 Elaine Auyoung has recently noted that too often literary scholars confuse "virtuosic performance of critical expertise" with teaching such expertise: "This time-honored approach to instruction presumes that students who lack critical acuity can develop it by observing what skilled critics, using acuity they already possess, are able to perceive in literary texts." And, I would suggest, such performances also mistake guidance into a particular text with teaching critical skills that can be applied to a variety of texts. Auyoung, "Becoming Sensitive," 158.

wholesale in the review, saying that he thinks Brod's interpretation seems "wholly correct."[59] If *Das Schloss* is an enigma to Van Praag, then Brod offers a shortcut to interpretation, specifying its "use."[60] This may be an extreme example, but it nevertheless shows how Brod helped early readers make sense of Kafka's texts.

The publishing history of Kafka in German further shows the way in which (German-language) readers have slowly been entrusted with increasingly complex forms of Kafka's novels. First, audiences were presented with the highly edited, more coherent texts of Brod's editions in the 1920s. Over time we were given increasingly more of the complexity of Kafka's original manuscripts, to end up with a facsimile edition of these manuscripts in their unfinished, fragmentary, and unedited shape, including deletions.[61] In the case of *Der Process* (The Trial, 1925) this new edition does not even sort its chapters, presenting them instead as separate booklets that could be read in any order. The publication history of Kafka's novels is thus a history of, in Lev Vygotsky's terminology, ever fewer scaffolding. "As caregivers and educators adjust the level of challenges for those who learn (how to read, for example), skill and challenge develop in tandem in what Vygotsky calls a 'zone of proximal development.'"[62] But even if Kafka's editors have (on a different timescale than Vygotsky describes) slowly adjusted the challenge for his German-language readers, paratexts such as introductions by editors and translators and explanatory notes remain in place to potentially scaffold the engagement of new readers.[63]

But what if form is not underspecified but rather overspecified, overly familiar, more akin to the bourgeois interiors that precipitate the rigid

---

59 Van Praag, "Opstellen en critieken," July 8, 1927.

60 This includes Brod's autobiographical novel in which a character based on Kafka by the name of Richard Garta appears. In a review of this book, Van Praag writes that it is only interesting in as far as it sheds light on Kafka. Van Praag, "Opstellen en critieken," April 19, 1929.

61 This edition, overseen by Roland Reuß and Peter Staengle, is not yet completed. See also Koelb, "Editions"; and Duttlinger, "Kafka in Oxford."

62 Kukkonen, *Probability Designs*, 154.

63 We might read the epic framing of *Berlin Alexanderplatz*, starting each chapter with the narrator's summary of what is about to happen, in a similar way as a scaffolding and thus as mitigating the more foreign and confrontational structure of montage. The adaptation of Kaiser's *Von morgens bis mitternachts* to film might also be read as a mode of scaffolding its original. Though certainly not devoid of formal complexity, the film adapts the story, as Cynthia Walk argues, "to the conventions of the detective film, the most popular serial film genre of the postwar period . . . redistributed into a proto-typical five-act crime scenario, representing 1) crime, 2) discovery, 3) escape, 4) chase, and 5) capture." Walk, "Cross-Media Exchange," 186.

habits that Benjamin wanted to get away from than to the unfamiliar city? On the face of it, Baum's *Menschen im Hotel* has a more familiar form than the ones discussed before. It relies on the familiar topos of a love story as well as the stock figures of the diva, the gentleman thief, and the sexy stenographer. Rather than underspecified, it seems overspecified; we know what to expect and how to proceed. Yet the serialized form in which Baum's *Menschen im Hotel* first appeared suggests a more dynamic form. As we will see, its serialization gave it the sense of a work in progress, of an evolving construction, one open to co-construction; its serialization was meant to elicit a more social reception; and its serialization brought its narrative into direct contact with readers' everyday concerns as expressed by the ads and various (news) articles and photographs it was surrounded with. Looking at Baum's text in its original context, then, allows us to see that this text, too, allowed for a far more dynamic engagement than one might initially expect.

The novel was published first in its entirety in serialized form in the biweekly *Berliner Illustrirte Zeitung* (*BIZ*), a newspaper that had a readership of approximately 1.8 million at the end of the 1920s.[64] Following the success of Baum's *Stud. chem. Helene Willfüer* (1928), the serialization of which started in 1928 but led into 1929, and which is said to have increased the circulation of the *BIZ* by 200,000, *Menschen im Hotel* was published in the *BIZ* from the end of March 1929 in fourteen instalments, ending at the end of June of that year.[65] Serialization has its effect on the structure of novels. The multiple plotlines of different characters in *Menschen im Hotel* seem, as Lawrence Jones points out about serial novels more generally, precipitated by the need to "fill 20 numbers and yet maintain action and narrative interest in each number."[66] Equally, the "need to catch readers' interests at the very beginning" and "to keep a forward momentum, often by creating suspense," is evident in *Menschen im Hotel*.[67] Baum's novel not only brings us straight into the action of the hotel from its first moments, but it also contains several suspenseful moments, such as Grusinskaja's attempted suicide and Gaigern's death.

The serialization of *Menschen im Hotel* also brings it in close kinship to *Berlin Alexanderplatz*. Döblin's novel was also serialized, although never

---

64 Deák, *Left-Wing Intellectuals*, 286. According to Peter de Mendelssohn the magazine's circulation reached 1.95 million in 1931 (De Mendelssohn, *Zeitungsstadt Berlin*, 110). The paper was published on Thursdays but bore the date of the next Sunday (De Mendelssohn, *Zeitungsstadt Berlin*, 364).

65 The first issue in which it appeared bore the date March 31, 1929. For the increase in circulation, see King, *Best-Sellers*, 12; and Barndt, *Sentiment und Sachlichkeit*, 65.

66 Jones, "Periodicals," n.p.

67 Jones, "Periodicals," n.p.

in its entirety.[68] In the *Frankfurter Zeitung*, as Malika Maskarinec points out, Döblin's epic was "largely reduced to the plot-related elements of the story of Biberkopf."[69] There was no need for the "heterogeneous elements" that make up an important part of Döblin's montage, "because they are inevitably supplied by the surrounding print in which the serial appeared."[70] She therefore argues that Döblin's montage has more to do with the literary history of the serialization of nineteenth-century novels than it does with film techniques as is the more common argument. Döblin's montage technique goes further than bringing in the obviously heterogeneous elements that Maskarenic focuses on in her reading of the beginning of book 2, if only because its novelty lies in bringing those elements of montage into the book itself. But her analysis does allow us to see how the serialization of Baum's novel equally embeds it in the extratextual experiences that are provided by the surrounding print.[71]

To take the first installment of *Menschen im Hotel* (in no. 13 of 1929) as an example: it is surrounded by all kinds of advertisements for alcohol, clothes, and personal care products, but also, for example, by photos of US President Herbert Hoover's inauguration. And affinities immediately light up between Baum's text and its extratextual companions. The advertisement placed in the middle of the story, for the new issue of Ullstein's other magazine *Uhu*, announcing "44 Fragen die ins Herz des modernen Eheproblems zielen" (44 questions that get at the heart of modern marriage problems) becomes conversant with Baum's characters Kringelein and Preyßing leaving their wives behind in town, to find excitement, and other women, in the city.[72] And if the first installment of *Menschen im Hotel* ends with a perspiring Grusinskaja doing her curtain calls, the advertisement on the next page, with a drawing of a female field hockey player, states that "wer Sport richtig treibt— / muß sein Haar richtig doppelt pflegen / denn Transpiration und Staub müssen gründlich entfernt werden, um das Haar nicht spröde und glanzlos zu machen" (they who perform sport properly— / must properly condition their hair twofold / because perspiration and dust must be removed thoroughly so as

---

68 Maskarinec, "Rethinking Montage," 125.
69 Maskarinec, "Rethinking Montage," 128.
70 Maskarinec, "Rethinking Montage," 128.
71 Maskarinec further argues that an emphasis on montage in *Berlin Alexanderplatz* over its plot "turns a blind eye to its highly gendered violence" (119). In reverse, criticism's (gendered) emphasis on the plot of *Menschen im Hotel* as "popular literature," whose storylines so clearly align with *Berlin Alexanderplatz*'s "absurdly sensationalist storyline: a story of thievery, betrayal, prostitution, and murder," overlooks its formal qualities (126). More research needs to be done on *Menschen im Hotel*'s serialized form and its context.
72 *Berliner Illustrirte Zeitung*, 38, no. 13 (1929), 521.

not to make the hair brittle and lackluster).[73] The text in serialized form thus was in direct conversation, intentionally or not, with readers' concerns expressed in (or provoked by) the extratextual advertisements and news articles.[74] Far from a static form, the serialized novel as embedded in the extratextual world of the newspaper afforded new and unexpected connections.

But to come back to the social affordances of modernist texts, the serialization of *Menschen im Hotel* opened it up to more social engagements in various ways. First, as mentioned above, the *BIZ* had a readership of close to two million, giving Baum's serial novel a wider readership than it would have had if it were published as a book only. Second, serialization allows for cliff-hangers, and the *BIZ*'s readers thus had time to anticipate, often together, the content of future installments. The evolving, as yet open-ended form of the novel elicited participation. Third, serialization means a more synchronized reception. The reception is paced over various days, weeks, months, or years, in which people read in similar time frames. As Patricia Okker and Nancy West write: "Unlike readers of bound novels who proceed at different paces, readers of serial fiction must experience the narrative together, reading installments and anticipating subsequent ones as a group."[75] Fourth, serialization means that readers think they have, and in the case of some famous examples such as Charles Dickens's *Martin Chuzzlewit* (1843–44) and Anthony Trollope's *The Last Chronicle of Barset* (1866–67) often did have, influence over the storytelling.[76] In Baum's memoirs, these last three aspects of serialization—anticipation, synchronized reading, and perceived influence on the narrative—are present in a letter she received from a group of her readers:

> Ich erinnere mich noch, daß ich eines Montagmorgens auf meinem Schreibtisch einen Brief vorfand. Persönlich. Durch Eilboten. "Drei Tage sind vergangen, seitdem Baron Gaigern gestorben ist, und wir

---

73 *Berliner Illustrirte Zeitung*, 38, no. 13 (1929), 524–25.

74 That the *BIZ* was not against blurring the lines between literary fiction and advertisement is clear from the same issue in which the first installment of *Menschen im Hotel* first appeared. When the *BIZ* imagines a magazine without advertisements, they use the main character of Baum's previous novel for a fake advertisement of cigarettes: "stud. chem. Helene Willfüer / hat für die nikotinarme Fabrik "Hektor" eine neue Schlankheitszigarette "Ford" erfunden, die garantiert über 1 Proz. Karlsbadersalz und echtes Marienbader Klima enthält" (stud. chem. Helene Willfüer / has invented a new slimming cigarette called "Ford" for the nicotine-low factory "Hektor," which is guaranteed to contain over 1 percent salt from Carlsbad and genuine Marienbad climate). *Berliner Illustrirte Zeitung* 38, no. 13 (1929), 548.

75 Okker and West, "Serialization," 733–34. See also Turner, "Telling."

76 Okker and West, "Serialization," 732–33.

können es noch immer nicht fassen." . . . "Wir die Unterzeichneten, können den Verlust dieses lieben, schönen jungen Menschen nicht ertragen, er hatte in unser eintöniges Dasein so viel Glanz und Abenteuer gebracht. Sehr geehrte Frau Baum, wir möchten, daß sie [sic] ihn in der nächsten Nummer wieder zum Leben bringen." Die guten Damen gaben mir dann allerlei Anregungen, wie ich das Wunder vollbringen könne. Es folgten dreißig Unterschriften—ein ganzer Frauenverein, ein Strickzirkel oder irgend so etwas.[77]

[I remember one Monday morning finding a letter on my desk. Private. By express messenger. "Three days have passed since Baron Gaigern died, and we still cannot believe it." . . . "We the undersigned, cannot bear the loss of this dear, beautiful young person, he had brought so much sparkle and adventure to our humdrum existence. Dear Mrs. Baum, we would like you to bring him back to life in the next issue." The good ladies then gave me all sorts of suggestions as to how I could accomplish this miracle. Thirty signatures followed—a whole women's club, a knitting circle or something like that.]

The anecdote is suggestive not only of the sociality of reading but also of the specific (perceived) affordance of serialization of influencing the narrative: can they save their favorite character? While we should hesitate in taking Baum's anecdote at face value—Baum, after years of working for Ullstein, a house famous for its early marketing strategies, was well aware of how publicity worked—we do have numerous similar anecdotes about readers attempting and succeeding to influence pieces published in serialization, especially from Victorian literature.[78] Moreover, the serialization was meant precisely to make the novel a topic of conversation. In his memoir of the Ullstein Publishing House, Hermann Ullstein, vice-president of the publishing house at the time, describes the serialization of Baum's novel as a commercial strategy in part relying on social pressure: "not having read it [in serialized form], you may have suffered from being unable to join in conversation in which its characters are being

---

77 Baum, *Es war alles ganz anders*, 384–85. My translation. Another anecdote of reading Baum together is recounted in Kerstin Brandt's *Sentiment und Sachlichkeit*. Ruth Clark Lert, Baum's daughter-in-law, recounts telling Baum in their first meeting about her first reading of the "scandalous" *Helene Willfüer*: "my best girlfriend and I would sit in the locked bathroom and read *Helene Willfüer* together" (114). Baum tells this story in generalized form in her memoirs (*Es war alles ganz anders*, 349; see also Barndt, *Sentiment und Sachlichkeit*, 114, n. 103).

78 See, e.g., Jones, "Periodicals," n.p.; Okker and West, "Serialization," 732–33.

discussed and the book itself praised or condemned."[79] Discussion of the novel and its characters was thus built into the novel's presentation through its serialization. It pushed for a more synchronized social reception. Just as the mosaic form of the novel gives space to various characters and shows how the hotel is a dynamic space animated by various engagements, so the novel's serialization intended to make reading the novel a dynamic, social experience, as well. That is, even if the novel's form was far more familiar in form than Kaiser's, Döblin's, or Benjamin's were, then through its serialized form it was nevertheless not only perceived to afford co-construction, but indeed also afforded collective exploration, and interacted dynamically with readers' extratextual lives through the ads, photographs, and articles of the *BIZ*.

If the serialization of Baum's novel suggested an on-going construction, it is not the only text in which this process is on display. The film adaptation of *Von morgens bis mitternachts*, for example, shows what Thomas Elsaesser has called the "tactical immediacy" of expressionism.[80] The roughly painted clothes, make-up, and décor deliberately betray the human *Handarbeit* (handwork) from which they stem. These brushstrokes show the artificiality of the film—as "houses," for example, consist of roughly painted canvases. *Malte Laurids Brigge*, too, in its emphasis on Malte's process of writing, and as a fictional collection of found papers, asks us to reflect on Rilke's writing and editing.

This *Handarbeit* brings us into closer contact with its creators. Vittorio Gallese, one of the researchers of the so-called Parma group that "discovered" the mirror neuron, suggests that art is often read as a trace of one or multiple artists: "The deer track stands for the deer despite its not being present."[81] He draws here on research in which motor simulation was evoked when people watched the visual works of Lucio Fontana and Franz Kline.[82] The research suggests that an imaginary mimicking is going on when we watch a painting, of the movements that we imagine have produced it. It suggests that the traces of human artistic skill at least also engage us motorically.

Questions about the importance of the traces of artists were also present in German intellectual circles of the 1920s in response to new media. In *i10* (1927–29), a short-lived multilingual, avant-garde magazine for which Benjamin wrote five articles, appeared a discussion around the topic of the difference between painting and the new media of

---

79   Ullstein, *Rise and Fall*, 96. I use here the German spelling of Hermann Ullstein's name rather than the English spelling "Herman" used in his English-language memoir.
80   Elsaesser, *Weimar Cinema and After*, 41.
81   Gallese, "Brain, Body, Habit," 389.
82   Umiltà et al., "Abstract Art"; and Sbriscia-Fioretti et al., "ERP Modulation."

film and especially photography. Initiated by László Moholy-Nagy, the magazine's editor for film and photography, a first article on the subject appeared by Ernő Kállai in the fourth issue (1927). Responses were printed in issue 6, by Piet Mondriaan, Wassily Kandinsky, Moholy-Nagy, and others. The important aspect for this discussion is that they were arguing about the extent to which the physical labor of the artist was still present in the technologies of photography and film. In short, Kállai's argument was that the difference between painting and photography lay in *Faktur*. In painting there is, he argues, a "Stofflichkeit und somit plastische Wirksamkeit der Faktur" (materiality, and therefore a plastic effect of the facture) that is absent in photography.[83] In other words, the texture of painting shows the engagement of an artist with his material; photography only captures some of that in collage, Kállai argues. Moholy-Nagy's critique of Kállai's argument about *Faktur* is clear and succinct when he writes that Kállai's definition of *Faktur* is too narrow. In the first paragraph of his response, Moholy-Nagy writes (for reasons of typography, he did not use capital letters):

> die art des herstellungsprozesses zeigt sich am fertigen objekt. wie er sich zeigt, nennen wir *faktur*. es wäre verfehlt, faktur nur das zu nennen, was als abtastbare oberfläche vorliegt, nur deswegen weil die früheren manuellen techniken meist gleichzeitig einen tastwert darstellten.
>
> [the nature of the production process is reflected in the finished object. how it appears is what we call facture. it would be wrong to call facture only what is present as a tactile surface, only because the earlier manual techniques usually constituted a tactility at the same time.][84]

That is to say that, at least for some of these writers, it was exactly the contact with another body present through the traces of physical engagement in *Faktur* that was at stake in photography. In the film version of *Von morgens bis mitternachts*, in Döblin's *Berlin Alexanderplatz*, in Baum's *Menschen im Hotel*, and more ambiguously in Rilke's *Malte Laurids Brigge*, such *Faktur* as production process is overtly present. If we are to believe Gallese's research, this means we are mimicking, even if only imaginarily, these movements of creation. But if this research is correct, it only highlights an aspect that should be evident anyway: that the foregrounding of construction envelops the gestures of a creative act. If we are initially overwhelmed by some of the experimental form of

---

83 Kállai, "Malerei und Fotografie," 153.
84 Moholy-Nagy, "Diskussion," 233. My translation.

modernism, we are also participating in these artists' skillful construction of an evolving form.

Conclusion

It is evident from the history of our discipline and modernism's reception in arts and culture more generally, that people have found ways into modernist texts. The relative difficulty of modernist form has not kept us from engaging, from making modernist form our own. If modernist form—even if I deem it to include more "popular" forms such as that of Baum's *Menschen im Hotel*—is more open than most other literary forms, it is a process that needs a particularly responsive reader, someone willing to give themselves over to a certain uncertainty of what a text will have to offer.[85] But if, as Baßler and Horn writing about *Berlin Alexanderplatz* say, "we keep at it" we experience the very process of familiarization that the likes of Malte, Biberkopf, and Grusinskaja also experience. What may have felt strange at first, slowly starts to make sense. It shows the kind of responsiveness, the slow, careful, and attentive attitude that reading unfamiliar form asks for. And it suggests that literature is open to a more social reception than it is often given credit for. The often-expressed openness or underspecification of modernist form may be overwhelming, but, with some help and effort, also allows us to engage closely and dynamically, and experience the same familiarization in habituating modernist form as we experience in making new urban environments our own.

Moreover, while my focus in the other chapters has been on how the content of these various texts explores familiarization and habituation, then my argument here has been that modernist form also brings our attention to the fact that our environments are constructed ones. Modernist forms express the material construction of our realities as well as the evolving, on-going, often social processes of meaning-making that underlie it, of bodies adjusting their skills to ongoing forms to make and unmake, tweak and scaffold them in the process. I have likened modernist form to the ecological niche as a set of affordances, because as the concept of the niche is meant to express, modernist form highlights its own on-going, evolving creation, and its openness to familiarization, participation, revivification, and co-construction.

---

85 For work on uncertainty within a cognitive literary framework, see McBriar, "Watchman."

Concluding Remarks

That warm encounters, aided by the topography of the big city, can make us more responsive to our surroundings is an idea that extends beyond Baum—and in some ways Benjamin—to other texts of the period, for example to Irmgard Keun's (1905–1982) *Das kunstseidene Mädchen* (The Artificial Silk Girl, 1932). Here its 18-year-old protagonist Doris, whose diary the novel is composed of, regularly visits Herr Brenner, a neighbor with whom she seems to have a sexual relationship. But because Brenner was blinded in the war, she also relays her daily experiences in Berlin to him.[1] She writes: "Ich sammle Sehen für ihn. Ich gucke mir alle Straßen an und Lokale und Leute und Laternen. Und dann merke ich mir mein Sehen und bringe es ihm mit" (I collect seeing for him. I walk around the streets and the restaurants and among people and lanterns. And then I try to remember my seeing and bring it to him).[2] She lends him her eyes; she tells him in much detail and in full color about her experiences on the *Kurfürstendamm* and the *Tauentzienstraße*, about KaDeWe and the men she sleeps with.[3] Later, when she hears he is about to be put into a home by his wife, she also takes him out into Berlin. But as much as she guides *him* through Berlin, first orally, then physically, these descriptions and his questions make her pay attention to her experiences as well. When he asks what she looks like, for example, she is reminded that she might have a fat stain on her behind.[4] When he asks about the stars, she not only lies to him about the presence of stars but also thinks: "Ich habe Sterne sehr gern, aber ich merke sie fast nie. Wenn man blind wird, weiß man ja wohl erst, daß man furchtbar viel vergessen hat zu sehen" (I love stars, but I hardly ever notice them. I guess when you're blind, you realize how much you forgot to see).[5] Who, we should ask, is teaching whom to see here? If Ingold and Gibson, as we saw in

---

1   Keun, *Das kunstseidene Mädchen*, 96. All translations of this source by Kathie von Ankum: Keun, *Artificial Silk Girl*, here, 63.
2   Keun, *Das kunstseidene Mädchen*, 97; Keun, *Artificial Silk Girl*, 64; translation altered.
3   The descriptions cover about 20 pages of a 215-page print. Keun, *Das kunstseidene Mädchen*, 96–116; Keun, *Artificial Silk Girl*, 63–80.
4   Keun, *Das kunstseidene Mädchen*, 97; Keun, *Artificial Silk Girl*, 64.
5   Keun, *Das kunstseidene Mädchen*, 115–16; Keun, *Artificial Silk Girl*, 76.

chapter 3, talk about an "education of attention," whose attention to the environment is being educated?

Keun's scene also points to how my reading of German-language modernist texts may be productively extended to readings of the role of disability and its imaginaries in German modernism. It extends my point about how different bodies, that is, different kinetic-affective engagements, point to different worlds, and how an attention to how other people engage with the world shows us new affordances and thus new ways of engaging. Further research on disability and its imaginaries in German modernism would be an important way of extending and further complicating my questions about recalcitrant worlds and how we come to inhabit them, especially about norms of engagement and how we relate to those norms. The mass disabling event of World War I, and the literature that engages with it, can be productively read through such a lens.

In this study, I have explored the importance given to embodied experiences in German modernism. I have investigated the ways in which its authors think about our *Umwelt*, that is, our kinetic-affective engagement with the environment, and the ways in which encounters with the unfamiliar and other people may elicit new engagements. Like with the blind neighbor from *Das kunstseidene Mädchen*, the unfamiliar environment that is the modern environment in these texts may be understood as debilitating us, or this lack of skill may be understood to help us open up to new ways of seeing and acting.[6]

The texts discussed in the preceding chapters have presented different ways of addressing the question of habituating modernism. If we cannot start over with exploring as newborns, how can we come to flourish within the ever-changing societies that we live in? Heidegger shows the difficulty of the task. If we are entangled in the socio-material environments that we grow up in, if knowledge is embedded, simply *deciding* to act differently and sustain that practice is very difficult, if not impossible.

Kaiser's play shows that money may be a temporary substitute for skill. His ecstatic experiences—in sports, dance, alcohol—offer an absorbed engagement away from the rigid and boring familiarity of small-town life with its modern conditions of labor and its repetitive gestures. Yet the cashier's ecstasy only marks an attempt at controlling and manipulating his environment that ultimately proves temporary and unsatisfactory. Such ecstasy that is inattentive to the immediate social and material environment proves empty. If Martin's film shows the ecstasy as something that is a challenge to the authorities, Kaiser's original play suggests that the cashier's crime is rather his inability to meaningfully connect to

---

6   Disabilities, importantly, are not objective states of the body, but are issues caused in the interaction with socio-material environments, environments that are often not accommodating.

other people: that being part of an environment means responsiveness, not control. In Kaiser's play thus lies the kernel of a social responsiveness that is further developed in the other texts.

Rilke's positive suggestion is task-oriented play. Malte does not use writing only to give meaning to his experiences in Paris: he also uses the virtual space of fiction to experiment with other people's practices. Like a bird sensitively attuning its movements to the evolving form of the nest, Malte builds himself a fictional niche of texts that do not support his habits but elicit a more dynamic self. We never get to see him get out of that virtual topology. Writing gets him away from thinking and into reenacting his environment, but it remains virtual and, consequently, non-committal. Malte does not seem to want to commit to any particular form of life, but ironically, that itself is the organizing task around which he organizes his practices.

Benjamin suggests that we find a way of revivifying our relation to the environment through an innervation of the body. He explores sensitive awareness and responsiveness to the environment and its effect on the body, in which immediate affect elicits actions and gets us out of our head and out of our habits. The question that arises is how we get reanimated into a state of play, action, and/or exploration. The modern environment and its technologies, the impulses and images it produces, seem to do just that for Benjamin, seem to solicit the primary affective-kinetic dynamics that form the basis of us as animated bodies. Benjamin also shows the importance of passion. The images of fire, of Don Juan and Casanova, and his excitement over Lācis, show that sexual excitement is not merely a metaphor for the kind of engagement he is after, but also sets the world aflame. For Benjamin, we should tune into the dynamically affected beings we are; turn to what excites us and turn away from what does not. If Malte wants to be no one, Benjamin wants us to realign ourselves with the environment under the terms that our affective-kinetic dynamics dictate.

The modern environment thus becomes an opportunity. An opportunity to assess our habitual practices and to do things differently. Nevertheless, this is difficult. On the basis of our explorations as children and later in life we have learned to find our way in the world and have found ourselves. It is no wonder, then, that Heidegger uses such a moment of crisis, of anxiety, for resoluteness. An environment that is *unzuhanden* is *the* place to recommit to our goals and practices. If Benjamin wants us to listen to our bodies' responses, Heidegger wants us to commit to one body of practices with full sensitivity and attention. Heidegger reminds us that it matters *for what* we adapt. Both he and Benjamin choose action over deliberation, but where Benjamin wants us to bypass thought to feel, to always make sure we still feel good about what we do, Heidegger wants us to commit to one way of life and perform it skillfully.

Döblin's text implicitly offers a counterexample to Heidegger's thesis. Biberkopf's stubborn adherence to being "anständig" gets him into continuous trouble. Rather than listening to his friends and being cleareyed about what his social environments afford him, he prefers to go at it alone. Other people are treated ambiguously in Döblin in the full knowledge that their influence can be both good and bad. But a knowledge of them, not theoretical but practical, is nevertheless essential. At worst, they show us how to avoid pitfalls, at best they help us achieve our goals. Sometimes, Döblin shows, we do need to adjust our ways of seeing to be able to flourish in our environments.

Baum opens up the apparent dichotomy between habit and responsiveness. She suggests that familiar others can sustain us in finding a meaningful engagement with the world, can help us revivify old practices for a new environment. If Kringelein is responsive in part because of his nature and in part because he is about to die, a seemingly more sustainable way into responsiveness is presented by Grusinskaja and Gaigern (and hinted at in Dr. Otternschlag) in whom others elicit a more positive past than the ones they are stuck in. Does Baum present us with the middle ground between Benjamin and Heidegger? She shows how the other who elicits a shared past, and the warmth that this shared past brings, can make us into more dynamic and responsive people. The best love, she suggests, can sustain a practice that brings us in touch both with who we were and who we can be given the new circumstances. The warmth between Grusinskaja and Gaigern both is grounded in their pasts and opens that past up to a different future. Even if this relation does not last, the dynamics of *Menschen im Hotel* shows the "daily webs that are spun between people, dropped, and picked up again" that Simmel concedes might exist in, and might be nurturing about, the modern environment.[7]

Moreover, if these texts especially investigate the ways in which we can make new environments our own, their forms seem to want to direct our attention to the ways in which our worlds are affordances, the dynamic product of the ongoing interaction between bodies and materials. They mimic not only the evolving forms of our human niches, emphasizing its co-constructed nature, but also the way in which our environments can be revivified under new engagements and familiarization. Even if Baum's *Menschen im Hotel* seems more familiar, its serialization brings it into a dynamic constellation with the extratextual concerns expressed in the ads and articles that surround it on the page and, through the gaps between installments, opens it up to ongoing social engagement.

This study has aimed to do what these texts struggle with and in many ways embrace, namely, to let the past rub against the present. Just

---

7 Simmel, "Soziologie der Sinne," 1026; Simmel, "Sociology of the Senses," 110."

as habits rub against the modern environment in the texts discussed in this monograph, and put both in relief, this study is itself an attempt at bringing modernist texts in conversation with contemporary theories of embodied cognition. Like Malte using medieval histories for a new world, so I have aimed not only to show how contemporary theories of embodied cognition could illuminate different aspects of modernism, but also how modernist texts can contribute to questions in cognition today. The experience of literature, like all experience, is a dynamic tool that can either die a silent death in one of the far corners of our memories or alight with meaning by new, relevant circumstances.

The modernist texts that this study investigates help bring questions of affect, ethics, other people, and human flourishing to the center of human animation. If we are the worldly animated bodies that Heidegger says we are, then our affective engagement with our social and material worlds is also always already entangled with ethical and existential questions. Habits and skills are not merely sets of bodily knowledge but are the ways in which we find ourselves in the world amongst other people. In other words, if meaning is use, if we enact the world, then investigations into embodied cognition are also always existentialist investigations.

Thus I submit that we need more studies into the existential questions that arise from contemporary approaches in the cognitive sciences such as enactivism. Yet we will not find answers to such questions merely in everyday, habitual use. Nor will we find them in developmental studies, which are focused on how children are first enveloped into the socio-cultural fold. Rather, what we need to explore further is the moment of adult embodied not-knowing. While, as we have seen, there are some exciting explorations of responsiveness to be found in Sheets-Johnstone's and Kiverstein's work, among others, we nevertheless need to spend more time investigating the moments in which our habits are frustrated; more time on the uncertain, the recalcitrant, the unexpected, and the unfamiliar. Modernism, whether literary, philosophical, or both, is a privileged place for such questions, because it provides testimony and investigation of the moments in which everyday habits are resisted by a recalcitrant world. As I have shown, modernist texts are interested precisely in the moments when movement breaks down, when the cogs in the wheel that is the dynamic coupling between environment and body gets stuck. They investigate the experience of people entering unfamiliar territory, of encountering the recalcitrant, and of those possessing habits that provide little grip on the current situation. At the same time, these texts provide explorations of how to get habituated to new situations. These authors are interested in how to behave when faced with an uncertainty about how the environment might respond. It is for this reason that I have turned to these texts to think about how we might resituate ourselves in changing environments.

This question might now be even more relevant than it was one hundred years ago. The more global our society, the more people choose to work, study, and/or start a life in foreign countries, the more people are uprooted by the effects of war, or by economic or environmental destruction, the more the question of how one finds a place for oneself in foreign societies determines our lives. An account of cognition that situates it socially, culturally, and materially has an important part to play in answering such questions, but it has to also look beyond its fascination with everyday habits, with embodied coping, and with skillful practices, to look at those moments in which the world becomes opaque to the touch.

At the same time, by focusing on embodied cognition in these modernist texts, this monograph has attempted to re-calibrate the focus in German modernist studies on the overwhelming, distancing, and isolating aspects of the modern environment. I do not wish to deny the importance of these aspects for understanding the modern experience and its literary responses. I only hope to have shown that they need not be necessary aspects but might have been, at least in part, also the result of unfamiliarity, of a lack of corporeal knowledge. Re-thinking the environment in these terms opens up these negative aspects to mitigation through use, habit, and skill. Thus by placing these texts in dialogue with contemporary theories of embodied cognition, we are able to put into relief how Baum, Döblin, Rilke, Kaiser, and Benjamin all explore the ways in which we can become responsive to the environment so as to take advantage of its possibilities and avoid its pitfalls.

This monograph has looked at questions of re-inhabiting as they were raised by these texts, reminding us that a familiarity with the ability to perform normative, skillful, and habitual movements is a site of privilege, the loss of which can be immensely unsettling. Foreign environments threaten our meaningful, everyday comportment and expose it as contingent. But if this is so then the same socio-material structures that can seem recalcitrant are also inviting to new ways of behaving; they can be used. The social and material environment can elicit the kind of (affective) responses that, if attended to, tell us who we are. Moreover, these responses let us coordinate our goals with the affordances of the socio-material environment and thus allow us to at least attune ourselves to, if not flourish in, the previously most unfamiliar of environments.

Appendix: Translation of "Duitsche Literatuur" (1929) by Chris de Graaff

GERMAN LITERATURE
By
CHR. DE GRAAFF
Walter Benjamin: "Einbahnstrasse."—Ernst Rowohlt Verlag, Berlin

WHEN one takes an overview of German literature since the renewal that began several years before the war with the predecessors of expressionism, then little remains of the truly new but a few verses. Prose continues, as it does here, in the same way or it does *not*, and stumbles with fits and starts. There is a large difference in style between Stefan George's poetry and that of Trakl, maybe even more difference than agreement. But a novel by the "expressionist" Max Brod deviates little in its essential stylistic qualities from a novel by Schnitzler. Several authors who during some few years were able to maintain an expressionist prose style soon kept silent or, like Kasimir Edschmid, returned to the old narrative style.

Prose turned out not to be resistant to radical attempts at renewal, a phenomenon that has already occurred in the 1880s, and which again shows that prose is more tied to tradition than lyricism is. Nobody writes a good page of prose without being settled, without a skilled professional seriousness. Moreover, no sustainable renewal is possible without solid ground, and because prose allows little or no "poetic liberties," it can find its foundations only in inherited idioms. In a time that must let go of all of the old, one can hardly expect a revival of prose; at best a very cautious regeneration.

The curious thing now is that in Germany, as with us, this slow recovery of the prose organs, which once again enables the writer to tense the muscles of his phrases, to make the heart beat audibly, flourishes most in the essay. The hope has been uttered that this exquisitely practiced, and yet so unsatisfying genre, will gradually develop into a new form of creativity. I doubt it, but I do believe that the contemporary novelist can learn a great deal from the essayist, not when it comes to ideas, but in terms of form, which to the real essayist always remains more important than his ideas.

Walter Benjamin rightly states:

Es gibt nicht Ärmeres als eine Wahrheit ausgedrückt[,] wie sie gedacht ward. In solchem Fall ist ihre Niederschrift noch nicht einmal eine schlechte Photographie. Auch weigert sich die Wahrheit (wie ein Kind, wie eine Frau, die uns nicht liebt) vorm Objektiv der Schrift, wenn wir uns unters schwarze Tuch gekauert haben, still und recht freundlich zu blicken.

[Nothing is poorer than a truth expressed as it was thought. Committed to writing in such a case, it is not even a bad photograph. And the truth refuses (like a child or a woman who does not love us), facing the lens of writing while we crouch under the black cloth, to keep still and look amiable.][1]

"Einbahnstrasse" is a collection of various kinds: short marginalia, ideas, meticulous descriptions of seemingly insignificant things, like a fairground, a dream, an incident from everyday life. Free journalism, if you will. The danger of the genre is obvious. Anyone who can causate to his heart's content about God and about merry-go-rounds, about Shakespeare and neon signs, is sometimes seduced to rattle, with so much freedom, the judgmental and prejudiced bourgeoisie. Benjamin does not always get away from that tendency to shock. He sometimes shows off—in a very German, saturnine way—with small contrivances. And he likes, in the manner of champagne socialists, to throw stones at glass houses without realizing that he himself far from lives in a fortress. But he writes good prose, on top of that he is spiritual and—a very rare characteristic among authors—has a nice intuition for the lives of children. What makes many of his notes so charming is the combination of an extraordinary acumen with a purely preserved sense of the primitive. Not only does he manage to enter the paradise that is childhood without disturbing its serenity; even when he describes a dream or a shooting gallery, reflects deeply on the magic of things, or fiercely chooses a side following his heart, one still feels a mysterious depth behind his words. He is one of the rare authors who can cover very "down to earth" and topical subjects without losing touch with the intuitive life. "Überzeugen ist unfruchtbar" [To convince is to conquer without conception] is his shortest comment. He is never just intellectual; behind the glittering owl-like glasses dream the eyes of a child.

New wisdom should not be sought in this booklet. Besides, how could the new ever be *wise*?

But new, personal, vital, inspiring expressions. True wisdom is always tied to its form. Benjamin thus gives his marginalia visual titles with every right. One of these notes is called "Torso."

1   The English translations of *Einbahnstraße* I take from Edmund Jephcott: Benjamin, *One-Way Street*.

Nur wer die eigene Vergangenheit als Ausgeburt des Zwanges und der Not zu betrachten wüsste, der wäre fähig, sie in jeder Gegenwart aufs Höchste [*sic*] für sich wert zu machen. Denn was einer lebte, ist bestenfalls der schönen Figur vergleichbar, der auf Transporten alle Glieder abgeschlagen wurden[,] und die nun nichts als den kostbaren Block abgibt, aus dem er das Bild seiner Zukunft zu hauen hat.

[Only he who can view his own past as an abortion sprung from compulsion and need can use it to full advantage in every present. For what one has lived is at best comparable to a beautiful statue that has had all its limbs broken off in transit, and that now yields nothing but the precious block out of which the image of one's future must be hewn.]

Another time he only records a contrivance, without working out the thought. And then he is often the most "anregend" [stimulating]. For example, he writes: "An Allem was mit Grund schön genannt wird, wirkt paradox, dass es erscheint" (In everything that is with reason called beautiful, appearance has a paradoxical effect).

This is by no means "profound." It could not be simpler and "a child can understand it."

Grown-ups who can only think with their level-headed minds and who have lost the childish sense of the magic of things, will shrug their shoulders.

For them Walter Benjamin did not write these. How could they enjoy miniatures like "Karusellfahrendes Kinds" [*sic*; Child on the Carousel], which I would like to quote here in full:

Das Brett mit den dienstbaren Tieren rollt dicht überm Boden. Es hat die Höhe, in der man am besten zu fliegen träumt. Musik setzt ein, und ruckweis rollt das Kind von seiner Mutter fort. Erst hat es Angst, die Mutter zu verlassen. Dann aber merkt es, wie es selber treu ist. Es thront als treuer Herrscher über eine [*sic*] Welt, die ihm gehört. In der Tangente bilden Bäume und Eingeborene Spalier. Da taucht, in einem Orient, wiederum die Mutter auf. Danach tritt aus dem Urwald ein Wipfel, wie ihn das Kind schon vor Jahrtausenden, wie es ihn eben erst im Karussell gesehen hat. Sein Tier ist ihm zugetan: Wie ein stummer Arion fährt er [*sic*] auf seinem stummen Fisch dahin, ein hölzerner Stier. Zeus [*sic*] entführt es als makelose [*sic*] Europa. Längst ist die ewige Wiederkehr aller Dinge Kinderweisheit geworden und das Leben ein uralter Rausch der Herrschaft, mit dem dröhnender [*sic*] Orchestrion in der Mitte als Kronschatz. Spielt es langsamer, fängt der Raum an zu stottern und die Bäume beginnen sich zu besinnen. Das Karussell wird unsicherer Grund. Und die Mutter taucht auf, der vielfach gerammte Pfahl, um welchen das landende Kind das Tau seiner Blicke wickelt.

[The platform bearing the docile animals moves close to the ground. It is at the height which, in dreams, is best for flying. Music starts, and the child moves away from his mother with a jerk. At first he is afraid to leave her. But then he notices how brave he himself is. He is ensconced, like the just ruler, over a world that belongs to him. Tangential trees and natives line his way. Then, in an Orient, his mother reappears. Next, emerging from the jungle, comes a treetop, exactly as the child saw it thousands of years ago—just now on the carousel. His beast is devoted: like a mute Arion he rides his silent fish, or a wooden Zeus-bull carries him off like an immaculate Europa. The eternal recurrence of all things has long become child's wisdom, and life a primeval frenzy of domination, with the booming orchestrion as the crown jewels at the center. As the music slows, space begins to stammer and the trees to come to their senses. The carousel becomes uncertain ground. And his mother appears, the much-hammered stake about which the landing child winds the rope of his gaze.]

I will admit that this is somewhat mannered. But those who have a feeling for the rhythm of this prose, for the calm tone, for the loving attention with which this simple and yet so profound children's adventure has been brought to the surface here—out of all of our forgetfulness—shining delicately and mysteriously, will recognize that such a page may be counted among the rare precious possessions of contemporary literature, even if the work is "merely essayistic."

Bibliography

Manuscript Sources

Berlin, Akademie der Künste, Walter-Benjamin-Archiv, Nr. 698 (Ms 865).
Berlin, Akademie der Künste, Walter-Benjamin-Archiv, Nr. 699, fols 1–2 (Ts 1674–1675).
Bern, Schweizerische Landesbibliothek, Ms. B 6, 74.

Printed Sources

Adams, Frederick, and Kenneth Aizawa. *The Bounds of Cognition*. Malden: Blackwell, 2008.
Adorno, Theodor W. *Minima Moralia: Reflexionen aus dem beschädigten Leben*. Berlin: Suhrkamp, 1951.
Agamben, Giorgio. *The Open: Man and Animal*. Translated by Kevin Attell. Stanford, CA: Stanford University Press, 2004.
Aho, Kevin A. *Heidegger's Neglect of the Body*. Albany: State University of New York Press, 2009.
Allison, Truett, Aina Puce, and Gregory McCarthy. "Social Perception from Visual Cues: Role of the STS Region." *Trends in Cognitive Sciences* 4, no. 7 (2000): 267–78.
Alsmith, Adrian J. T., and Frédérique de Vignemont. "Embodying the Mind and Representing the Body." *Review of Philosophy and Psychology* 3, no. 1 (2012): 1–13.
Armstrong, Paul B. *Stories and the Brain: The Neuroscience of Narrative*. Baltimore: Johns Hopkins University Press, 2020.
Auyoung, Elaine. "Becoming Sensitive: Literary Study and Learning to Notice." *PMLA* 138, no. 1 (2023): 158–64.
Baldwin, Dare A. "Infants' Ability to Consult the Speaker for Clues to Word Reference." *Journal of Child Language* 20, no. 2 (1993): 395–418.
Barbisan, Léa. "Eccentric Bodies: From Phenomenology to Marxism—Walter Benjamin's Reflections on Embodiment." In "Discontinuous Infinities," edited by Jan Sieber and Sebastian Truskolaski. Special issue, *Anthropology and Materialism*, Special Issue I (March 2017): 1–14.
Barndt, Kerstin. *Sentiment und Sachlichkeit: Der Roman der neuen Frau in der Weimarer Republik*. Cologne: Böhlau, 2003.
Baßler, Moritz, and Melanie Horn. Afterword to *Gesammelte Werke* by Alfred Döblin, edited by Christina Althen. Vol. 10, *Berlin Alexanderplatz: Die Geschichte vom Franz Biberkopf*, 523–44. Frankfurt am Main: Fischer Klassik, 2014.

Bateson, Mary Catherine. "Mother-Infant Exchanges: The Epigenesis of Conversational Interaction." In *Developmental Psycholinguistics and Communication Disorders (Annal of the New York Academy of Sciences)*, edited by D. Aaronson and R. W. Rieber, 101–13. New York: New York Academy of Sciences, 1975.

Baum, Vicki. *Es war alles ganz anders: Erinnerungen*. Berlin: Ullstein, 1962.

———. *Grand Hotel*. Translated by Basil Creighton. New York: New York Review Books, 2016.

———. *Menschen im Hotel*. Cologne: Kiepenhauer & Witsch, 2007.

Bayerdorfer, Hans-Peter. "Der Wissende und die Gewalt: Alfred Döblins Theorie des epischen Werkes und der Schluss von Berlin Alexanderplatz." *Deutsche Vierteljahrsschrift für Literaturwissenschaft und Geisteswissenschaft* 44, no. 2 (1970): 318–53.

Bayliss, Andrew P., Alexandra Frischen, Mark J. Fenske, and Steven P. Tipper. "Affective Evaluations of Objects Are Influenced by Observed Gaze Direction and Emotional Expression." *Cognition* 104, no. 3 (2007): 644–53.

Bayliss, Andrew P., Matthew A. Paul, Peter R. Cannon, and Steven P. Tipper. "Gaze Cueing and Affective Judgments of Objects: I Like What You Look At." *Psychonomic Bulletin and Review* 13, no. 6 (2006): 1061–66.

Beasley-Murray, Tim. *Michail Bakhtin and Walter Benjamin: Experience and Form*. London: Palgrave Macmillan, 2007.

Becker, Sabina. *Urbanität und Moderne: Studien zur Großstadtwahrnehmung in der deutschen Literatur 1900–1930*. St Ingbert: W. J. Röhrig, 1993.

Behnke, Elizabeth A. "Edmund Husserl's Contribution to Phenomenology of the Body in *Ideas II*." In *Issues in Husserl's Ideas II*, edited by Thomas Nenon and Lester Embree, 135–60. Dordrecht: Kluwer, 1996.

Benjamin, Walter. 8 June 1931. In *Benjamin und Brecht: Denken in Extremen*, edited by Erdmut Wizisla, 47. Berlin: Suhrkamp, 2017.

———. *Gesammelte Briefe*. Edited by Christoph Gödde and Henri Lonitz. Vol. 3, 1925–30. Frankfurt am Main: Suhrkamp, 1997.

———. *Gesammelte Schriften*. Vol. 1, edited by Rolf Tiedemann and Hermann Schweppenhäuser. Frankfurt am Main: Suhrkamp, 1991.

———. *Gesammelte Schriften*. Vol. 2, edited by Rolf Tiedemann and Hermann Schweppenhäuser. Frankfurt am Main: Suhrkamp, 1991.

———. *Gesammelte Schriften*. Vol. 3, *Kritiken und Rezensionen*, edited by Hella Tiedemann-Bartels. Frankfurt am Main: Suhrkamp, 1991.

———. *Gesammelte Schriften*. Vol. 4, edited by Tillman Rexroth. Frankfurt am Main: Suhrkamp, 1991.

———. *Gesammelte Schriften*. Vol. 6, edited by Rolf Tiedemann and Hermann Schweppenhäuser. Frankfurt am Main: Suhrkamp, 1991.

———. *Gesammelte Schriften*. Vol. 7, *Nachträge*, edited by Rolf Tiedemann and Hermann Schweppenhäuser. Frankfurt am Main: Suhrkamp, 1991.

———. *Illuminations: Essays and Reflections*. Edited by Hannah Arendt. Translated by Harry Zohn. New York: Schocken Books, 2007.

———. *Kritische Gesamtausgabe*. Edited by Christoph Gödde and Henri Lonitz. Vol. 8, *Einbahnstraße*, edited by Detlev Schöttker and Steffen Haug. Frankfurt am Main: Suhrkamp, 2009.

———. *One-Way Street*. Edited by Michael W. Jennings. Translated by Edmund Jephcott. Cambridge, MA: Belknap, 2016.

———. *Selected Writings*. Vol. 2, edited by Michael W. Jennings, Howard Eiland, and Gary Smith, translated by Rodney Livingstone and Others. Cambridge, MA: Belknap, 2005.

Bernini, Marco. *Beckett and the Cognitive Method: Mind, Models, and Exploratory Narratives*. Oxford: Oxford University Press, 2022.

———. "Supersizing Narrative Theory: On Intention, Material Agency and Extended Mind Workers." *Style* 48, no. 3 (2014): 349–66.

Bistis, Margo. "Simmel and Bergson: The Theorist and the Exemplar of the 'Blasé Person.'" *Journal of European Studies* 45, no. 4 (2005): 395–418.

Bloch, Ernst. "Revueform in der Philosophie." In *Erbschaft dieser Zeit*, 276–79. Zurich: Oprecht & Helbling, 1935.

Boa, Elizabeth. "Women Writers in the 'Golden' Twenties." In *The Cambridge Companion to the Modern German Novel*, edited by Graham Bartram, 123–37. Cambridge, UK: Cambridge University Press, 2004.

Bolens, Guillemette. *The Style of Gestures: Embodiment and Cognition in Literary Narrative*. Baltimore: Johns Hopkins University Press, 2012.

Boos, Sonja. "Reading Gestures: Body Schema Disorder and Schizophrenia in Kafka's Modernist Prose." *Modernism/modernity* 26, no. 4 (2019): 829–48.

Brandstetter, Gabriele. *Tanz-Lektüren: Körperbilder und Raumfiguren der Avantgarde (Um einen dritten Teil erweiterte Auflage)*. Freiburg i. Br.: Rombach, 2013.

Britten, Robert. "'Blick und Gebärde': Embodied Perception in *Die Aufzeichnungen des Malte Laurids Brigge*." *Monatshefte* 114, no. 1 (2022): 66–84.

Bronstein, Michaela. *Out of Context: The Uses of Modernist Fiction*. Oxford: Oxford University Press, 2018.

Bruineberg, Jelle, Ludovic Seifert, Erik Rietveld, and Julian Kiverstein. "Metastable Attunement and Real-Life Skilled Behavior." In *Synthese* 199 (2021): 12819–42.

Buchanan, Brett. *Onto-Ethologies: The Animal Environments of Uexküll, Heidegger, Merleau-Ponty, and Deleuze*. Albany: State University of New York Press, 2008.

Buck-Morss, Susan. *The Dialectics of Seeing: Walter Benjamin and the Arcades Project*. Cambridge, MA: MIT Press, 1989.

Burke, Michael, and Emily Troscianko, eds. *Cognitive Literary Science: Dialogues between Literature and Cognition*. Oxford: Oxford University Press, 2017.

Butterworth, G. "Joint Visual Attention in Infancy." In *Theories of Infant Development*, edited by J. Gavin Bremner and Alan Slater, 317–54. Malden: Blackwell, 2004.

Caillois, Roger. *Man, Play, and Games.* Translated by Meyer Barash. London: Thames & Hudson, 1961.

Cappuccio, Massimiliano L., ed. "Unreflective Action and the Choking Effect." Special issue, *Phenomenology and the Cognitive Science* 14, no. 2 (2015).

Caracciolo, Marco. "Embodiment at the Crossroads: Some Open Questions between Literary Interpretation and Cognitive Science." *Poetics Today* 34, no. 1–2 (2013): 233–53.

———. *The Experientiality of Narrative: An Enactivist Approach.* Berlin: De Gruyter, 2014.

Caracciolo, Marco, and Karin Kukkonen. *With Bodies: Narrative Theory and Embodied Cognition.* Columbus, OH: Ohio State University Press, 2021.

Caracciolo, Marco, Cécile Guédon, Karin Kukkonen, and Sabine Müller. "The Promise of an Embodied Narratology: Integrating Cognition, Representation and Interpretation." In *Emerging Vectors of Narratology*, edited by Per Krogh Hansen, John Pier, Philippe Roussin, and Wolf Schmid, 435–60. Berlin: De Gruyter, 2014.

Caravà, Marta, and Claudia Scorolli. "When Affective Relation Weighs More Than the Mug Handle: Investigating Affective Affordances." *Frontiers in Psychology* 11 (2020): 1–5.

Carman, Taylor. "On Being Social: A Reply to Olafson." *Inquiry* 37, no. 2 (1994): 203–23.

Carroll, Noël. "Comments on *Strange Tools* by Alva Noë." *Philosophy and Phenomenological Research* 94, no. 1 (2017): 214–21.

Cave, Terence. *Thinking with Literature: Towards a Cognitive Criticism.* Oxford: Oxford University Press, 2016.

Cerbone, David R. "Heidegger and Dasein's 'Bodily Nature': What is the Hidden Problematic?" *International Journal of Philosophical Studies* 8, no. 2 (2000): 209–30.

Ciaunica, Anna, and Aikaterini Fotopoulou. "The Touched Self: Psychological and Philosophical Perspectives on Proximal Intersubjectivity and the Self." In *Embodiment, Enaction, and Culture: Investigating the Constitution of the Shared World*, edited by Christoph Durt, Thomas Fuchs, and Christian Tewes, 173–92. Cambridge, MA: MIT Press, 2017.

Clark, Andy, and David Chalmers. "The Extended Mind." *Analysis* 58, no. 1 (1998): 7–19.

Colombetti, Giovanna. *The Feeling Body: Affective Science Meets the Enactive Mind.* Cambridge, MA: MIT Press, 2014.

Craig, Robert. "Rainer Maria Rilke's Dark Ecology." *Oxford German Studies* 51, no. 3 (2022): 256–71.

Csikszentmihalyi, Mihaly. *Applications of Flow in Human Development and Education: The Collected Works of Mihaly Csikszentmihalyi.* Dordrecht: Springer, 2014.

———. *Flow: The Psychology of Optimal Experience.* New York: Harper & Row, 1990.

Das, Santanu. *Touch and Intimacy in First World War Literature*. Cambridge: Cambridge University Press, 2006.
De Cauwer, Stijn. "Beyond the Stimulus Shield: War Neurosis, Shock and Montage in Alfred Döblin's *Berlin Alexanderplatz*." *Neophilologus* 99, no. 1 (2014): 97–112.
De Jaegher, Hanne, and Ezequiel Di Paolo. "Participatory Sense-Making: An Enactive Approach to Social Cognition." *Phenomenology and the Cognitive Sciences* 6, no. 4 (2007): 485–507.
De Waelhens, Alphonse. "Philosophy of the Ambiguous." Introduction to *The Structure of Behaviour*, by Maurice Merleau-Ponty, xviii–xxvii. Translated by Alden L. Fisher. London: Methuen, 1965.
Deák, István. *Weimar Germany's Left-Wing Intellectuals: A Political History of the* Weltbühne *and Its Circles*. Berkeley: University of California Press, 1968.
Dewey, John. *Art as Experience*. New York: Perigee, 2005.
Di Paolo, Ezequiel A., Marieke Rohde, and Hanne de Jaegher. "Horizons of the Enactive Mind: Values, Social Interaction, and Play." In *Enaction: Toward a New Paradigm for Cognitive Science*, edited by John Stewart, Olivier Gapenne, and Ezequiel A. Di Paolo, 33–87. Cambridge, MA: MIT Press, 2010.
Döblin, Alfred. "An Romanautoren und ihre Kritiker: Berliner Programm." In *Aufsätze zur Literatur*, 15–18. Olten: Walter-Verlag, 1963.
———. "Aufmerksamkeitsstörungen bei Hysterie." *Archiv für Psychiatrie und Nervenkrankheiten* 45, no. 2 (1909): 464–88.
———. "Der Bau des epischen Werks." In *Aufsätze zur Literatur*, 103–32. Olten: Walter-Verlag, 1963.
———. *Berlin Alexanderplatz*. Translated by Michael Hofmann. London: Penguin, 2018.
———. "The Construction of the Epic Work." In *German Masquerade: Writings on Politics, Life, and Literature in Chaotic Times*, vol. 4, *Literature*, edited and translated by C. D. Godwin, 213–30. https://beyond-alexanderplatz.com/german-masquerade/.
———. *Gedächtnisstörungen bei der Korsakoffschen Psychose*. . . . Berlin: Tropenverlag, 2006.
———."Der Geist des naturalistischen Zeitalters." In *Aufsätze zur Literatur*, 62–83. Olten: Walter-Verlag, 1963.
———. *Gesammelte Werke*. Edited by Christina Althen. Vol. 10, *Berlin Alexanderplatz: Die Geschichte vom Franz Biberkopf*. Frankfurt am Main: Fischer Klassik, 2014.
———. *Gesammelte Werke*. Edited by Christina Althen. Vol. 11, *Unser Dasein*. Frankfurt am Main: Fischer Klassik, 2017.
———. *Das Ich über der Natur*. Berlin: Fischer Verlag, 1928.
———. "Mein Buch 'Berlin Alexanderplatz.'" In *Schriften zu Leben und Werk*, edited by Erich Kleinschmidt, 215–17. Frankfurt am Main: Suhrkamp, 1975.

———. "The Spirit of a Naturalistic Age." In *German Masquerade: Writings on Politics, Life, and Literature in Chaotic Times*. Vol. 2, *Politics and Society*, edited and translated by C. D. Godwin, 75–87. https://beyond-alexanderplatz.com/german-masquerade/.

———. "To Novelists and Their Critics." In *German Masquerade: Writings on Politics, Life, and Literature in Chaotic Times*. Vol. 1, *Pre-War and Aftermath*, edited and translated by C. D. Godwin, 10–12. https://beyond-alexanderplatz.com/german-masquerade/.

Dreyfus, Hubert L. *Being-in-the-World: A Commentary on Heidegger's Being and Time, Division I*. Cambridge, MA: MIT Press, 1997.

———. "Interpreting Heidegger on Das Man." *Inquiry* 38, no. 4 (1995): 423–30.

———. "Responses." In *Heidegger, Authenticity, and Modernity: Essays in Honor of Hubert L. Dreyfus, Vol. 1*, edited by Mark Wrathall and Jeff Malpas, 305–41. Cambridge, MA.: MIT Press, 2000.

———. "The Return of the Myth of the Mental." *Inquiry*, 50 (2007): 371–77.

Duttlinger, Carolin. *Attention and Distraction in Modern German Literature, Thought, and Culture*. Oxford: Oxford University Press, 2022.

———. "Kafka in Oxford." *Oxford German Studies* 50, no. 4 (2021): 416–27.

———. "Modernist Writing and Visual Culture." In *The Cambridge Companion to the Literature of Berlin*, 89–110. Cambridge: Cambridge University Press, 2017.

———. "Network – Figure – Labyrinth: New Routes into Walter Benjamin." *The Future of Benjamin* (blog), edited by Nitzan Lebovic. https://importance-of-benjamin.cas2.lehigh.edu/content/network-%E2%80%93-figure-%E2%80%93-labyrinth-new-routes-walter-benjamin.

Eiland, Howard, and Michael William Jennings. *Walter Benjamin: A Critical Life*. Cambridge, MA: Belknap, 2014.

Eisner, Lotte. *The Haunted Screen: Expressionism in the German Cinema and the Influence of Max Reinhardt*. London: Secker & Warburg, 1973.

Eldridge, Richard. Introduction to *The Oxford Handbook of Philosophy and Literature*, edited by Richard Eldridge, 3–15. Oxford: Oxford University Press, 2009.

Elsaesser, Thomas. *Weimar Cinema and After: Germany's Historical Imaginary*. London: Routledge, 2000.

Engel, Manfred. Afterword to *Die Aufzeichnungen des Malte Laurids Brigge*, by Rainer Maria Rilke, 319–50. Stuttgart: Reclam, 1996.

Engler-Coldren, Katharina, Lore Knapp, and Charlotte Lee. "Embodied Cognition around 1800." Special issue, *German Life and Letters* 70, no. 4 (2017).

Evans, Jules. *The Art of Losing Control: A Philosopher's Search for Ecstatic Experience*. Edinburgh: Canongate, 2017.

———. "Mihalyi Csikszentmihalyi on Flow and Ecstasy." *The History of Emotions Blog*. June 11, 2014. https://emotionsblog.history.qmul.ac.uk/2014/06/mihayli-csikszentmihayli-on-flow-and-ecstasy/.
Felski, Rita. *Hooked: Art and Attachment*. Chicago: University of Chicago Press, 2020.
———. *The Uses of Literature*. Malden, MA: Blackwell, 2008.
Fick, Monika. *Sinnenwelt und Weltseele: Der Psychophysische Monismus in der Literatur der Jahrhundertwende*. Tübingen: Max Niemeyer, 1993.
Fischer, Luke. *The Poet as Phenomenologist: Rilke and the "New Poems."* New York: Bloomsbury, 2015.
Fischer, M. H., and A. E. Kornmüller, "Optokinetisch ausgelöste Bewegungswahrnehmungen und optokinetischer Nystagmus." *Journal für Psychologie und Neurologie* 41 (1930).
Fore, Devin. "Döblin's Epic: Sense, Document, and the Verbal World Picture." *New German Critique* 33, no. 3 (2006): 171–207.
Franck, Didier. "Being and the Living." In *Who Comes after the Subject?*, edited by Eduardo Cadava, Peter Connor, and Jean-Luc Nancy, 135–47. London: Routledge, 1991.
Gallagher, Shaun. *Enactivist Interventions: Rethinking the Mind*. Oxford: Oxford University Press, 2017.
———. *How the Body Shapes the Mind*. Oxford: Oxford University Press, 2005.
———. "Inference or Interaction: Social Cognition without Precursors." *Philosophical Explorations* 11, no. 3 (2008): 163–73.
———. "Mindful Performance." In *The Extended Theory of Cognitive Creativity: Interdisciplinary Approaches to Performativity*, edited by Antonino Pennisi and Alessandra Falzone, 43–58. Cham: Springer, 2020.
———. "The Practice of Mind: Theory, Simulation or Primary Interaction?" *Journal of Consciousness Studies* 8, no. 5–7 (2001): 83–108.
———. "Understanding Interpersonal Problems in Autism: Interaction Theory as an Alternative to Theory of Mind." *Philosophy, Psychiatry, and Psychology* 11, no. 3 (2004): 199–217.
Gallagher, Shaun, and Daniel D. Hutto. "Primary Interaction and Narrative Practice." In *The Shared Mind: Perspectives on Intersubjectivity*, edited by Jordan Zlatev, Timothy P. Racine, Chris Sinha, and Esa Itkonen, 17–38. Amsterdam: John Benjamins, 2008.
Gallagher, Shaun, and Rebecca Seté Jacobson. "Heidegger and Social Cognition." In *Heidegger and Cognitive Science*, edited by Julian Kiverstein and Michael Wheeler, 213–45. New York: Palgrave Macmillan, 2012.
Gallagher, Shaun, and Andrew N. Meltzoff. "The Earliest Sense of Self and Others: Merleau-Ponty and Recent Developmental Studies." *Philosophical Psychology* 9 (1996): 213–36.
Gallagher, Shaun, Ben Morgan, and Naomi Rokotnitz. "Relational Authenticity." In *Neuroexistentialism: Meaning, Morals, and Purpose in the Age*

of *Neuroscience*, edited by Owen Flanagan and Gregg D. Caruso, 126–45. Oxford: Oxford University Press, 2018.

Gallese, Vittorio. "Brain, Body, Habit, and the Performative Quality of Aesthetics." In *Habits: Pragmatic Approaches from Cognitive Science, Neuroscience, and Social Theory*, edited by Fausto Caruana and Italo Testa, 376–94. Cambridge: Cambridge University Press, 2021.

Garrington, Abbie. *Haptic Modernism: Touch and the Tactile in Modernist Writing*. Edinburgh: Edinburgh University Press, 2015.

Gelderloos, Carl. "Das Ich über der Natur." In *Döblin Handbuch: Leben – Werk – Wirkung*, edited by Sabina Becker, 276–80. Stuttgart: J. B. Metzler Verlag, 2016.

Gibbs Jr., Raymond W. "Embodied Dynamics in Literary Experience." In *Cognitive Literary Science: Dialogues between Literature and Cognition*, edited by Michael Burke and Emily T. Troscianko, 219–37. Oxford: Oxford University Press, 2017.

Gibson, James J. *The Ecological Approach to Visual Perception*. New York: Psychology Press, 2015.

Gide, André. *Journal des faux-monnayeurs*. 16th ed. Paris: Éditions de la Nouvelle Revue Française, [1929?]).

Godfrey-Smith, Peter. "On the Status and Explanatory Structure of Developmental Systems Theory." In *Cycles of Contingency: Developmental Systems and Evolution*, edited by Susan Oyama, Paul E. Griffiths, and Russell D. Gray, 283–98. Cambridge, MA: MIT Press, 2001.

Goldman, Alvin I. "A Moderate Approach to Embodied Cognitive Science." *Review of Philosophy and Psychology* 3, no. 1 (2012): 71–88.

Goodwin, Charles. "Action and embodiment within situated human interaction." *Journal of Pragmatics* 32, no. 10 (2000): 1489–1522.

Gopnik, Alison, and Andrew N. Meltzoff. *Words, Thoughts, and Theories*. Cambridge, MA: MIT Press, 1997.

Graaff, Chr. de. "Duitsche Literatuur." *Algemeen Handelsblad*, May 18, 1929. https://resolver.kb.nl/resolve?urn=ddd:010658936:mpeg21:a0278.

Groeneveld, Leanne. "Modernist Medievalism and the Expressionist Morality Play: Georg Kaiser's *From Morning to Midnight*." *Acta Univ. Sapientiae, Film and Media Studies* 16 (2019): 81–101.

Haan, W. de. "Franz Biberkopfs Zondeval." *Het Vaderland*, February 6, 1931. https://resolver.kb.nl/resolve?urn=ddd:010013344:mpeg21:a0232.

Haas, Willy. [N.t.]. In *Alfred Döblin im Spiegel der zeitgenössischen Kritik*, edited by Ingrid Schuster and Ingrid Bode, 219–25. Bern: Francke Verlag, 1973.

Hansen, Mark B. N. *Embodying Technesis: Technology beyond Writing*. Ann Arbor: University of Michigan Press, 2000.

Hansen, Miriam. "Benjamin, Cinema and Experience: 'The Blue Flower in the Land of Technology.'" *New German Critique* 40 (1987): 179–224.

———. "Of Mice and Ducks: Benjamin and Adorno on Disney." *South Atlantic Quarterly* 92, no. 1 (1993): 27–61.

Haugeland, John. *Dasein Disclosed: John Haugeland's Heidegger*. Cambridge, MA: Harvard University Press, 2013.

———. "Truth and Finitude: Heidegger's Transcendental Existentialism." In *Heidegger, Authenticity, and Modernity: Essays in Honor of Hubert L. Dreyfus, Vol. 1*, edited by Mark Wrathall and Jeff Malpas, 43–77. Cambridge, MA: MIT Press, 2000.

Head, Henry, and Gordon Holmes. "Sensory Disturbances from Cerebral Lesions." *Brain* 34, no. 2–3 (1911): 102–254.

Heidegger, Martin. *The Basic Problems of Phenomenology*. Translated by Albert Hofstadter. Bloomington: Indiana University Press, 1988.

———. *Being and Time*. Translated by Joan Stambaugh. Albany, NY: State University of New York Press, 2010.

———. *Gesamtausgabe*. Edited by Friedrich-Wilhelm von Herrmann. Vol. 29/30, *Die Grundbegriffe der Metaphysik: Welt – Endlichkeit – Einsamkeit*. Tübingen: Klostermann, 1983

———. *Die Grundprobleme der Phänomenologie*. Frankfurt am Main: Vittorio Klostermann, 2005.

———. *Sein und Zeit*. Tübingen: Max Niemeyer, 2006.

———. *Zollikon Seminars: Protocols – Conversations – Letters*. Edited by Medard Boss. Translated by Franz Mayr and Richard Askay. Evanston: Northwestern University Press, 2001.

———. *Zollikoner Seminare: Protokolle – Gespräche – Briefe*. Frankfurt am Main: Vittorio Klostermann, 1987.

Herman, David. "Re-Minding Modernism." In *The Emergence of Mind: Representations of Consciousness in Narrative Discourse in English*, edited by David Herman, 243–72. Lincoln: University of Nebraska Press, 2011.

———. *Storytelling and the Science of Mind*. Cambridge, MA: MIT Press, 2013.

Herwig, Malte. "The Unwitting Muse: Jakob von Uexküll's Theory of Umwelt and Twentieth-Century Literature." *Semiotica* 134, no. 1 (2001), 553–92.

Hessel, Franz. "Walter Benjamin: Einbahnstraße. Ernst Rowohlt Verlag." In *Kritische Gesamtausgabe*, by Walter Benjamin. Edited by Christoph Gödde and Henri Lonitz. Vol. 8, *Einbahnstraße*, edited by Detlev Schöttker and Steffen Haug, 511–13. Frankfurt am Main: Suhrkamp, 2009.

Heyes, Cecilia. *Cognitive Gadgets: The Cultural Evolution of Thinking*. Cambridge, MA: Belknap Press, 2018.

———. "Where Do Mirror Neurons Come From?" *Neuroscience & Biobehaveriol Reviews* 34, no. 4 (2010): 575–83.

Hillard, Derek. "Rilke and Historical Discourse or the 'Histories' of Malte Laurids Brigge." *German Studies Review* 29, no. 2 (2006): 299–313.

Hillebrand, Bruno, ed. *Nietzsche und die deutsche Literatur. Part I: Texte zur Nietsche-Rezeption 1873–1963*. Berlin: De Gruyter, 2016.

Høffding, Simon "A Phenomenology of Expert Musicianship." PhD diss., University of Copenhagen, 2015.

———. *A Phenomenology of Musical Absorption*. Basingstoke, UK: Palgrave Macmillan, 2018.
Hofmann, Michael. Afterword to *Berlin Alexanderplatz*, by Alfred Döblin, 447–58. London: Penguin, 2018.
Horn, Eva. "Literary Research: Narration and the Epistemology of the Human Sciences in Alfred Döblin." *MLN* 118, no. 3 (April 2003): 719–39.
Hubbs, Nadine. *Rednecks, Queers, and Country Music*. Berkeley: University of California Press, 2014.
Huder, Walther. Afterword to *Von morgens bis mitternachts: Stück in zwei Teilen*, by Georg Kaiser, 78–88. Ditzingen: Reclam, 2020.
Husserl, Edmund. *Experience and Judgement: Investigations in a Genealogy of Logic*. Edited by Ludwig Landgrebe. Translated by James S. Churchill and Karl Ameriks. Evanston, IL: Northwestern University Press.
Huyssen, Andreas. "The Notebooks of Malte Laurids Brigge." In *The Cambridge Companion to Rilke*, edited by Karen Leeder and Robert Vilain. Cambridge: Cambridge University Press, 2010.
———. "Paris/Childhood: The Fragmented Body in Rilke's Malte Laurids Brigge." In *Twilight Memories: Marking Time in a Culture of Amnesia*. New York: Routledge, 1995.
Ingold, Tim. *The Perception of the Environment: Essays on Livelihood, Dwelling and Skill*. New York: Routledge, 2000.
IJzerman, Hans, Marcello Gallucci, Wim T. J. L. Pouw, Sophia C. Weißgerber, Niels J. van Doesum, and Kipling D. Williams. 2012. "Cold-Blooded Loneliness: Social Exclusion Leads to Lower Skin Temperatures." *Acta Psychologica* 140, no. 3 (2012): 283–88.
IJzerman, Hans Rocha. *Heartwarming: How Our Inner Thermostat Made Us Human*. New York: Norton, 2021.
Jähner, Harald. *Erzählter, montierter, soufflierter Text: Zur Konstruktion des Romans "Berlin Alexanderplatz" von Alfred Döblin*. Frankfurt am Main: Peter Lang, 1984.
Jensen, Thomas Wiben, and Sarah Bro Pedersen. "Affect and Affordances: The Role of Action and Emotion in Social Interaction." *Cognitive Semiotics* 9, no. 1 (2016): 79–103.
Jentsch, Tobias. "Franz Karl Biberkopf als Sein-zum-Tode: Das 'Lied des Todes' in Alfred Döblins *Berlin Alexanderplatz* als vorlaufendes Todesbewusstsein Heideggers," *Neophilologus* 84, no. 3 (2000): 423–42.
Johnson, Susan C. "The Recognition of Mentalistic Agents in Infancy." *Trends in Cognitive Sciences* 4, no. 1 (2000): 22–28.
Jones, Lawrence. "Periodicals and the Serialization of Novels." In *Encyclopedia of the Novel*, edited by Paul Schellinger, Christopher Hudson, and Marijke Rijsberman. London: Fitzroy Dearborn, 1998.
Jules. "Das Kunstwerk und sein Kritiker: Walter Benjamin und seine dreizehn Thesen." In *Kritische Gesamtausgabe*, by Walter Benjamin, edited by Christoph Gödde and Henri Lonitz. Vol. 8, *Einbahnstraße*, edited

by Detlev Schöttker and Steffen Haug, 508–10. Frankfurt am Main: Suhrkamp, 2009.

Kaiser, Georg. "Der kommende Mensch." In *Stücke, Erzählungen, Aufsätze, Gedichte*, by Georg Kaiser, edited by Walther Huder, 679–83. Cologne: Kiepenheuer & Witsch, 1966.

———. "Über mein Werk." In *Werke*, edited by Walther Huder. Vol. 4, *Filme, Romane, Erzählungen, Aufsätze, Gedichte*, 563. Frankfurt am Main: Propyläen, 1971.

———. *Von morgens bis mitternachts: Stück in zwei Teilen*, edited by Walther Huder. Ditzingen: Reclam, 2020.

Kállai, Ernő. "Malerei und Fotografie." *i10*, 4 (1927): 148–57.

Keil, Thomas. *Alfred Döblins "Unser Dasein": Quellenphilologische Untersuchungen*. Würzburg: Königshausen & Neumann, 2005.

Keun, Irmgard. *The Artificial Silk Girl*. Translated by Kathie von Ankum. London: Penguin, 2019.

———. *Das kunstseidene Mädchen*. Berlin: Deutsche Verlags-Aktiengesellchaft, 1932.

Kiesel, Helmuth. *Geschichte der literarischen Moderne: Sprache, Ästhetik, Dichtung im zwanzigsten Jahrhundert*. Munich: C. H. Beck, 2004.

King, Lynda J. *Best-Sellers by Design: Vicki Baum and the House of Ullstein*. Detroit: Wayne State University Press, 1988.

———. "*Menschen im Hotel/Grand Hotel*: Seventy Years of a Popular Classic." *Journal of American & Comparative Cultures* 23, no. 2 (2000): 17–23.

Kiverstein, Julian. "Empathy and the Responsiveness to Social Affordances." *Consciousness and Cognition* 36 (2015): 532–42.

Kiverstein, Julian, and Michael Wheeler, eds. *Heidegger and Cognitive Science*. New York: Palgrave MacMillan, 2012.

Kleinschmidt, Erich. "Materielle und psychische Welt: Wissenspoetik bei Alfred Döblin." In *Internationales Alfred-Döblin-Kolloquium Emmendingen 2007: 'Tatsachenphilosophie'; Alfred Döblins Poetik des Wissens im Kontext der Moderne*, edited by Sabina Becker and Robert Krause, 185–93. Bern: Peter Lang, 2008.

Klotz, Volker. *Die erzählte Stadt: Ein Sujet als Herausforderung des Romans von Lesage bis Döblin*. Munich: Hanser, 1969.

Koelb, Clayton. "Editions." In *Franz Kafka in Context*, edited by Carolin Duttlinger, 293–301. Cambridge: Cambridge University Press, 2018.

Kracauer, Siegfried. *From Caligari to Hitler: A Psychological History of the German Film*. New York: Princeton University Press, 1947.

Krell, David Farrell. *Daimon Life: Heidegger and Life-Philosophy*. Bloomington: Indiana University Press, 1992.

Kukkonen, Karin. *4E Cognition and Eighteenth-Century Fiction: How the Novel Found Its Feet*. Oxford: Oxford University Press, 2019.

———. *A Prehistory of Cognitive Poetics: Neoclassicism and the Novel*. Oxford: Oxford University Press, 2017.

———. *Probability Designs: Literature and Predictive Processing.* Oxford: Oxford University Press, 2019.

Lakin, Jessica L., Tanya L. Chartrand, and Robert M. Arkin. "I Am Too Just Like You: Nonconscious Mimicking as an Automatic Behavioral Response to Social Exclusion." *Psychological Science* 19, no. 8 (2008): 816–22.

Landauer, Gustav. *Aufruf zum Sozialismus.* Berlin: Paul Cassirer, 1919.

———. *Call to Socialism.* Soesterberg: Aspekt, 2022.

———. "Twenty-Five Years Later: On the Jubilee of Wilhelm II." In *Revolution and Other Writings: A Political Reader*, edited and translated by Gabriel Kuhn, 62–67. Pontypool: Merlin Press, 2010.

Lavazza, Andrea, and Howard Robinson, eds. *Contemporary Dualism: A Defense.* London: Routledge, 2014.

Legerstee, Maria. "The Role of Person and Object in Eliciting Early Imitation." *Journal of Experimental Child Psychology* 51 (1991): 423–33.

Lehleiter, Christine. "Reading Minds: German Studies and the Neurohumanities." Special issue, *Seminar: A Journal of Germanic Studies* 58, no. 1 (2022).

Leidinger, Armin. *Hure Babylon: Großstadtsymphonie oder Angriff auf die Landschaft? Alfred Döblins Roman Berlin Alexanderplatz und die Großstadt Berlin: Eine Annäherung aus kulturgeschichtlicher Perspektive.* Würzburg: Königshausen & Neumann, 2010.

Lethen, Helmut. *Cool Conduct: The Culture of Distance in Weimar Germany.* Translated by Don Reneau. Berkeley: University of California Press, 2002.

———. *Verhaltenslehre der Kälte: Lebensversuche zwischen den Kriegen.* 8th ed. Frankfurt am Main: Suhrkamp, 2018.

Levin, David Michael. "The Ontological Dimension of Embodiment: Heidegger's Thinking of Being." In *The Body: Classic and Contemporary Readings*, edited by Donn Welton, 122–49. Oxford: Blackwell, 1999.

Lévinas, Emmanuel. Totalité et infini: Essais sur l'extériorité. The Hague: Martinus Nijhoff, 1961.

Levine, Caroline. *Forms: Whole, Rhythm, Hierarchy, Network.* Princeton, NJ: Princeton University Press, 2015.

Lewis, Cara L. *Dynamic Form: How Intermediality Made Modernism.* Ithaca, NY: Cornell University Press, 2020.

Mach, Ernst. *Grundlinien der Lehre von den Bewegungsempfindungen.* Leipzig: Engelmann, 1875.

Maillard, Christine. "Unser Dasein." In *Döblin Handbuch: Leben – Werk – Wirkung*, edited by Sabina Becker, 280–85. Stuttgart: J. B. Metzler Verlag, 2016.

Mann, Thomas. "An Appeal to Reason," In *The Weimar Republic Sourcebook*, edited by Anton Kaes, Martin Jay, and Edward Dimendberg, 150–59. Berkeley: University of California Press, 1994.

———. *Deutsche Ansprache: Ein Appell an die Vernunft.* Berlin: Fischer, 1930.

Martens, Gunter. *Vitalismus und Expressionismus: Ein Beitrag zur Genese und Deutung expressionistischer Stilstrukturen und Motive*. Stuttgart: Kohlhammer, 1971.

Marx, Ursula. "Von Gästen und Vandalen: Eine Typologie des Wohnens." In *Benjamin und Brecht: Denken in Extremen*, edited by Erdmut Wizisla, 48–61. Berlin: Suhrkamp, 2017.

Maskarinec, Malika. "Rethinking Montage: Berlin Alexanderplatz's Paper Trails." *Deutsche Vierteljahrsschrift für Literaturwissenschaft und Geistesgeschichte* 95 (2021):115–35.

Matthias, Bettina. *The Hotel as Setting in 20th-Century German and Austrian Literature*. Rochester, NY: Camden House, 2006.

McBriar, Shannon. "'Watchman, What of the Night?': Reading Uncertainty in Djuna Barnes's *Nightwood*." In *Worlding the Brain: Neurocentrism, Cognition and the Challenge of the Arts and Humanities*, edited by Stephan Besser and Flora Lysen, 142–55. Leiden: Brill, 2024.

McBriar, Shannon, and Meindert Peters. "Transatlantic Cognitive Cultures." Special issue, *Symbiosis* 25, no. 2 (2021).

McCracken, Scott. "The Completion of Old Work: Walter Benjamin and the Everyday." *Cultural Critique* 52 (2002): 145–66.

Meltzoff, Andrew N., and Rechele Brooks. "'Like Me' as a Building Block for Understanding Other Minds: Bodily Acts, Attention, and Intention." In *Intentions and Intentionality: Foundations of Social Cognition*, edited by Bertram F. Malle et al., 171–91. Cambridge, MA: MIT Press, 2001.

Meltzoff, Andrew N., and M. Keith Moore. "Imitation, Memory, and the Representation of Persons." *Infant Behavior and Development* 17 (1994): 83–99.

———. "Imitation of Facial and Manual Gestures by Human Neonates." *Science* 198 (1977): 75–78.

Menary, Richard. "Writing as Thinking." *Language Sciences* 29, no. 5 (2007): 621–32.

Merleau-Ponty, Maurice. *Phenomenology of Perception*. Translated by Donald. A. Landes. London: Routledge, 2012.

———. *The Structure of Behaviour*. Translated by Alden L. Fisher. London: Methuen, 1965.

Midgley, David R. *The German Novel in the Twentieth Century: Beyond Realism*. Edinburgh: Edinburgh University Press, 1993.

Mildenberg, Ariane. *Modernism and Phenomenology: Literature, Philosophy, Art*. London: Palgrave Macmillan, 2017.

Miller, Tyrus. *Modernism and the Frankfurt School*. Edinburgh: Edinburgh University Press, 2014.

Moholy-Nagy, László. "Diskussion über Ernst Kallai's Artikel 'Malerei und Fotografie.'" *i10* 6 (1927): 233–34.

Moi, Toril. "The Adventure of Reading: Literature and Philosophy, Cavell and Beauvoir." *Literature and Theology* 25, no. 2 (2011): 125–40.

Moretti, Franco. *Signs Taken for Wonders: Essays in the Sociology of Literary Forms*. London: Verso, 1988.

Morgan, Ben. "A 5th E: Distributed Cognition and the Question of Ethics in Benjamin and Vygotsky, and Horkheimer and Dewey." In *Distributed Cognition in Victorian Culture and Modernism*, edited by M. Anderson, P. Garrett, and M. Sprevak, 232–50. Edinburgh: Edinburgh University Press, 2020.

———. "Benjamin, Heidegger and the Anthropology of Everyday Life." In *Walter Benjamins anthropologisches Denken*, edited by Carolin Duttlinger, Ben Morgan, and Anthony Phelan, 95–124. Freiburg: Rombach, 2012.

———. "Walter Benjamin Re-Situated." *Paragraph* 41, no. 2 (2018): 218–32.

Morgan, Ben, Ellen Spolsky, and Sowon Park, eds. "Situated Cognition." Special issue, *Poetics Today* 38, no. 2 (2017).

Morrison, India. "Keep Calm and Cuddle On: Social Touch as a Stress Buffer." *Adaptive Human Behavior and Physiology* 2, no. 4 (2016): 344–62.

Müller, Lothar. "Die Großstadt als Ort der Moderne: Über Georg Simmel." In *Die Unwirklichkeit der Städte: Großstadtdarstellungen zwischen Moderne und Postmoderne*, edited by Klaus R. Scherpe, 14–36. Hamburg: Rowohlt, 1988.

Muschg, Walter. Afterword to *Berlin Alexanderplatz: Die Geschichte vom Franz Biberkopf*, by Alfred Döblin, 413–30. Munich: DTV, 1995.

Newen, Albert, Leon de Bruin, and Shaun Galllagher, eds. *The Handbook to 4E Cognition*. Oxford: Oxford University Press, 2018.

Newman-Norlund, Roger D., Matthijs L. Noordzij, Ruud G. J. Meulenbroek, and Harold Bekkering. "Exploring the Brain Basis of Joint Attention: Co–Ordination of Actions, Goals and Intentions." *Social Neuroscience* 2, no. 1 (2007): 48–65.

Noë, Alva. *Action in Perception*. Cambridge, MA: MIT Press, 2004.

———. "Art and Entanglement in Strange Tools: Reply to Noël Carroll, A. W. Eaton and Paul Guyer." *Philosophy and Phenomenological Research* 94, no. 1 (2017): 238–50.

———. *Strange Tools: Art and Human Nature*. New York: Hill & Wang, 2015.

Noland, Carrie. Introduction to *Migrations of Gesture*, edited by Carrie Noland and Sally Ann Ness, ix–xxviii. Minneapolis: University of Minnesota Press, 2008.

Nottelmann, Nicole. *Die Karrieren der Vicki Baum: Eine Biographie*. Cologne: Kiepenheuer & Witsch, 2007.

Okker, Patricia, and Nancy West. "Serialization." In *The Encyclopedia of the Novel*, edited by Peter Melville Logan, 730–38. Malden, MA: Wiley, 2011.

Olafson, Frederick A. "Heidegger à la Wittgenstein or 'Coping' with Professor Dreyfus." *Inquiry* 37, no. 1 (1994): 45–64.

———. *Heidegger and the Philosophy of Mind*. New Haven, CT: Yale University Press, 1987.

Overgaard, Søren. "Heidegger on Embodiment." *Journal of the British Society for Phenomenology* 35, no. 2 (2014): 116–31.

Pascal, Roy. "Georg Simmels *Die Großstädte und das Geistesleben*: Zur Frage der 'Moderne.'" In *Gestaltungsgeschichte und Gesellschaftsgeschichte*, edited by Helmut Kreuzer, 450–60. Stuttgart: Matzler, 1969.
Peters, Meindert. "Benjamin in *i10*: Journalistic Networks, Exchange, and Reception behind a Dutch, Multi-Lingual, Avant-Garde Magazine." In "Der Journalist als Produzent: Walter Benjamins publizistische Texte und die Medienlandschaft der Zwischenkriegszeit," edited by Carolin Duttlinger and Daniel Weidner, special issue *Monatshefte* 115, no. 2 (2023): 189–203.
———. "Heidegger's Embodied Others: On Critiques of the Body and 'Intersubjectivity' in *Being and Time*." *Phenomenology and Cognitive Science* 18, no. 2 (2019): 441–58.
Petersen, Klaus. "Mythos in Gehalt und Form der Dramen Georg Kaisers." *Neophilologus* 60, no. 2 (1976): 266–79.
Petry, Walter. "Aufschrift und Marke nicht vergessen: Zur 'Einbahnstraße' von Walter Benjamin. Ernst Rowohlt Verlag, Berlin." In *Kritische Gesamtausgabe*, by Walter Benjamin. Edited by Christoph Gödde and Henri Lonitz. Vol. 8, *Einbahnstraße*, edited by Detlev Schöttker and Steffen Haug, 502–3. Frankfurt am Main: Suhrkamp, 2009.
Pisters, Patricia. *The Neuro-Image: A Deleuzian Filmphilosophy of Digital Screen Culture*. Stanford, CA: Stanford University Press, 2012.
Praag, Siegfried van. "Opstellen en critieken." *Centraal Blad voor de Israëlieten in Nederland*. April 19, 1929.
———. "Opstellen en critieken." *Centraal Blad voor de Israëlieten in Nederland*. July 8, 1929.
Proust, Marcel. *Finding Time Again*. Translated by Ian Patterson. Vol. 6, *In Search of Lost Time*. London: Penguin, 2003.
———. *Le temps retrouvé*. Vol. 8, *À la recherche du temps perdu*. Paris: Gallimard, 1954.
Ratcliffe, Matthew. "The Phenomenology of Mood and the Meaning of Life." In *The Oxford Handbook of Philosophy of Emotion*, edited by Peter Goldie, 349–72. Oxford: Oxford University Press, 2009.
———. *Rethinking Commonsense Psychology: A Critique of Folk Psychology, Theory of Mind and Simulation*. Basingstoke, UK: Palgrave MacMillan, 2007.
Richter, Gerhard. *Thought-Images: Frankfurt School Writers' Reflections from Damaged Life*. Stanford, CA: Stanford University Press, 2007.
Rietveld, Erik, and Julian Kiverstein. "A Rich Landscape of Affordances." *Ecological Psychology* 26, no. 4 (2014): 325–52.
Rilke, Rainer Maria. *Die Aufzeichnungen des Malte Laurids Brigge*. Stuttgart: Reclam, 1996.
———. *Auguste Rodin*. Wiesbaden: Insel, 1949.
———. *Briefe aus Muzot 1921 bis 1926*. Edited by Ruth Sieber-Rilke and Carl Sieber. Leipzig: Insel, 1935.
———. *Briefe über Cézanne*. Edited by Clara Rilke. Frankfurt am Main: Insel, 1962.

———. "Die Bücher zum wirklichen Leben." In *Werke: Kommentierte Ausgabe in vier Bänden*, edited by Manfred Engel et al. Vol. 4, *Schriften*, edited by Horst Nalewski, 651–52. Frankfurt am Main: Insel, 1996.

———. *Gesammelte Briefe in 6 Bänden*. Edited by Ruth Sieber-Rilke and Carl Sieber. Vol. 2, *Briefe aus den Jahren 1904 bis 1907*. Leipzig: Insel, 1939.

———. *Letters of Rainer Maria Rilke: 1910–1926*. Translated by Jane Bannard Greene and M. D. Herter Norton. New York: Norton, 1949.

———. *Neue Gedichte*. Leipzig: Insel Verlag, 1923.

———. *The Notebooks of Malte Laurids Brigge*. Translated by Robert Vilain. Oxford: Oxford University Press, 2016.

———. *Sämtliche Werke*. Edited by Rilke-Archiv, Ruth Sieber-Rilke, and Ernst Zinn. Wiesbaden: Insel Verlag, 1966.

———. *Worpswede*. Frankfurt am Main: Insel, 1987.

Rokotnitz, Naomi. "Colluding in the Conspiracy of Their Fiction." In "Transatlantic Cognitive Cultures," edited by Shannon McBriar and Meindert Peters. Special Issue, *Symbiosis* 25, no. 2 (2021): 183–211.

———. *Trusting Performance: A Cognitive Approach to Embodiment in Drama*. London: Palgrave Macmillan, 2011.

Rotha, Paul. *The Film Till Now: A Survey of the Cinema*. London: Jonathan Cape, 1930.

Ruprecht, Lucia. *Gestural Imaginaries: Dance and Cultural Theory in the Early Twentieth Century*. Oxford: Oxford University Press, 2019.

———. "Gesture, Interruption, Vibration: Rethinking Early Twentieth-Century Gestural Theory and Practice in Walter Benjamin, Rudolf von Laban, and Mary Wigman." *Dance Research Journal* 47, no. 2 (2015): 23–41.

Ryle, Gilbert. *The Concept of Mind*. Harmondsworth, UK: Penguin, 1963.

Saint-Amour, Paul K. "Weak Theory, Weak Modernism." In "Weak Theory, Weak Modernism," edited by Paul K. Saint-Amour. Special issue, *Modernism/modernity* 24, no. 3 (2018): 437–59.

Sartre, Jean-Paul. *L'être et le néant: Essai d'ontologie phénoménologique*. Paris: Gallimard, 1965.

Sbriscia-Fioretti, Beatrice, et al. "ERP Modulation during Observation of Abstract Paintings by Franz Kline." *PLoS One* 8, no. 10 (2013): 1–12.

Scheler, Max. *The Nature of Sympathy*. Translated by Peter Heath. London: Routledge & Kegan Paul, 1954.

Scheutz, Matthias, ed. *Computationalism: New Directions*. Cambridge, MA: MIT Press, 2002.

Schleich, Carl Ludwig. "Cocainism." In *The Weimar Republic Sourcebook*, edited by Anton Kaes, Martin Jay, and Edward Dimendberg, 723–24. Berkeley: University of California Press, 1994.

———. "Kokainismus." *Das Tage-Buch* 2 (1921): 1310–15.

Schoenbach, Lisi. *Pragmatic Modernism*. Oxford: Oxford University Press, 2011.

Schöttker, Detlev. *Konstruktiver Fragmentarismus: Form und Rezeption der Schriften Walter Benjamins*. Frankfurt am Main: Suhrkamp, 1999.

Schöttker, Detlev, and Erdmut Wizisla, eds. *Arendt und Benjamin: Texte, Briefe, Dokumente*. Frankfurt am Main: Suhrkamp, 2006.
Schueler, H. J. "The Symbolism of Paradise in Georg Kaiser's Von Morgens bis Mitternachts." *Neophilologus* no. 68 (1984): 98–104.
Schwan, Stephan, and Sermin Ildirar. "Watching Film for the First Time: How Adult Viewers Interpret Perceptual Discontinuities in Film." *Psychological Science* 21, no. 7 (2010): 970–76.
Schwartz, Frederic. *Blind Spots: Critical Theory and the History of Art in Twentieth-Century Germany*. New Haven, CT: Yale University Press, 2005.
Shapiro, Lawrence, and Shannon Spaulding. *The Routledge Handbook of Embodied Cognition: Second Edition*. London: Routledge, 2024.
Sheets-Johnstone, Maxine. *The Primacy of Movement: Expanded Second Edition*. Amsterdam: John Benjamins, 2011.
Shimamura, Arthur P. "Psychocinematics: Issues and Directions." In *Psychocinematics: Exploring Cognition and the Movies*, edited by Arthur P. Shimamura, 1–26. Oxford: Oxford University Press, 2013.
Simmel, Georg. *Die Großstädte und das Geistesleben*. Frankfurt am Main: Suhrkamp, 1995.
———. "The Metropolis and Mental Life." In *The Sociology of Georg Simmel*, edited and translated by Kurt H. Wolff. New York: Free Press of Glencoe, 1950.
———. "Sociology of the Senses." Translated by Mark Ritter and David Frisby. In *Simmel on Culture: Selected Writings*, edited by David Frisby and Mike Featherstone. London: Sage, 1997.
———. "Soziologie der Geselligkeit." In *Verhandlungen des ersten deutschen Soziologentages*, 1–16. Tübingen: J. C. B. Mohr, 1910.
———. "Soziologie der Sinne." *Die Neue Rundschau* 18, no. 9 (September 1907): 1025–36.
Smith, Barry. "Toward a Realistic Science of Environments." *Ecological Psychology* 21, no. 2 (2009): 121–30.
Sokel, Walter H. *The Writer in Extremis: Expressionism in Twentieth-Century German Literature*. Stanford, CA: Stanford University Press, 1959.
Solomon, Robert C. *The Passions: Emotions and the Meaning of Life*. Cambridge, MA: Hackett, 1993.
Sparenberg, Tim. "Georg Simmels soziale Physik und die moderne Literatur." *Zeitschrift für Germanistik* 20, no. 3 (2010): 522–42.
Stambaugh, Joan, trans. *Being and Time*, by Martin Heidegger. Albany: State University of New York Press, 2010.
Sutton, John, Doris McIlwain, Wayne Christensen, and Andrew Geeves. "Applying Intelligence to the Reflexes: Embodied Skills and Habits between Dreyfus and Descartes." *Journal of the British Society for Phenomenology*, 41 (2014): 78–103.
Taussig, Michael. "Physiognomic Aspects of Visual Worlds." *Visual Anthropology Review*, 8 (1992): 15–28.

The Little Mermaid. Directed by Ron Clements and John Musker. Walt Disney Pictures. 1989.
Thompson, Evan. *Mind in Life: Biology, Phenomenology, and the Sciences of Mind*. Cambridge, MA: Harvard University Press, 2010.
Tiemersma, Douwe. *Body Schema and Body Image: An Interdisciplinary and Philosophical Study*. Amsterdam: Swets & Zeitlinger, 1989.
Trevarthen, Colwyn. "Communication and Cooperation in Early Infancy: A Description of Primary Intersubjectivity." In *Before Speech: The Beginning of Interpersonal Communication*, edited by Margaret Bullowa, 321–48. Cambridge: Cambridge University Press, 1979.
———. "The Foundations of Intersubjectivity: Development of Interpersonal and Cooperative Understanding of Infants." In *The Social Foundation of Language and Thought: Essays in Honor of Jerome S. Bruner*, edited by D. R. Olsen, 316–41. New York: Norton, 1980.
Turner, Mark. *The Literary Mind*. Oxford: Oxford University Press, 1998.
———. "Multimodal Form-Meaning Pairs for Blended Classic Joint Attention." *Linguistics Vanguard* 3, no. 1 (2017): 1–7.
Turner, Mark W. "'Telling of my Weekly Doings': The Material Culture of the Victorian Novel." In *A Concise Companion to the Victorian Novel*, edited by Francis O'Gorman. London: Blackwell, 2005.
Uexküll, Gudrun von. *Jakob von Uexküll: Seine Welt und seine Umwelt*. Hamburg: Wegner, 1964.
Uexküll, Jakob von. *A Foray into the Worlds of Animals and Humans: with "A Theory of Meaning."* Translated by Joseph D. O'Neil. Minneapolis: University of Minnesota Press, 1910.
———. "The Metropolis and Mental Life." In *The Sociology of Georg Simmel*, edited and translated by Kurt H. Wolff. New York: Free Press of Glencoe, 1950.
———. "Die Umrisse einer kommenden Weltanschauung." *Die Neue Rundschau* 18 (1907): 641–61.
———. *Umwelt und Innenwelt der Tiere*. Berlin: Springer, 1909.
———. *Umwelt und Innenwelt der Tiere*. Edited by Florian Mildenberger and Bernd Herrmann. 1921. Reprint. Berlin: Springer, 2014.
———. "Wie sehen wir die Natur und wie sieht die Natur sich selber?" *Die Naturwissenschaften* 10 (1922): 265–71, 296–301, 316–22.
Uexküll, Jakob von, and Georg Kriszat. *Streifzüge durch die Umwelten von Tieren und Menschen: Ein Bilderbuch unsichtbarer Welten*. Berlin: Springer, 1934.
Ullstein, Herman. *The Rise and Fall of the House of Ullstein*. London: Nicholson & Watson, [ca. 1944].
Umiltà, Maria Alessandra, et al. "Abstract Art and Cortical Motor Activation: An EEG Study." *Frontiers in Human Neuroscience* 6 (2012): 311.
Van Hulle, Dirk. *Modern Manuscripts: The Extended Mind and Creative Undoing from Darwin to Beckett and Beyond*. New York: Bloomsbury, 2013.

Varela, Francisco J., Evan Thompson, and Eleanor Rosch. *The Embodied Mind: Cognitive Science and Human Experience*. Cambridge, MA: MIT Press, 1991.
Vilain, Robert. Explanatory Notes to *The Notebooks of Malte Laurids Brigge*, by Rainer Maria Rilke, 159–93. Oxford: Oxford University Press, 2016.
Von Morgens bis Mitternachts. Directed by Karlheinz Martin. Filmmuseum München. 1920.
Walk, Cynthia. "Cross-Media Exchange in Weimar Culture: *Von morgens bis mitternachts.*" *Monatshefte* 99, no. 2 (2007): 177–93.
Webber, Andrew J. Introduction to *The Cambridge Companion to the Literature of Berlin*, 1–12. Cambridge: Cambridge University Press, 2017.
Wheeler, Michael. *Reconstructing the Cognitive World: The Next Step*. Cambridge, MA: MIT Press, 2005.
Whitehead, Alfred North. *The Aims of Education and Other Essays*. New York: Macmillan, 1929.
Whitworth, Michael H. *Modernism*. Malden: Blackwell, 2007.
Widdig, Bernd. *Culture and Inflation in Weimar Germany*. Berkeley: University of California Press, 2001.
Williams, Raymond. *The Country and the City*. London: Chatto & Windus, 1973.
Williams, Rhys W. "Culture and Anarchy in Georg Kaiser's 'Von morgens bis mitternachts.'" *The Modern Language Review* 83, no. 2 (1988): 364–74.
Willink, Luc. "Nieuw Uitgaven." *Het Vaderland*, January 30, 1931. https://resolver.kb.nl/resolve?urn=ddd:010013332:mpeg21:a0224.
Wolff, Janet. "The Invisible Flâneuse: Women and the Literature of Modernity." *Theory, Culture, Society* 2, no. 3 (1985): 37–46.
Zahavi, Dan. "Beyond Empathy: Phenomenological Approaches to Intersubjectivity." *Journal of Consciousness Studies* 8, no. 5–7 (2001): 151–67.
Zukow-Goldring, Patricia. "Assisted Imitation: First Steps in the Seed Model of Language Development." *Language Sciences* 34 (2012): 569–82.
Zunshine, Lisa, ed. *Introduction to Cognitive Cultural Studies*. Baltimore: Johns Hopkins University Press, 2010.
———, ed. *The Oxford Handbook of Cognitive Literary Studies*. Oxford: Oxford University Press, 2015.

Index

4E cognition, 5, 138n47

Adams, Frederick, 7n16
Adorno, Theodor W., 133n36, 168n50
affordances, 7–8, 17–18, 53, 56–58, 66, 93–109, 113–18, 124, 150, 159, 167, 173, 175–81, 189, 193, 195, 197, 199
Agamben, Giorgio, 2, 3n7
Aho, Kevin A., 25n12, 31
Aizawa, Kenneth, 7n16
alienation, 4, 10–15, 82, 85, 147, 169
Allison, Truett, 34n44
Anderson, Miranda, 16n47
Andreas-Salomé, Lou, 68n57
animation, 6, 132, 171, 198
Anthony the Great, Saint, 55
anxiety, 9, 15, 23, 40–43, 45–47, 52, 55–56, 72, 75, 83, 91–92, 105, 111–12, 116, 118, 127, 135, 164, 196
Aragon, Louis, 182
Armstrong, Paul B., 175
Arnim, Bettina von, 62n37
Askay, Richard, 30n24
attunement, 3n6, 16, 117n54, 139, 149–50, 151, 167, 170, 175n10
authenticity, 9, 23, 31n28, 34, 37–38, 40–44, 65–66, 68–69, 88, 99, 117, 168
Auyoung, Elaine, 185n57, 185n58

Baker, Josephine, 161
Bakhtin, Michail, 122n7
Baldwin, Dare A., 34n44
Barbisan, Léa, 121n3
Barndt, Kerstin, 187n65, 190n77
Baßler, Moritz, 92, 93, 103, 117, 179–80, 193

Bateson, Mary Catherine, 22n5
Baudelaire, Charles, 61, 66, 70, 139–40
Baum, Vicki, works by:
  Es war alles ganz anders, 145n3, 189–90; *Menschen im Hotel*, 3, 5, 9, 10, 13, 19, 76, 84, 143, 144–72, 174, 176, 187–91, 192, 193, 194, 197, 199; *Stud. chem. Helene Willfüer*, 187, 189n74, 190n77
Bayerdorfer, Hans-Peter, 93n7
Bayliss, Andrew P., 167n48
Beasley-Murray, Tim, 122n7
Beckett, Samuel, 179n28
Behnke, Elizabeth A., 132
Bekkering, Harold, 166n47
Benjamin, Walter, correspondence with Gershom Scholem, 182–83
Benjamin, Walter, works by:
  Einbahnstraße and its *Nachtragsliste*, 3, 4, 8–9, 10, 15, 19–20, 70, 76, 81, 88, 89–90, 119, 120–43, 146–47, 169, 170, 174, 176, 181–85, 187, 191, 194, 195, 196–97, 199, 201–4; *Das Kunstwerk im Zeitalter seiner technischen Reproduzierbarkeit*, 121, 122n7, 141n52, 142; *Passagen-werk*, 11–12, 122n7; *Über einige Motive bei Baudelaire*, 12, 139–40
Bernini, Marco, 16n48, 178n21
Bistis, Margo, 13n42, 15n46
Bloch, Ernst, 181
Boa, Elizabeth, 145n4, 170n52, 170n54
Bolens, Guillemette, 16n47
Bosch, Hieronymus, 55
Boss, Medard, 21

Brandstetter, Gabriele, 163n37
Brecht, Bertolt, 127
Britten, Robert, 51n6, 59–60
Brod, Max, 185–86
Bronstein, Michaela, 175n12
Brooks, Rechele, 22n5
Bruin, Leon de, 5n11
Bruineberg, Jelle, 117n54
Buchanan, Brett, 23n7
Buck-Morss, Susan, 138
Burke, Michael, 16n47, 61n31
Butterworth, G., 22n6

Caillois, Roger, 78–80
Cairns, Douglas, 16n47
Cannon, Peter R., 167n48
Cappuccio, Massimiliano L., 8n25
Caracciolo, Marco, 16n47, 62n34, 64n48, 174n4
Caravà, Marta, 105n40
Carman, Taylor, 31n28
Carroll, Noël, 64
Cartesian dualism, 3, 5
Casanova, Giacomo, 137, 196
Cave, Terence, 7n20, 18, 93–94, 103, 175, 176, 180
Cavell, Stanley, 105
Cerbone, David R., 24–25
Cézanne, Paul, 55, 58
Chalmers, David, 59n26
Charles the Bold, Duke of Burgundy, 61, 67–68
Charles VI (emperor), 61
Charles VI (king), 61, 62
Christensen, Wayne, 122, 123, 127–29, 130, 131, 132
Ciaunica, Anna, 164n43
Clark, Andy, 59n26
cognitivism, 3, 5
Colombetti, Giovanna, 22n6, 123, 153–54
computationalism, 5
Craig, Robert, 56n19
Csikszentmihalyi, Mihaly, 72–73, 74–75, 76–77, 78n19, 79, 81, 86–87, 88, 89, 123, 135n40

Darwin, Charles, 95

Das, Santanu, 18n55
De Cauwer, Stijn, 180–81
De Jaegher, Hanne, 22n6, 51, 65
De Waelhens, Alphonse, 21, 24n10
Deák, István, 187n64
Dewey, John, 18n55, 63n42
Di Paolo, Ezequiel, 22n6, 51, 65
Dickens, Charles, works by:
    Martin Chuzzlewit, 189
Didi-Huberman, Georges, 180
direct perception theory, 109n48, 153, 159
disability, 18–19, 92n5, 195
Dmitry I, False (tsar), 61, 67
Döblin, Alfred, works by:
    "An Romanautoren und ihre Kritiker: Berliner Programm," 93–94, 107n44, 107n45
    "Aufmerksamkeitsstörungen bei Hysterie," 100; "Der Bau des epischen Werks," 178–79;
    Berlin Alexanderplatz, 3, 5, 8, 10, 13, 17, 69, 70, 72, 75, 88, 90, 91–119, 120, 122, 123, 126, 135, 137, 144n1, 153, 156, 169, 170, 176–181, 186n63, 187–88, 191, 192, 193, 197, 199; *Gedächtnisstörungen bei der Korsakoffschen Psychose*, 100n27;
    "Der Geist des naturalistischen Zeitalters," 91, 102, 118; *Das Ich über der Natur*, 95–96, 102; "Mein Buch 'Berlin Alexanderplatz'," 95n14
Dowden, Stephen D., 65, 179
Dreyfus, Hubert L., 28, 30, 31n26, 31n28, 37n50, 39n53, 40–41, 42, 73n3, 128, 151
Duchamp, Marcel, 83
Duttlinger, Carolin, 130n26, 186n61

ecstasy, 9, 30, 45, 58, 72–82, 85–89, 122, 132n34, 134n39, 140–41, 195
Eiland, Howard, 183n47
Eisner, Lotte, 82–83, 84
Eldridge, Richard, 46n66
Elsaesser, Thomas, 191

INDEX ♦ 227

embodied cognition, 3–6, 8, 10, 15, 16, 50–52, 64n48, 93, 118, 127–28, 136, 139, 175, 198–99
Eming, Jutta, 7n20
empathy, 36n49, 179
Engel, Manfred, 50, 52, 55n17, 59n24, 66
Engler-Coldren, Katharina, 16n47
Evans, Jules, 76–77, 79, 81, 86, 88
expressionism, 83, 191, 201

Felski, Rita, 18, 173, 175, 176, 184–85
Fenske, Mark J., 167n48
Fick, Monika, 61
Fischer, M. H., 53n12
flâneur, 11–12, 15
Flaubert, Gustave, 55
flow, 63–64, 72–73, 74–78, 81, 85, 86, 88, 89, 123n11, 135n40
Fontana, Lucio, 191
Fore, Devin, 103, 176–77, 180
Fotopoulou, Aikaterini, 164n43
Franck, Didier, 24n11
Freud, Sigmund, 12
Frischen, Alexandra, 167n48

Gallagher, Shaun, 5n11, 6, 7, 8, 22–23, 26–28, 32–40, 44, 68n58, 117, 130n28, 153n20, 159, 166–67
Gallese, Vittorio, 191–92
Garrington, Abbie, 18n55
Geeves, Andrew, 122, 123, 127–29, 130, 131, 132
Gelderloos, Carl, 95n15
Gibbs, Raymond W. Jr., 62
Gibson, James J., 7–8, 51, 53, 66, 93, 99, 102, 106, 124–25, 177, 194–95
Gide, André, 120, 134, 136, 139
Godfrey-Smith, Peter, 8n23
Godwin, C. D., 178n22
Gogh, Vincent van, 139
Goodwin, Charles, 167n48
Gopnik, Alison, 34n44
Graaff, Chris de, 182–84
Groeneveld, Leanne, 72n1, 75–76

Guédon, Cécile, 64n48

Haas, Willy, 107
habituation, 2, 3, 5, 10, 18n55, 72, 84, 104, 115, 134, 136, 193, 195
Hansen, Mark B. N., 121n3, 122n5, 139–40
Hansen, Miriam, 121–22, 132, 137
Haug, Steffen, 120n2
Haugeland, John, 41, 43
Head, Henry, 26
Heidegger, Martin, works by: *Die Grundbegriffe der Metaphysik*, 23n7, 149, 150, 151; *Die Grundprobleme der Phänomenologie*, 21, 39, 46, 56, 58; *Sein und Zeit*, 3, 7, 9, 16, 20, 21–47, 49, 52, 55, 73, 83, 88, 90, 91, 93, 99, 105n40, 121, 122n8, 123, 149–51, 166, 177, 195, 196–97, 198; *Zollikoner Seminare*, 21, 22n3, 25, 27, 29, 44, 129, 136
Herman, David, 2n5, 16–17
Herrmann, Bernd, 2n4
Herwig, Malte, 52
Hessel, Franz, 182, 184
Heyes, Cecilia, 8, 160, 166n46
Hillard, Derek, 61n30, 62n36
Hillebrand, Bruno, 87n41
Høffding, Simon, 64n48, 73n3, 130n28
Hofmann, Michael, 179
Holmes, Gordon, 26
Hoover, Herbert, 188
Horn, Eva, 103–4
Horn, Melanie, 92, 93, 103, 117, 179–80, 193
Hubbs, Nadine, 174n7
Huder, Walther, 79–81
Hulewicz, Witold, 59, 63
Husserl, Edmund, 7, 133n37, 146, 155
Hutto, Daniel D., 33n33
Huyssen, Andreas, 12–13, 60

IJzerman, Hans Rocha, 160–61
Ildirar, Sermin, 175n8

Ingold, Tim, 106, 113–14, 117, 173, 177–78, 179, 194–95
intersubjectivity, 22–23, 28–40, 44–45, 109–110, 153–54, 159

Jacobson, Rebecca Seté, 22–23, 28, 32–40, 44
Jähner, Harald, 91, 177–78, 180
James, William, 18n55
Jennings, Michael W., 183n47
Jensen, Thomas Wiben, 105n40
Jentsch, Tobias, 93n7
Job, the Book of, 61, 66, 70, 92
John XXII (pope), 61
Johnson, Susan C., 34n44
Jones, CJ, 7n20
Jones, Lawrence, 187, 190n78
Jooss, Kurt, 163n37
Joyce, James, 179n28
Joyce, James, works by: *Ulysses*, 11
Juan, Don, 134n39, 137, 196

Kafka, Franz, 10, 179n28, 185–86
Kaiser, Georg, works by: "Der kommende Mensch," 87; "Über mein Werk," 88; *Von morgens bis mitternachts*, 3, 8, 9, 72–90, 170, 174, 181n41, 186n63, 191, 195–96, 199
Kállai, Ernő, 192
Kandinsky, Wassily, 192
Keil, Thomas, 95
Keun, Irmgard, works by: *Das kunstseidene Mädchen*, 194–95
Kiesel, Helmuth, 92
King, Lynda J., 144, 187n65
Kiverstein, Julian, 7, 35n47, 41n59, 93, 94, 99, 100, 102–3, 105n40, 106, 109–10, 113–15, 117, 149–50, 154, 173, 174n4, 198
Kleinschmidt, Erich, 100n27
Kline, Franz, 191
Klotz, Volker, 91, 93
Knapp, Lore, 16n47
Koelb, Clayton, 186n61
Kornmüller, A. E., 53n12
Kracauer, Siegfried, 12, 83, 84
Krell, David Farrell, 24n11, 25

Kriszat, Georg, works by: *Streifzüge durch die Umwelten von Tieren und Menschen*, 2, 49, 52–53
Kschessinska, Mathilde, 167n49
Kukkonen, Karin, 16n47, 18, 64n48, 175, 178n21, 186n62

Lācis, Asja, 137–38
Landauer, Gustav, 81, 87n41, 87n44
Lavazza, Andrea, 5n12
Lee, Charlotte, 16n47
Legerstee, Maria, 22n5
Lehleiter, Christine, 16n47
Leib (Heidegger), 21–22, 23–30, 35, 40, 44–45, 136
Lethen, Helmut, 19, 170
Levin, David Michael, 25n12
Lévinas, Emmanuel, 32
Levine, Caroline, 18, 175
Lewis, Cara L., 175n11
The Little Mermaid, 24
Loos, Adolf, 139
Luxembourg, Pierre de, 61

Mach, Ernst, 53n12
Maillard, Christine, 95n15
das Man (Heidegger), 7, 31–32, 34, 35, 41, 42, 44, 45, 151
Mann, Thomas, 81, 179n28
Martens, Gunter, 87
Martin, Karlheinz, works by: *Von morgens bis mitternachts*, 72–74, 78, 79, 82–85, 86, 88–90, 186n63, 191, 192, 195
Marx, Ursula, 124, 127n18
Maskarinec, Malika, 178n21, 188
Matthias, Bettina, 144n2, 147, 156, 168n50
Mauthner, Fritz, 177
May, Theresa, 42
Mayr, Franz, 30n24
McBriar, Shannon R., 16n47, 193n85
McCarthy, Gregory, 34n44
McCracken, Scott, 122n7
McIlwain, Doris, 122, 123, 127–29, 130, 131, 132
Meltzoff, Andrew N., 22n5, 34n44, 166n45

Menary, Richard, 59n26
Mendelssohn, Peter de, 187n64
Merleau-Ponty, Maurice, 7, 21, 26, 35n48, 44
Meulenbroek, Ruud G. J., 166n47
Midgley, David R., 180
Mikhailovich of Russia, Grand Duke Sergei, 167n49
Mildenberg, Ariana, 18n55
Mildenberger, Florian, 2n4
Miller, Tyrus, 182
mimicry, 62, 78–80, 165–68
mirror neurons, 166
modernism, 3–5, 8, 9, 10–13, 15–20, 23, 40, 42, 45, 46, 63n42, 65, 76, 79, 80, 82, 121, 123, 147, 168, 173–76, 179, 182, 189, 193, 195, 198–99; and alienation, 4, 10–16; and weakness, 18–19
Moholy-Nagy, László, 182, 192
Moi, Toril, 46n66, 105
Mondriaan, Piet, 192
montage, 91, 118, 176–81, 186n63, 188
mood (Heidegger), 149–51
Moore, M. Keith, 22n5, 166n45
Moran, Joe, 48, 175
Morgan, Ben, 16n47, 43n62, 68n58, 117, 122, 123n9, 138n47
Morrison, India, 160–61, 163–64
Müller, Lothar, 12
Müller, Sabine, 64n48
Muschg, Walter, 93
Muybridge, Eadweard, 83

Nagaia, Marie, 67
Neppach, Robert, 83
new objectivity, 19, 170
Newen, Albert, 5n11
Newman-Norlund, Roger D., 166n47
Nietzsche, Friedrich, 87
Noë, Alva, 51, 54, 55–56, 63–65, 70
Noland, Carrie, 133n36
Noordzij, Matthijs L. 166n47
Nottelmann, Nicole, 145n3

Okker, Patricia, 189, 190n78
Olafson, Frederick A., 31n28, 39n53

Overgaard, Søren, 24–25, 35n48

Park, Sowon, 16n47
Pascal, Roy, 12n37
Paul, Matthew A., 167n48
Pavlova, Anna, 145
Pedersen, Sarah Bro, 105n40
Peters, Meindert, 16n47, 182n45
Pisters, Patricia, 16n47
popular literature, 169–70, 188n71
Praag, Siegfried van, 185–86
Proust, Marcel, 171
Puce, Aina, 34n44

Rank, Otto, 83
Rastelli, Enrico, 131
Ratcliffe, Matthew, 22n6, 149–50
recalcitrance, 4, 9–10, 17, 23, 40–41, 45–47, 49, 51–55, 57, 58, 64, 70, 83, 85, 90, 92, 195
responsiveness, 10, 13, 87, 94, 106, 107, 109, 113, 115–16, 118–19, 122, 123, 132–34, 136–38, 141–42, 144, 146, 150, 153–55, 163–64, 166, 168, 169, 171, 175, 181, 185, 193, 196, 197, 198
Reuß, Roland, 186n61
Richter, Gerhard, 132, 182n43
Rietveld, Erik, 7, 35n47, 41n59, 93, 99, 100, 102–3, 113–15, 117, 173, 174n4
Rilke, Rainer Maria: correspondence with Lou Andreas-Salomé, 68n57; correspondence with Witold Hulewicz, 59, 63; correspondence with Clara Rilke-Westhoff, 176; correspondence with Gudrun and Jakob von Uexküll, 1–3
Rilke, Rainer Maria, works by: *Die Aufzeichnungen des Malte Laurids Brigge*, 3, 5, 8, 9, 12, 17, 44, 46–47, 48–71, 75, 82, 89, 91–93, 99, 117, 120, 138, 141, 165, 168–69, 173, 176, 178, 191, 192, 196, 198, 199; *Auguste Rodin*, 58; *Briefe über Cézanne*, 58; *Neue Gedichte*, 58n20; "Puppen," 65n52
Rilke-Westhoff, Clara, 176

Robinson, Howard, 5n12
Rodin, Auguste, 58
Rohde, Marieke, 51, 65
Rokotnitz, Naomi, 16n47, 68n58, 69, 117
Rosch, Eleanor, 6–7
Rotha, Paul, 84
Ruprecht, Lucia, 18n55, 121n3, 132n31, 133, 163n37
Ryle, Gilbert, 128

Saint-Amour, Paul K., 18–19
Sartre, Jean-Paul, 21, 24n10, 25, 37, 44
Sbriscia-Fioretti, Beatrice, 190n82
Scheerbart, Paul, 126
Scheler, Max, 34–35
Scheutz, Matthias, 5n12
Schleich, Carl Ludwig, 81–82
Schneckenburger, Max, 97n21
Schoenbach, Lisi, 18n55
Scholem, Gershom, 182–83
Schöttker, Detlev, 120n2, 122n8, 182n43
Schueler, H. J., 86–87
Schwan, Stephan, 175n8
Schwartz, Frederic, 130n26, 182n43
Schwerin, Luise Countess of, 1n2
Scipio, 132–33, 134, 135–36
Scorolli, Claudia, 105n40
Seifert, Ludovic, 117n54
serialization, 146n7, 187–91, 197
Shapiro, Lawrence, 5n11
Sheets-Johnstone, Maxine, 4n8, 5–6, 51–52, 123, 132, 133n37, 136–38, 146, 148–50, 154–55, 198
Shimamura, Arthur P., 175n8
shock, 12, 15, 94, 139, 176, 183–84, 202
Simmel, Georg, 10–15, 94, 147, 152, 176, 179, 181, 197
Simmel, Georg, works by: *Die Großstädte und das Geistesleben*, 10–11, 179; "Soziologie der Geselligkeit," 15n46; "Soziologie der Sinne," 13–15
Smith, Barry, 99
smooth coping, 8, 9, 52, 73, 75

Sokel, Walter H., 87–88
Sparenberg, Tim, 12n37
Spaulding, Shannon, 5n11
Spolsky, Ellen, 16n47
Staengle, Peter, 186n61
stimulus shield, 10, 180
Sutton, John, 122, 123, 127–29, 130, 131, 132

Taussig, Michael, 121, 136
Thompson, Evan, 6–7, 8n22
Tiemersma, Douwe, 26n16
Tipper, Steven P., 167n48
Trefilova, Vera, 167n49
Trevarthen, Colwyn, 22, 33, 45, 167
Trollope, Anthony, works by: *The Last Chronicle of Barset*, 189
Troscianko, Emily, 16n47, 61n31
Trotsky, Leon, 15, 134–36, 138–39
Turner, Mark, 33n38, 63n41

Uexküll, Gudrun Baroness von, 1
Uexküll, Jakob Baron von, 2–4, 7–8, 16, 23n7, 41n59, 49, 51, 52–53, 60–61, 66, 95–96, 99, 102, 116
Uexküll, Jakob Baron von, works by: *Streifzüge durch die Umwelten von Tieren und Menschen*, 2, 49, 52–53; "Die Umrisse einer kommenden Weltanschauung," 4n10; *Umwelt und Innenwelt der Tiere*, 2;
Ullstein, Hermann, 190–91
Umiltà, Maria Alessandra, 191n82
Umwelt, 1–3, 7–8, 17, 23n7, 41, 46, 51, 52–53, 55–58, 61, 64, 65, 66, 68, 95, 99, 102, 136, 195

Van Hulle, Dirk, 17, 178n21
Varela, Francisco J., 6–7
Victorian literature, 190
Vilain, Robert, 50, 55n17
Vygotsky, Lev, 186

Wagner, Lily, 146
Walk, Cynthia, 89, 186n63
Webber, Andrew J., 12
West, Nancy, 189, 190n78

Wheeler, Michael, 7n21, 25n14
Whitehead, Alfred North, 185n57
Whitworth, Michael H., 10–11
Widdig, Bernd, 13
Wigman, Mary, 163n37
Wilhelm, Karl, 97n21
Williams, Raymond, 11n32
Williams, Rhys W., 72n1, 74, 81, 84n36, 86
Wittgenstein, Ludwig, 34, 99
Wizisla, Erdmut, 122n8, 127n19

Wolff, Janet, 12
Woolf, Virginia, works by: *Mrs Dalloway*, 11
World War I, 9, 18n55, 81, 121, 126, 127, 140, 148, 195

Zahavi, Dan, 7n19, 32n29, 37n50
Zuhandenheit (Heidegger), 7, 9, 23–24, 26, 41, 46, 196
Zukow-Goldring, Patricia, 113–14
Zunshine, Lisa, 16n47